FATHER, WHO ART

Drew O'Brien

For Scott, always, and my first team:

Tom, Joyce, Chuck, Jeri, and Earl & Mary

FATHER, WHO ART

1.

"Just make sure you support his head—you remember, Gem," Gem's wife, Kelly, said.

But just as Gem felt the softness of the blanket and his newborn grandson squirming beneath it, the maternity room at Cedars began to close in on him. And the pulling sensation caused his heart to race and he was slipping into a tunnel. Cold sweat broke out on his forehead. '*No, you don't want to hurt your grandson,*' Gem thought.

"Gem, you're going to ruin our selfie—smile."

The digital click of the iPhone shutter set his teeth on edge. He had to get out of that room—the sky! He needed to see the sky immediately just like the first time he felt this when he was fifteen. Gem grabbed Kelly's arm and placed it around the baby. Kelly pulled the baby to her.

"Gem, you okay?"

"Just gotta get some air."

He bolted out the door. Kelly shrugged toward their daughter Angela, whose brow furrowed underneath her mane of raven, corkscrew locks inherited from Kelly. Some of her curls were still pasted to her forehead by the sweat of recent labor. The baby cried and Angela began to open her rose-patterned hospital gown. Her Nordic-god-of-a husband Chuck stood up, turned his back, and waved his digital camera around.

"Should I go and see…" he pointed to the door.

Kelly shook her head. She stepped over and handed the baby to Angela whose breast was bared for the baby's feeding.

Chuck cleared his throat and lumbered over and sat in the gray vinyl visitor chair.

"You'll get used to it, Chuck," Kelly said.

By the time the elevator doors opened and Gem pushed past the other occupants and out onto Third Street, he breathed as if he had just run two miles. His mind felt disconnected from his body. The grinding and clanking sounds of Third Street seemed miles away. He raised his face to the sky. He glanced past the dark towers of Cedars-Sinai and struggled to find one blue patch. A billboard of Angelyne in her pink, busty glory blocked most of his view but he landed on a corner of hazy cornflower blue. That was enough to prod deeper breaths. His heart began to slow. It wasn't that he didn't recognize a panic attack; it was the question of why now. And the thought to hurt his newborn grandson, the trigger for it, sent shudders through him again. It was as if the last thirty-seven years had evaporated and he was fifteen again. Had he not lived those years: thirty with his gloriously smart Stanford music grad wife, twenty-nine as one of the top TV agents in L.A.? All the richness, love, and joy of their lives seemed to have dissolved into breathless panic. It was as if he were fifteen again, or worse, younger.

No! This was not going to steal his mind and his life. Goddamn it, no! But as a bus blared past him and a horn honked somewhere, he wasn't so sure. He looked up at the massive wall of alternating black and gray windows of the Cedars-Sinai Medical Group tower and began to count the gray ones. This drew his attention away from his anxiety panic. *'But what if I just go up there and push Kelly and the baby out the window? Seven-eight-nine. What if I jabbed a hypodermic into Chuck's eye. Ten-eleven-twelve.'*

'I've got the power...' the techno-blues wail of Snap distracted him as his office Blackberry rang. He punched on his Bluetooth and immediately heard the nervous voice of his executive assistant, Marcie.

"Mr. O'Connell, sorry to disturb you with the baby and all".

"Yeah. What's up?"

"Katherine just walked off the set. She's pissed about Al's guarantee being so much higher than hers. She's sitting in your office."

"My office?"

"I know, I told her you were at a meeting over at Paramount but she insisted that you—and I'm quoting here-- get your ass in here."

Gem sighed. As he was about to respond, his home cell phone rang. 'You are everything…and everything is you…'

"Hang on, Marcie. I got another call."

"Gem" Kelly said. Her tone was flat.

"Yep."

"Where are you?"

"Just down on Third Street getting some fresh air. That room was stuffy."

"You coming back up to see your grandson anytime soon?"

"I can't. Katherine's in my office having a meltdown over her guarantee. I gotta go put out that fire."

"Okay but you still sound odd."

"Odd?"

"It wasn't like you to storm out of here. Not like you *now*, anyway."

Gem's stomach and chest felt like a balloon full of ninja butterflies. He looked up and started counting the windows to prevent another wave of the anxiety. His Bluetooth beeped in his ear and he remembered Marcie was still holding.

"I'm headed to the office. Tell the kids I'll be back when I can. I love you and them."

"Love you, too."

"You don't look so good, fella," a graveled voice said behind him. Gem turned toward the voice and watched as a man in a crusty baseball cap reached down and shook his penis. Gem jumped back.

"You almost hit my shoes, buddy!"

The man tucked and zipped, showing the stained elbows on his torn, herringbone sport coat. He reached up and scratched his matted salt and pepper beard. Pointing at the building, he gazed at Gem with strangely clear, blue-green eyes.

"The hospital's right here. You should check in 'cause you're kinda' all pale and shitty."

Gem reached into his pocket for some change and the homeless man shook his head.

"I don't need nothin' from you. I got all I need right here."

He pounded his chest with hands gnarled from arthritis and cracked red and scaly. The man turned back toward a shopping cart stacked with a broken lamp, a bag of dog food, dirty rags and plastic odds and ends. He paused and said over his shoulder:

"You're so tense you oughtta try meditating. I do it every morning and afternoon. Good for ya."

Gem shook his head and walked toward the hospital parking structure.

2.

His therapist already knew something unusual was up at the point he walked into her office and shook her hand. Gem's hand was frigid from angst and he caught Dr. Friedman's quick glance as she clutched his hand with her French-manicured fingers. The thoughts hadn't assaulted him in a couple decades and he was unnerved.

"You look great," Dr. Friedman said. "What's it been—twenty-six years or so?"

"Yeah."

Dr. Friedman dropped Gem's hand and held out her arms for a hug. Gem hugged her briefly.

"Good to see you again, kid." Dr. Friedman said.

Gem did notice that even though she was a few years older than he, she looked ten years younger. What's her secret, he thought? He glanced around the room and saw the framed cover of Los Angeles Magazine with Dr. Friedman's photo and the title: Your Brain on Laughter: Blazing the Therapy Trail with Humor. Another framed cover of Psychology Today featured Dr. Friedman and the title: The Science of Humor in Therapy. On the opposite wall hung a black poster with large, newspaper font letters that read: Lighten Up.

"You have been busy," Gem said. He pointed to the magazine covers.

"All those referrals over the years from you for some of your high-profile actors didn't hurt."

"Glad I could help. What a surprise, neurotic actors."

"They're not kidding about this humor therapy approach," she said as she pointed at the magazine covers.

"Not long after our sessions years back, I took a stand-up comedy workshop for kicks. I bombed my first open mic night, but I realized the possibility of humor as part of therapy and ta-dah—I was correct. My article in the NIH is still cited in industry studies and magazines. Now I even provide clinical training to new therapists at UCLA and make comedy study a requirement. Sit already, this is about you, not me."

Gem sat. His fingers drummed the arm of the sofa with its tapestry fabric. As if of their own accord, the tips of his fingers thudded out in repetitive rhythm.

"Eine Kleine Nachtmusik again?" Dr. Friedman asked. "I remember that." One of the reasons Gem liked Dr. Friedman was her wry, low-key delivery.

'Ba-dum-chee' he thought.

"What's with the fingers already? Are you washing your hands too often again, too?"

Gem shook his head and dropped his chin to his chest, feeling the putty of neck flesh insult his chest with the reminder of his fifty-two years. He scratched the crown of his head and rapidly smoothed out the coarse gray hair over the thinning spot. He pulled his flattened palm forward toward his forehead. He had to work the pomade hard this morning to fix what Kelly called the 'debate head': the blocky JFK square of the sides and crown of his hair, and the thinning Nixon widow's peak. Now he felt the need to fix it, again, and again, again.

"I think your hair looks fine," Dr. Friedman said. "Looks like you got it bad right now."

Gem sighed and raised his eyes to meet Dr. Friedman's. Those inquisitive, pushy, and yet gentle hazel eyes had been able to bore into his mind and heart since he first saw her back in '91. Just after Curt was born, she diagnosed it then: obsessive anxiety disorder with some compulsion thrown in.

"It's started again," he admitted. "We were at Cedars the other day with Angela and Chuck and the baby. They handed me little Tyler and …" his face flushed hot.

"I got it, I got it—thumb into his soft spot, or throwing him across the room…whatever…"

10

Gem nodded. To hear his thoughts spoken aloud by someone made him feel guilty and disgusted with himself.

"I held Tyler just long enough for Kelly to snap a selfie of the three of us, and then handed him to Kelly. My heart pounded and I had to leave the room."

"You're not going to commit infanticide, or smother your wife, or any of those other ideas that pop into your head. The very fact those ideas trigger your anxiety should remind you that you're not capable of violence."

"I know that, Dr. Friedman, I know it. I remember from before. But what the hell? Why are they flooding in again with my first grandkid?"

"'Why' is a question I don't recognize—you know that already. Leave that for priests and rabbis. 'How' and 'What' are more important to me. And that's where we are going to focus."

Gem took a deep breath, letting the spicy scent of the patchouli candles sitting on the glass side table anchor him. He crossed his arms but uncrossed them quickly as he felt the little paunch under his yellow polo shirt. He sat up straight and pulled his shirt loose.

"Let's see, I'm—never mind. How old are you again?" Dr. Friedman asked.

"Fifty-two...and five months..."

Dr. Friedman chuckled.

"Funny that we added every week and month to our age as kids and now we're doing that in middle age."

"Late middle age—people don't live to be a hundred and four very often," Gem replied.

"It's not the number we rack up. It's what we are doing each hour and day. Quality. But the best part is, I now know why the obsessive anxiety is creeping back up."

"Really? You do?" Gem's first hint of optimism crept in his voice.

Dr. Friedman nodded. She placed her iPad on the glass coffee table next to the bust of Cloris Leachman as Nurse Diesel in 'High Anxiety' and a collection of Dr. David Viscott paperbacks. Gem glanced at the glowing screen to see if he could make out any notes. Her soft heels clicked across the bamboo office floor to an antique cherry credenza that had the

11

theatre faces of drama and comedy carved in baroque style in each corner. The skirt of her sapphire fitted suit accented her legs well. She still moved lithely and gracefully. Or was that peacefully, he thought. Someone at complete ease with herself. She looked through the shelves of the credenza. She slid books aside and shifted a stack of paper.

"Did you end up signing that actress?" she said over her shoulder. "I keep up on 'The Variety' for all my biz patients. You always seem to have something cooking."

"Oh yeah. We already have her signed to a thirteen-episode deal at Sony. I negotiated obscene options for two more seasons."

Dr. Friedman pulled a large, leather folio from the credenza. She dusted it off, closed the credenza, and walked back to her chair. Her brows furrowed as she sat.

"You don't sound very enthusiastic about it."

"Meh. I'm a bit bored with it all now. I'm thinking it's time to sell the agency and just retire."

"And do what exactly?"

"Maybe travel more."

"Haven't you been all over the world—at least the Variety says so."

"Yeah, I guess. Work and pleasure. OK, maybe buy a winery up north. Raise gmo free bean sprouts. I don't know."

"Right".

Dr. Friedman extended her index finger and raised her thumb in a gun shape. She picked up the iPad and made a note.

"What? What?"

"Relax. I just texted my dad to meet me tonight at seven-thirty."

"How old is he now?"

"Eighty-four but still spry as a forty-year old. We really didn't think he'd bounce back after mom died."

"Your mom died?"

"Three years ago. They were high school sweethearts and we all thought it would kill him. But it didn't. He's still my hero."

"Hmmm." was all Gem could say.

She held up the folio and unlatched it. Before her thin fingers had withdrawn the item, Gem blurted out.

"You still have *that?*"

Dr. Friedman smiled and nodded. She pulled out a manuscript bound like a screenplay by orange cardboard with two brads. The orange covers were soiled and rumpled as she flipped it open.

"You were my first male patient right after I was licensed. Color me sentimental."

"Oh, come on, not that old shit again." Gem shifted in his seat.

"It's time to get to this, like it or not."

"That has no bearing on my life now. I made it through and prospered."

"You're like a Power of Positive Thinking bumper sticker. Your problem right now isn't your anxiety disorder. That's going to be with you the rest of your life. The problem is what's triggering it."

Gem stood up and held his hands out in protest.

"Nothing in there is going to change anything."

She tossed the manuscript toward him. He flinched and caught it.

"What is this—shock therapy? Is a lobotomy next?" he asked.

Dr. Friedman chuckled.

"Good one. The anxiety is creeping in because it's time for you to confront yourself."

"Confront? Confront what? I have all the money I need, a wife who adores me, a grandkid now and—"

"Better, let's say you need to be honest with yourself about the main person in your story there."

"Maybe boredom with work is making me anxious. Right?"

Dr. Friedman stepped over and pulled the manuscript from his hands. She held it up to his face.

"Here's a mirror for you. If you want to move through this and come out with less anxiety and more peace, we gotta work this together. And whether you like it or not, we have to finally deal with your father. For whatever reason, he's your main trigger for anxiety—always has been."

Dr. Friedman attempted to hand Gem the manuscript. Gem folded his arms and shook his head. All this was long dead and buried and was going to stay that way. Dr. Friedman placed the manuscript on the glass table and returned to her chair.

"I told you years back we could talk about anything and everything. Did I hold anything back?" Gem asked.

"Only about him."

It was Gem's turn to throw the manuscript. He picked it up and threw it to the floor. He slumped back onto the couch. The song, THAT song, played through his mind. Out of nowhere along with the violent thoughts, the song coursed through his mind again. *'Who needs wings to fly?...'* He wasn't so sure he wasn't cracking up. Many friends of his had hit this same point in their lives but what they said held them together were some choice words their fathers had said every day or maybe the feeling of being loved and wanted they got from their mothers. Gem had three things he could recall from his childhood: fear, anxiety, and sadness. A creepy song and violent thoughts were his support.

Dr. Friedman, cognizant of Gem's heightening anxiety, picked up the manuscript and smoothed the pages.

"Twenty-five years ago you were an unpublished writer and you brought me this final story of yours. You were full of anxiety because Kelly had just delivered—your boy?"

"Yeah. Curt."

"And the anxiety you presented was violent, obsessive thoughts toward your baby and Kelly. You also felt you had no direction and all your abandonment issues were stirred up. We focused on those things but I suspected more. Something in this last story of yours was going to help us understand what triggered the thoughts and anxiety."

"Let's keep it straight—it's all true. My childhood spent yearning for Dad. Lou Hawk, Nonfiction 435, eight AM, final assignment. I was just twenty-one when I wrote it. No one ever read it but her and that's the way it needed to be. What the hell did I know about anything?"

"You thought it might help your therapy. But then you made me promise never to read it because it wasn't finished. I honored that even though I thought that request was bullshit."

"It's as done as it will ever be. I'm no writer and that's that."

"I'm not being literal," Dr. Friedman said. "I'm talking about the unfinished—the unresolved—story inside you. *That father thing.* "

"No," Gem said with a weak plead in his voice.

"Okay, fine. We won't bother with this."

She tossed the manuscript on the side table. She folded her hands and leaned toward Gem.

"But you're not off the hook. Tell me right now. What did your father do to you?"

"Nothing."

"Did he molest you?"

"No."

"Did he beat you?"

"No."

"Did he beat your mom?"

"No."

"Then what did he do, Gem? Why is he such an obstacle to your peace of mind?"

Gem shook his head. Dr. Friedman stood up and went back over to the credenza. She pulled open the doors and reached in to find a manila folder bulging with notes. She walked back over and sat.

"Well lookee here, your old file. I took a read before you got here. Twenty-five years ago, you put discussing your father off limits."

She opened the folder and turned to a page marked with a Post-it flag.

"You said, and I'm quoting here, 'Any conversation or discussion about my dad will be pointless, inconsequential, and fruitless.' 'Fruitless'. Could ya' plotz? Well, twenty-five years ago when I was a newly licensed therapist with my PhD from Cal, I caved to that. But not this time. I'm in charge now, and I'm the one that makes the rules this time."

Gem nodded. The thought of hurting his grandson was just too horrifying. He had to deal with the root of it all and he knew where to find it—in the manuscript. Dr. Friedman set down the manila folder and picked up the manuscript again.

"I told you back then that you'd be back with me over this father thing."

15

"But I got over the anxiety then. I just got busier and busier with work and raising Curt and then Angela. I really thought I had licked it."

"An anxiety disorder can subside for years and then resurface. That's not unusual. Finding the triggers is the hard part. You in or not?"

"You have always been so pushy."

"Can you take any time off?"

"Why?"

"I think it's time for an intensive."

"What—check into the psyche ward?"

"No. I have picked up some new therapy tricks over at UCLA's neuroscience department. It's a cut above the cognitive approach we used when we worked together last time. It does take time. We're talking daily for several hours over a couple weeks."

Gem dropped his head to his chest. He noticed his fingers strumming again and pulled them into a fist. He sighed.

"I can make the time. Can we make it easy and conference via Skype?"

"No. I need to see you in the office here away from any possible multi-tasking temptations."

Gem sighed. "Okay. I'll make the time."

"Good. We're going to navigate this father mystery of yours with this new approach. Nothing is off limits."

Gem jumped up. His chest heaved.

"He was killed. What the hell is there left to say?"

"That much I already know. But I also know there's much more to it."

She tapped the cover of the manuscript. Each tap was a hammer to Gem's brain.

"Well?" she said.

"Okay-yes. I got to get a handle on this anxiety again."

Dr. Friedman smiled smugly and nodded. A digital version of the 1980's Styx song 'Grand Illusion' suddenly played from her iPad. She reached over and muted it.

"Time's up. We'll get you scheduled for two weeks, four hours daily, starting next Monday. You and I got some 'splainin' to do."

Dr. Friedman ran her fingertips across her iPad. She stood up and straightened her skirt.

"Stay here a second."

She stepped out of the office into the reception area. A computer printer hummed to life. She returned after a moment and handed Gem a slip of paper.

"Here's a referral to Dr. Schwartz. He can prescribe some Ativan if the anxiety becomes too intense. Your call—with the new approach we're going to take, I don't think you'll need it."

The traffic heading west tightened up at Avenue of the Stars. Gem stopped his BMW 730i at the red light. He glanced up at the silver tower of 9797 Santa Monica Boulevard and recalled the temp job he had in the accounting department of Ultimate Talent, one of the many talent agencies that were swallowed up by CAA over the years. Talk about anxiety—every call he answered was a stressed agent who had just been screamed at by their TV or film client. It was all about the money and usually, a guarantee payment was overdue. He learned quickly that the surest way to an actor's heart was through their paycheck. In a short time in the accounting department, he had learned contracts, talent fees, the union codes, even what the agents had asked and got when they negotiated. Four years at USC and two in its prestigious film school producer program couldn't compare to that time at UT. He had quickly learned the basic corporate maxim that dominates the entertainment business: 'Show me the money and I'll show you the power.' But there was a price to that wisdom and Gem had learned that, too. Whatever talent and inspiration that had propelled him into the USC film school was lost those summer days at UT. Money and deals came to him so much easier than any plot and story he could conceive. Add to that a lack of desire to direct a film, and an average at best set of technical skills, there was no other option for him in the business but to become an agent. Thanks to Pat Vennari, the super TV agent who mentored him and became another surrogate father, he grew into a powerhouse.

He dropped his eyes back to the signal light that was once again turning from green to red. He hadn't taken his foot off the brakes. He punched on his iPhone and after a few tones, he heard Kelly's sweet voice.

"Are you on your way back to the office or coming home on time tonight?"

"I left Dr. Friedman's a half hour ago and the traffic is just pissing me off. I'm heading home."

"Great. 'Cause I went by Sherwin Williams and grabbed a couple samples. Really light and pretty."

"Cuppy," Gem called Kelly her pet name. Short for 'cupcake', it was inspired by the Hostess package they shared on their first date when they were interns at Columbia Pictures. "You don't need to go overboard. It's going to be weeks before the kids leave the baby with us and we really don't need a nursery. A crib in our bedroom is fine."

"Cupper," Kelly called him her version of 'cupcake', "We have five more bedrooms in this house than we need. Converting one to a granny nursery is no big deal."

"Just as long as you leave Curt's room alone. You never know when he'll stay overnight for six months."

"I doubt Shana is going to let him do that."

"That's right—she's paying the rent."

They both chuckled. Curt had inherited his mother's brains and music propensity but not his father's smarts and drive. At twenty-five, he was still trying to form a garage band with his modicum of acoustic guitar talent while working at the Best Buy at the Beverly Connection as a CD stock clerk.

"So I'm going to take a couple weeks off starting Monday."

"No shit!!! Are we're going to work on the nursery together? Or did you want to go back to Edinburgh? Or better, Funchal?! Wait—Vienna. I could even write the trip off if I do a guest lecture at the Conservatoire--"

"Before you dial Jeannie and book the trip, Cuppy, it's not going to really be a vacation. Dr. Friedman has a new therapy technique for me to try and it's an intensive, daily thing. Four hours a day for two weeks starting Monday."

"Oh. That does sound intense. I'm glad she has a strategy. But we can spend nights going out, maybe even dancing or a concert or play. If you feel like it."

"We'll see. Right now, I feel like ramming the four cars in front of me so that I can make the next light. I'll see you when I get home."

As he hung up, he thought about the support Kelly would give him through this ordeal. Once again, he fell in love with his wife. This time, he fell for her strength and spirit. In a word, she was fierce. No one was as level-headed as she was back during the '92 riots when they lived in one of the Park LA Brea towers.

He opened the steel door of the apartment with its metallic, hollow clank and fifty years of enamel paint the day the riots broke out. Kelly ran to him.

"So glad you're safe. Now we all are." They held each other but as he looked over her shoulder, he noticed his mother-in-law, Ruth, visibly shaking. Clarence, his father-in-law, still in his work apron, gripped Ruth's trembling shoulder with his massive arm.

"The brothers are going crazy out there, just crazy." Ruth said.

"We got the diner closed up just when Kelly got there and picked us up," Clarence added. "A couple of the joints nearby could stand a little torchin'."

"Clarence! It's no time for your smart-aleck humor," Ruth hollered and slapped his shoulder.

"I'm just sayin'," he answered.

Ruth and Clarence ran Ruth's Chicken House, one of the best fried chicken restaurants in Los Angeles. They had been written up in the L.A.Times several times and they were most proud about representing how hard work and hope could bring success no matter their skin color. The restaurant stood on Pico about a mile and half from Gem and Kelly's place at Park La Brea. It was also a couple walking blocks from Ruth and Clarence's home on south La Brea where his lovely Kelly grew up.

"I just asked Jesus to bring us safe home and to bless all the angry brothers and sisters," Ruth said. "My soul's aching for everybody." She kissed the top of Curt's head.

"Fools burning and stealing from their own folks. That I just don't get," Clarence added.

Gem didn't know what to say. He started wondering if he could ask for longer hours at the talent agency where he was a junior television agent, or work weekends on a second job in case his parents-in-law lost their diner to the riots. He leaned over and kissed Ruth's forehead and patted Clarence's shoulder.

"Mama, tell you what," Kelly said. "Let's go up to the roof and take a look and see what we can make out."

"Yeah, girl" Ruth said. "Sort of keep an eye out."

Just as the four of them stepped through the heavy door to the rooftop deck, Gem saw the plumes of smoke. Every direction they looked—toward Beverly Hills, toward Pico and Ruth's Chicken House, toward the Hollywood sign, or toward downtown—smoke whirled in gray-brown tornadoes toward the sky.

"Lord Almighty Jesus," Ruth whispered.

Above the sound of breaking glass, screeching breaks, and sirens, a stranger sound met their ears. Laughter and, implausibly, clinking glasses. Gem, Kelly, Clarence, and Ruth exchanged confused glances. On all sides of the rooftop crowds of neighbors stood. But one group off to the side was pouring drinks from a pitcher and laughing. Kelly shook her head, kissed her mama, and walked over toward the group. Gem followed quickly behind.

"Are you all for real?" she addressed them.

"What?" a short woman of about twenty-two with magenta hair hissed.

"People are hurt—losing their homes or businesses— maybe even their lives. And you all are thinking this is a party or something?"

Gem gently tugged Kelly's tensed forearm with its curving, brown-sugar loveliness. She yanked it away and before he knew it, Kelly snatched the drink pitcher from the woman. She went to throw it over the side, caught herself, and then hurled it against the concrete rooftop wall.

"You can't just do that to our margaritas" a man with a goatee cried.

"Now you fools know what's going on out there in the rest of the world. Fools!"

Kelly turned to join her mom and dad. Gem paused long enough to take in the looks of shock on the group's faces. The man with the goatee was the first to respond. He laughed.

Characteristic of Kelly, she not only was up early the next morning cleaning up the mess, but she also bought a Lenox drink pitcher from May Company and dropped it by the apartment of the goofballs.

Gem also recalled the day years later when Curt came home from school and tearfully told Kelly about getting in trouble.

"I guess I shoulda' stood up for the Pledge of Allegiance, Mama, but Mr. Macy told me next time he'd send me back to Africa."

Gem was incensed when he got home from work that night and heard about it. What moron would say such a thing to a seven-year-old? Kelly patted his shoulder.

"This one I got, Cupper."

Kelly turned up at Curt's school the next morning and confronted a slouching Mr. Macy and the principal about it.

"My son is an American, Irish on his WHITE father's side and proud African American on my side. You are not only ignorant but a bigot, sir."

She turned to the principal. "How many times has this clown gotten away with treating kids like this? How many more times will he?"

Kelly folded her arms as the principal flipped the propeller of an aluminum replica of The Spirit of St. Louis on his desk. Macy slouched further in his chair.

"Mrs. O'Connell, I assure you that we take this matter seriously."

And they did. Mr. Macy was dismissed shortly after the meeting. Like so many other times, Gem was so proud to call Kelly his wife and the kids' mother. Recalling those times heartened him through the Los Angeles traffic till he finally pulled into the cobblestone driveway of their Brentwood home. While he waited for the mid-century ranch garage door to open, he glanced left past the white ranch fence that surrounded the quarter acre front yard that was once a sweeping green fescue bordered by lush beds of geraniums, pansies, and roses. Now it resembled a dry riverbed. The dusty look of river rock and drought-tolerant, spiky plants made him wince. When the El Nino returns and fills up the reservoirs, he thought, we'll get our lawn back. Kelly stood at the open garage service door. Her arms were folded and Gem thought he was in trouble. He checked his watch as the garage door clanged shut.

"I'm not—"

"No, you're not late," Kelly said.

Kelly sighed as they hugged and kissed. Gem recognized her sigh as irritation. Kelly held up her iPhone.

"Read the text from Curt."

Gem looked down at her iPhone in its leopard case. He shook his head.

"He couldn't call to tell us that. A text? Really?"

"I got the text on my way home from class so I barely have had time to digest it," Kelly replied. "I got the urge to go Lorena Bobbit on him. Looks like we raised a real fool."

"I thought Shana had some good Latina Catholic sense," Gem said.

"I say we have Betty keep dinner warm and we go for a surprise visit," Kelly said.

"Isn't he on shift till seven? That's about forty-five minutes."

"My boy texts me that he's knocked up his live-in girlfriend with our grandchild, he's going to get a visit from Mama Bear."

"Oh jeez. We're going ghetto then."

"Umm hmm," Kelly said. Gem loved the southern folksy cadence of Kelly and her family and always found non-African Americans who attempted the cool dialect to be hopeless imitators. He could never get the accent or phrasing right so never tried. He admired that her years at Stanford and UCLA teaching music theory never obliterated that wondrous soul in her. He was almost envious that she was anchored by that accent that left no question where she was raised and by whom. But he also knew that he didn't mess with his wife when she flipped into it in anger.

As they pulled into the parking structure, where the Best Buy rose like a five story, glass shark fin from the corner of Beverly and Third Street, Kelly interrupted her rant that had begun as they pulled out of their driveway.

Even in all her anger, Gem still trusted her motherly instincts more than any tepid fatherly abilities he possessed. It was a long learning curve and Kelly, coming from that loving, tough, and tender household had really taught him how to be a father. Hell, she taught him how to live and be as complete as he could be, all things considered. 'No', he thought, as a wave of anxiety began to play across his chest. Their car had just entered the parking space two feet past a cement post when Kelly threw open the passenger door and headed toward Best Buy.

"There he is—stocking away CD's. My fool of a boy."

Gem followed behind her and didn't even have a second to greet Curt when she yanked Curt's iPod earbuds from his ears and grabbed his right ear. For his part, Curt's green eyes flared in surprise by the pinch and seeing his mother's face. The stack of Beyoncé CD's he was stocking fell crisply against the bin.

"We got something to talk about."

"Mom," Curt managed to get out from between clenched teeth.

Kelly led him to the glass doors and Gem kept his eyes trained on Curt's navy blue polo shirt that twisted and contorted against Kelly's steel grip. He averted his eyes from the customers on either side of the store. He dropped his head and stepped through the automatic doors. When Gem joined them in a dead end corner next to bright blue bike racks, Kelly was shaking Curt's iPod toward his face. His son's chin was against his chest, his gold-brown corkscrews of hair bobbing as he nodded.

"..And since that's how much you respect us, you better sure as hell get your low-class ass back in there and apply for a management job. 'Cause that baby—my grandchild--is going to come first before any tired dream you have of being a bass player. You hear?"

"Yes, Mama, the whole parking structure can hear you."

"Yeah? Is that right?"

Kelly turned toward a couple walking past and pointed to her son.

"See him? He's about the biggest fool you'll ever see!"

"Mama!"

23

"Kelly," Gem dared. It was Kelly's eyes' turn to flare their usually gentle black-brown at Gem.

"Well you want to add something here, then?"

"Son, your mom's right. That baby has to come first. We'll help along the way but you and Shana have to make it work."

"I plan on sitting down with her parents and getting their permission to propose."

"Oh, we get the text and they get a sit down talk, huh?" Kelly fumed. She threw the iPod at Curt's chest, folded her arms and walked away shaking her head. Gem's instinct was to follow her because, like in all other situations in their lives with the kids, Kelly handled everything. Curt looked inquisitively at his dad, but Gem simply froze. His mind drew a blank. He had no wise words or fatherly advice from his own past that would help. His early life screamed at him in times like these. He could argue, strategize, and out-negotiate anybody in Hollywood, but when it came to his kids, he was more useless than an intern. Emotional stuff baffled him and he relied on Kelly to help him sort through and understand. Gem reached out and grabbed his son by the shoulders.

"I'm glad you're starting to plan. It's also a good thing that Shana is an RN since you will need more money than you can imagine."

"Dad, I'm sure this is also going to disappoint you but we figure I'll stay home with the baby and work on my music when she's ready to go back to work. I'll pull some sort of work-at-home gig, too, to bring in some more bucks. We can do this."

"You better. Grandma over there is going to demand the best for her grandchild."

Curt rubbed his sore ear. He looked toward Kelly, nodded, and then shrugged. He popped an earbud into his left ear.

"I'm still on shift for a half hour or so."

Gem nodded and was relieved he wouldn't have to offer anymore feeble guidance. Curt started to walk away and Gem grabbed his shoulders. He turned his son's cheek toward his mouth and kissed it.

"Love you, boy—man."

Curt nodded again. He turned and popped the other earbud into his right ear. Gem watched his son step back inside the store and the swarm of laughing co-workers surround him.

Gem joined Kelly and they walked toward their car. She began to cry.

"This is so not right. He's got talent and now he's gone and done this."

"You want to head to Santa Barbara for the weekend?" he asked her. "I need a break after this and before the bullshit starts."

Kelly snorted back her tears. She wiped her eyes as they slid into the seats of the car.

"Cupper, you don't have to go to therapy if you don't think it will work. Call Dr. Friedman and cancel."

"The therapy isn't the bullshit. I just don't think I'm ready to deal with that old stuff again."

She rubbed his back. She touched his chin and raised his face toward hers.

"You're afraid, that's all. There's nothing back there that you can't deal with. I'm with you every step of the way."

They kissed softly. Gem started the car.

"Getting away sounds good," Kelly said. "Summerland even better than Santa Barbara since it's quieter."

3.

Kelly stoked the log in the glowing fireplace. Gem watched from behind as the firelight cast a silhouette through her cream-colored negligee. His eye traced the line of her right breast, down to her waist until it faded at her lovely hip. The metallic clang of the poker being replaced snapped him out of his lusty reverie. She turned toward him and brushed soot from her hands.

"You know my prime rib wasn't quite up to The Big Yellow House's par. A bit too well done for medium."

Gem shrugged and patted the white sateen sheet. A cool ocean breeze blew in from the open window. Kelly smiled and joined him.

"The chicken and dumplings were no match for your mom's," he said.

Kelly snapped off the bedside lamp and kissed Gem with the velvet gentleness of nearly three decades of love. Gem's hands moved of their own accord as if in a familiar dance of pleasure. He stroked his wife's décolletage, now a golden brown from the firelight. As the touching and kissing began to increase and they lay together naked, Gem gently pulled Kelly closer. They began to make love.

"Oh, shit," he said.

"Cupper?"

Though Gem's breathing had increased along with the passionate kissing, and his arms and legs began to tighten with sexual tension, his penis failed him. He rolled off Kelly with a grunt of failure. Embarrassed, he pulled the sheet over his useless organ.

"Cuppy," he said quietly. "Now this again. Sorry."

Kelly rolled onto her side and laid her arm across his lightly-haired chest, now peppered with gray. She kissed his shoulder then blew a raspberry into it.

"Oh, that's gonna get me in the mood."

She chuckled and laid her head on his shoulder. Her warmth reassured Gem.

"Whether we have sex in five minutes or never again, it doesn't really matter to me. You are my Cupper forever. It's not like that's the most important thing in our lives."

"Dr. Axelrode offered me a Viagra prescription at my last check-up. Maybe I should have—"

Kelly closed his lips with her index finger.

"No, let it be. This is where we are in life—older—and it's the way it's supposed to be."

It was Kelly's turn to grunt and sigh.

"What?" Gem asked.

"I just thought of that fool son of ours. Didn't we figure we might have conceived him here?"

"Too bad the family jewels worked so well then."

They laughed with a quiet joy and humor ripened over years.

"Who needs wings to fly?..." The graveled male voice sang the song. It bounced off the industrial green walls.

Gem's heart pounded as he followed the song. He passed jail cells through which scraggly faces and mean eyes peered. A horrible stink—like sewage drying in the sun—infected his nose. His legs moved sluggishly, fighting every step.

"Come on, Gemmy. Who needs wings to fly?..."

He gripped an aluminum baseball bat. He pounded on the bars of each cell he passed.

"Shut up!" he screamed.

"Who needs wings to fly? Who needs wings to FLY???"

Gem stood inside a jail cell. He faced a wall covered in graffiti and sludge and who knows what else. A hand grabbed his shoulder and swung him around. His father's face, twisted in a snarl, red and covered with oozing blisters and blackened flesh, stared at him.

27

"You belong with me Gemmy. You have wings to fly!"

Gem gasped for breath as he started awake. The room was dark except for a lace curtain that billowed and caught the moonlight. In a moment, he realized he was in the cottage at Summerland. Kelly lay on her side next to him, her breathing quiet and steady. Sweat seemed to paste his hair and back to the sheets for a moment. A sense of lightness crept up from his abdomen and his heart began to pound. Without a typical violent thought that preceded it, the pressing agony of anxiety gripped him. He had to move, he had to run, and he was trapped. With just enough composure to slide out of the bed without disturbing Kelly, he pulled on his sleep pants. In a panic to get outside, he grabbed Kelly's robe and crept out the door of the cottage.

Moist ocean air chilled his chest and neck but the sensation of being pulled into a tunnel in his mind did not abate. As if he were now watching a movie of himself, he felt his bare feet slap the hard pavement as he ran toward and then over the pedestrian bridge that crossed the 101. When they met soft dirt, he knew he was just steps away from the beach. He had to get there—no choice at this point. His father's gnarled face from his nightmare popped into his head and now he broke out into a full run. Sand kicked up around him and he could now see the silver crests of the waves. Keeping his eyes on the waves as they rolled in from the ink-black ocean, he sat down in the sand. The moon struggled to break through the thick clouds but its muted rays cast everything in a pewter light. No stars to anchor him tonight. Soft wind and the rumbling roar of the surf played in his ears. Still, though, he felt trapped a million miles inside his mind.

Am I flipping out? He thought. *We got some 'splaining to do,'* he heard Dr. Friedman's calm confidence. That along with the pressure of sand on his butt and thighs began to soothe him. Still he fought the aloneness of his anxiety and worse, a sense that he was almost back *then.* As if the last thirty-nine years had never occurred. Like this was death. He shuddered and kept his eyes steady on the crashing waves. The first anxiety attack he could recall was in his teens, and he focused on the stars to help "pull" his mind back into his body. Though the stars were a frightening mystery to him then, not the source of endless fascination for his atheist mind as they were now, staring up at them somehow grounded him. Waves would have to do tonight. He began to count each wave, and then let his mind begin to calculate the frequency of their crests. Time began to have no meaning and he suddenly felt a puff of sand hit his back.

"I been walking up and down this beach, you know," Kelly's voice said from behind. "You scared the crap outta me."

He turned around and saw Kelly. The ocean breeze pressed the folds of her negligee against her thighs and small abdomen. She pulled his violet plaid robe from off her shoulders and held it toward him.

"I think this will match your outfit a little better."

He looked down to see the hair of his chest peeking through a border of satin and lace and jumped to his feet. The robe slid easily from his shoulders and he thrust it toward Kelly.

"That would have been a cute scene if a cop wandered up," he said.

She slipped the robe over her shoulders.

"It was a little tight across the chest for you."

Normally that would have evoked a chuckle. But he was far away from himself still and the last thing he felt was normal. He tied his robe and sat back down. Kelly plopped down next to him.

"Do you want to pray?"

He turned toward her and squinted, his eyes full of incredulity. She chuckled with a girlish grin.

"You *are* becoming your mother," he shot back.

"Oh Jesus saves Green stamps!" she laughed. "As Mama says, I still got a room reserved with you in hell. At least I made you smile."

"She blames me for you giving up Jesus—I think that puts me in hell's basement."

"The God I believe in doesn't require anything other than love and forgiveness and letting everyone be. I guess that still sends me to hell, doesn't it?"

He nodded and dropped his chin. She rubbed his back.

"You seriously scared me, though. You haven't run out in panic for years. It's all back, isn't it?"

Gem felt tears begin to sting his eyes. He grabbed Kelly's hand and like the waves, it reeled him back closer to himself.

"You going to be able to make it through this again?" he asked. "Maybe you should get out this time. I would understand."

Kelly pulled her hand from his. She wrapped her arms around him and kissed his cheek.

"In sickness or health and all that shit," she said. "I meant that and always will. We can do this."

He wiped the edges of his eyes. He pressed his head deep into her embrace.

"I would have negotiated better options for you. This is a lousy deal."

Kelly wrapped her arms around him, kissed him again, and stood. She brushed sand off her body.

"You want to fight this alone for a while or head back with me?"

Gem stood up and reached for Kelly's hand. She brushed the sand off his back and butt with her left hand and finished with a little pinch. He grinned.

"I guess we'll hit breakfast tomorrow in Santa Barbara then Chumash?" he said.

"OK, but I'm only going in for quarter Keno. No craps."

They walked arm and arm back to their cottage. Gem's head still felt light, but the panic was receding to low-level anxiety. When they reached the cottage, the firelight had dwindled down to an orange glow of embers. As Kelly removed her robe, he traced the outline of her small shoulders. He grabbed her and kissed her deeply.

"I love you so much."

His body responded this time and his anxiety was forgotten for a while.

The Monday following their weekend away, Gem sat in Dr. Friedman's office. It was 9:05 and Dr. Friedman frowned at him. He held up his left index finger toward her.

"No, it's a twenty-five percent increase over the initial term," he spoke into his Bluetooth. "Tell him I just looked over the contract—he's our attorney for Christ's sake. He can manage Fox legal."

Dr. Friedman stood, straightened her hunter green skirt, and walked over to Gem. He turned away and kept speaking.

"You can get me later, all right? This is a working staycation so I'll be around. Nothing before one thirty, though, got it?"

Dr. Friedman clicked off his Bluetooth and pulled it from his ear. She slid it into her skirt pocket.

"If you're a good boy, you'll get this back when we're finished today. Now let's get going."

Dr. Friedman peeled open the orange cardboard cover and glanced at the title page. She read:

"'Looking for Dad'. Hmmm. Clever title."

Gem reached for the manuscript and Dr. Friedman slapped his hand away. He could feel the burn of embarrassment set his face ablaze. Writing may have been something he abandoned, but having someone read his words and be critical from the outset made him feel naked. He realized that was probably part of this therapy so he leaned back into the sofa cushion and tried to relax. Dr. Friedman read a few pages before she paused and looked at him over her horned-rim reading glasses.

"First person—a perfect therapeutic choice. But wait."

She handed the manuscript to Gem. She nodded.

"What?" He asked.

"I think it will best if you read it aloud. We can then pause and discuss pertinent issues relating to your father as they arise. Will that bother you?"

"Of course it will bother me but isn't that what I'm here for? Unless you think it would be smarter for you to read the whole thing through and then we talk. I could just take today and finish up--"

"Hell no. You know me well enough to understand that I like to avoid psycho-babble and jargon, right?"

Gem nodded. He wiped away a bead of sweat from his left temple. Socializing always made him sweat a bit and therapy sessions always seemed to amplify it. He handed the manuscript back to her.

"This is no time for avoidance behavior," she said.

She raised her left index finger, the nail polished a pale periwinkle. She tapped her upper left brow.

"It's good that you're sweating, too. Means you're feeling vulnerable and that's a good place to start."

Dr. Friedman fanned the manuscript to reach the end. She then went back to the beginning and pinched sections of pages together to roughly divide the manuscript into five sections.

"This is about 130 pages it looks like. You stopped numbering them manually after 49 for some reason."

Gem shrugged. "Really?"

"Yep."

Dr. Friedman slid her hand about midway through the manuscript and her eyebrows furrowed. She reached into the section and Gem suddenly heard the crinkling sound of cellophane. Dr. Friedman extracted a cellophane package with faded and chipped paint but held rigid by a thin, white piece of cardboard stained with oil and dark material. She held it up by one corner and grimaced.

"Oh my God!" Gem said. "A cupcake wrapper! *The* cupcake wrapper!"

Recoiling, Dr. Friedman extended the remnant toward Gem, clutching it with her thumb and forefinger to avoid further contact. He took it carefully.

Gem now regarded the cupcake package with its worn "H" and "S's" from the Hostess label. He turned it gently.

"You're not going to believe it but I have wondered about this for years," he said softly.

Dr. Friedman looked at him over her reading glasses.

"Seems quite important to you-why?"

"It's the cupcake wrapper from our first date—Kelly and me. I thought it got thrown away years ago. And it must be the last time I read this, too."

"Sweet. Then it's a good talisman to remind you of your happy life now. You might as well hang on to it because as we dig into all this, I'm sure you'll need it."

Gem nodded and gingerly placed the wrapper on the side table. Dr. Friedman handed the manuscript back to Gem. "Read."

4.

I gave up on a father in the sky or anywhere else for that matter. God, karma, meditation, the whole spiritual bit when I watched my girlfriend die of cancer last year. We both would have been twenty-one as I write this. I'm going to graduate in June, I have a new girl named Kelly, and my old girlfriend is dead.

I prayed and prayed to Him to save her. But the day before she died, I finally realized I was just talking to myself. She died and that was the end. Either God was punishing me again for no reason, God didn't have the power, I was paying again for some past-life karma, or God and the rest of it was just something I bought into to feel safe. I didn't want to fear death, or worse, that all of it was pointless atoms at play. But just because I believed in something like billions of other people didn't make it real. I threw out the saints with the holy water, the meditation with enlightenment, and all the other hocus-pocus mystical crap at that moment. Done. That was years after I found out who my father really was. 'Father, who art' that had once meant something peaceful later became something terrifying.

When I was little, though, faith gave me a feeling of warmth. Almost as if I was wrapped in a blanket all the time. I had faith in the priests, in their satin robes they wore at Mass, in the tabernacle, and Jesus, of course. I believed I could talk to Jesus any time I needed something. I had my dad and mom still then, too. Every Sunday, it was St. Joan of Arc's in Lomita for church, and then the parish hall for doughnuts and punch. I can still recall the taste of fruit punch mixed with the crunch of a sugary doughnut. But all that was going to change once the astronauts walked on the moon.

I remember the moon landing so well because it was the last

34

time I sat between my mom and dad to watch TV.

"Gemmy, can you believe what we're watching?" Dad asked me as I sat on his lap. Mom and Dad had turned out all the lights in the living room so that we could better see the screen of our black and white set.

"The moon is so far away," Mom added. "It's a true miracle."

Just as the screen showed the first astronaut step out of the lunar module, I couldn't resist. I jumped up off my Dad's lap and ran out the front door. The moon was real bright so I was just sure I would see the lunar module and the astronauts, too. But all I saw was the big, white moon. Nothing else. I stared for a couple of minutes before Mom showed up behind me.

"What are you doing?"

I pointed at the moon and sighed. I dropped my head and started for the front porch.

"Oh, you thought you could see the astronauts," she said behind me. "Sorry, Gemmy."

The next day, Dad screamed with excitement in the bleachers as I hit another home run for my pee wee league team, The Tigers. The worst part about hitting home runs was the run around the bases. As I made my way toward first base, I saw Dad jumping up and down and scattering his bag of sunflower seeds all over the other spectators. It made me laugh as I continued on to the other bases, jogging slowly. Running was the only thing I didn't like about playing ball. It was so boring.

I never quite understood why Dad got so happy for something that was so easy for me to do. I always kept my eye on the ball, whether at bat or fielding at third base. My hands followed wherever I looked and each time the ball cracked against the bat or stung as it hit my glove, it made sense to me. I never thought about not following the ball. But it made Dad so happy and that's all I ever wanted was for him to be happy with me.

As I huffed and rounded third towards home, my team, in a swarm of black and orange jerseys, came running toward me from the dugout. They screamed wildly. That was the other thing I didn't really care about: winning or losing the game. What was so hard about following the ball and winning? The same things happened to me at school. I was in first grade and whether it was adding in math, or reading aloud and answering questions about what we read, or handwriting, all of it was easy for me. I handed my first report card to

Dad the day after our last little league game in fall.

"Your first report card?" he asked.

Dad was so proud when I brought home my first report card—all A's. I shrugged and went in to watch 'The Three Stooges' on Channel 52 Corona.

"Gemmy, you going to watch 'Star Trek' with me tonight?" Dad asked.

Watching 'Star Trek' or any TV show with my dad was the most joyful time in my life. It was even better than bedtime stories my mom sometimes told me as a little kid. Except for Disneyland when Dad would take me on the Matterhorn, or cracking peanuts together at a Dodger game, watching TV with Dad was like nothing else.

"Can't wait to see what happens with Captain Kirk and Spock, Daddy."

"Sorry, son, you'll have to stand back."

A policeman pulled me aside one night the following week as I stood at our front door. Just as I noticed that the whole neighborhood seemed to have gathered on the front sidewalk, partially highlighted from the red police car light, Mom pulled me back into the house. Two police officers pushed past us and pulled Dad between them and down the porch. The handcuffs shined and reflected the yellow, anti-bug bulb we had in our front porch light. Another policeman carried a cardboard box of stuff he had taken from the rafters in the garage.

"Daddy. No!" I screamed. Mom pulled me further into the house and slammed the front door. She started to cry. It all made me so sad that first I cried, too. But the confusion of it all started to make me angry.

Not long after Dad was taken away, Mom grew more and more quiet. She stopped curling and spraying her thick, honey-blonde hair and only sometimes wore her favorite lipstick, Avon misted apple. Her gray-green eyes that were usually surrounded by soft, gold-brown eye shadow seemed to be puffy and red most days. Mom was once the prettiest lady on the block. But no longer.

She wouldn't tell me why Dad was taken away. I did have a theory: he got caught playing doctor with two little neighbor girls. He was too old to do that—even I knew it was bad at the time. I also saw some bad pictures when the police came back and looked through the house another time. I wanted to tell Mom but the policeman said I shouldn't say anything to anybody about it. I assumed he meant Mom, too, so I obeyed. But Mom stopped talking about Dad after a month or so, and I wasn't allowed to ask anything about him, either. I missed him, but Mom didn't seem to care about what I felt one way or another. She spent a lot of time in bed when she wasn't working at the rectory during school days. We began going to church more often, even in the middle of the week.

Not that I minded then. When we walked into the church, there was something about the three-story-high ceiling with its open, oak beams and white plaster. I imagined angels could be floating about because it was so high. And the hand-carved wood Stations of the Cross with arched windows above told the story of the Crucifixion. The wall behind the altar was as high as the ceiling and it almost glowed from the red satin draped from the ceiling to the floor. Jesus up on the crucifix looked so real and odd with the satin behind it. But when the choir sang "Alleluia," and the priest raised his hands from his robe of white and purple, the white wafers became Jesus. I didn't think of it as transubstantiation in the house of God; it was more like the magic from 'Bewitched' or 'I Dream of Jeannie'. That's when I realized I wanted to be a priest—to have that magic power. Maybe if I were a priest, I could make Mom happy again, too. Or so I thought.

One particular day, to get Mom out of bed, I decided to surprise her. I took the hall hamper and covered it with a green bath towel. A new roll of toilet paper and two bobby pins crossed over the top held up a green washcloth to make a tabernacle. I added a crown of loose leaf paper I had cut into a thin strip with triangles on top. The last thing I did was grab a half roll of Necco wafers and another green bath towel. I wrapped the bath around my shoulders and pinned it with a safety pin.

"Mom, come here for a sec I wanna show you something," I hollered.

"I'm tired, Gemmy. What?"

"Just please come here for a sec."

Mom sighed and the bed creaked. Her feet clomped and then paused at her bedroom door. She cracked it open slowly. I grabbed a Necco and raised it over my head:

"This is my body. The body of the new and everlasting covenant…" I said recalling some of the words from Mass.

Mom stepped out her bedroom door, pulling the belt of her light-blue, quilted robe to tighten it. Her hair was a mess but her eyes suddenly sparkled. She smiled as she put her hands on her hips.

"What are you doing?"

"Performing Mass. I'm going to be a priest when I grow up."

She reached over and touched the tabernacle. Her eyes surveyed the green towel on the makeshift altar. I thought she might be angry with me when she ran her hands down my shoulders and ended at the safety pin holding my towel cassock.

"You do all this for me?"

I nodded. I gestured for her to kneel.

"Kneel down so I can give you communion."

She kneeled. I pushed her hair back in place. Now she was ready.

"Body of Christ," I said.

Mom closed her eyes and leaned her head back.

"Amen," she said.

I placed the Necco wafer on her tongue. She closed her mouth and grimaced. Her eyes popped open.

"Wintergreen. Yuk," she said.

I shrugged. It was communion to me. I had performed the Mass magic. She sat on the floor.

"You really want to be a priest?"

I nodded with excitement, so happy that my priest magic could make Mom feel happy again. Pretty soon, I built the hamper altars and performed Mass not just when Mom was sad in bed but also on St. Patrick's Day, Easter, and just about every other holiday. Every time, Mom smiled and felt better. I really believed I had the magic of a priest.

But all that was before the voice started in my head. It wasn't some crazy voice telling me I was Napoleon or Jesus. It was a voice that was strange to hear at first, but then I grew more comfortable with it. The voice always told me what was real, the truth, I guess. But not the philosophical or religious ideas of truth—just the bare facts of what I was seeing or thinking. The first time I heard the voice was also the first Christmas without Dad.

"Silent Night, Holy Night..." the entire church choir showed up Christmas Eve and sang on our front lawn. Mom and I stood at the open front door. Even though the night air was cold and damp, we stayed until the choir finished 'Oh Holy Night.'

"Gem, run inside and get the box of See's."

I brought out the two-pound box of chocolate candies Mom got as a gift from the rectory and made my way over to the choir members. Mrs. Wagner, my godmother, and one of the other ladies in the choir, went and stood next to Mom. Mrs. Wagner's thick shoulders hunched over and it looked as if she were crying. It embarrassed me so I looked down at her thick legs sticking out from her brown skirt. Sausages in knee-highs, I thought, and that made me giggle.

"Is that a Bordeaux?" Mr. Farrington asked as he plucked one of the chocolates from the box.

"Hand me a scotchmallow, will you?" I heard Mrs. Smith say.

"Hey, Gem," Mom said from behind. "Mrs. Wagner just saw Santa's sleigh. You better get in your room and wait."

I would have dropped the box of candy if Mr. Farrington hadn't caught it. Santa was almost at my house and I had to hide in the bedroom or he wouldn't stop.

"Don't you all gotta go? Santa won't come if you don't leave!" I said.

"Hurry, Gem. He's almost here."

I ran past my Mom and into the house. Slamming the door of my bedroom, I hurried over to the shutters and cracked them for a look. I saw Mom on the porch.

"Close the shutters, Gem, and turn off your light!" she said.

My heart pounded and I listened for Santa's sleigh bells as I turned off the bedroom light. The orange, red, green, white, and blue of our outside Christmas lights glowed warm and soft behind the closed slats of my shutters. I leaned against the wall, my heart racing as I thought about what Santa might bring: an Etch-a-Sketch? New watercolor paints? Sillysand? A new Wilson baseball glove? I felt so nervous that I started counting the slats of the maple shutters. Over and over again until I grew tired and closed my eyes. Something thudded against the wall. Breath squeezed from my lungs: Santa!

I couldn't resist. I had to see his sled, and the reindeer. I pulled the bar on the shutter and a present wrapped in green paper with red bells seemed to float past my eyes. I tried to see if it was Santa carrying the present, but instead of his red coat, I saw something else: a brown sport coat. Confused, I opened the shutter enough to see Mr. Farrington pass through the open front door. Just behind him came Mrs. Wagner with a present wrapped in blue foil and a yellow ribbon. Could they be helping Santa unload?

I opened the other shutter that faced the lawn, and there was Mrs. Nielsen's blue Camaro. Its passenger door stood open and presents were heaped on the front seat. Where was Santa's sleigh? The reindeer? I thrust the shutters closed. What did all this mean? I felt nervous again and started counting the slats. But this time, when I'd reach the last one, number fifteen, I counted backwards.

A few minutes later, Mom opened my bedroom door and said Santa had come. When I stepped into the living room, six people from the choir stood next to the tree that was loaded underneath with presents. They smiled at me.

"Merry Christmas, Gem!"

I almost felt like Charlie Brown when his scraggily tree was magically transformed into a decorated, full tree. I couldn't talk and I felt paralyzed by the excitement.

Mrs. Wagner grabbed the present wrapped in the blue foil tied with the yellow ribbon and handed it to me.

"Here's your first present from Santa!"

That snapped me out of my stupor. I saw her carry this present up the porch and into the house a little while ago. Santa's sled wasn't anywhere nearby. Was she lying to me?

A six-year-old is supposed to believe in Santa, the voice suddenly said in my head. *Pretend you still believe in him or you may not get to keep the presents.*

What was that voice in my head? Was it the guardian angel Mom said was always near me? Was it something else? Was I bad for thinking like that? These mixed up ideas jumped around inside me even as I tore into the blue foil. What was wrong with me?

"Thank you, Mrs. Wagner," I said. "I wonder what Santa brought me."

The next time I heard the voice was a few months later. Mom was getting sadder and sadder, but I didn't know why. Mom was often tired from the work at the rectory and now as a cafeteria helper at Bishop Montgomery High School. She talked about the rent, how much food cost, and how we were eating up all the savings but I didn't really understand.

Whenever I would ask about Dad now, she would put her hand over my mouth, and then cross herself. I prayed every night for God to bring Dad back, and I would have talks with Mary and Jesus about it, but nothing worked.

About seven months after Dad was taken away, Mom had to go to a courthouse in downtown Los Angeles. Mrs. Wagner came and sat with me for the day. Mrs. Wagner said Mom had to go to a special hearing because Dad did some sick things that they were going to put him away for. She told me to pray for him. I prayed to God, Jesus, and

Mary that they would let Dad come home.

Mom returned home around the time I was watching "Beach Blanket Bingo" on Channel 7. Mrs. Wagner practically jumped off the couch to greet Mom at the door. I looked up and saw Mom wiping tears from her eyes and shaking her head. Mrs. Wagner held her a moment.

"Well does Daddy getta come home ?"

Mom shook her head, burst into tears, and ran out of living room. Mrs. Wagner looked at me and shook her head.

"You're going to have to be more grown up about all this and watch what you ask your mother."

Mrs. Wagner stepped past me and down the hall to Mom and Dad's bedroom. She opened the door and I could hear muffled crying and talking after she closed it. I just didn't understand why Dad couldn't come back home if he was sick.

"A big change in the weather is on its way," Dr. George Fishbeck, the local weatherman, said on TV. He held his right hand over his heart and smiled widely under his moustache. When the movie started again and Annette was talking to Frankie about some caper, I forgot about Dad for awhile.

As time passed, I stopped asking about Dad. It usually made me angry whenever I thought about him. And all the time I prayed, nothing changed. When Mom got sick, I didn't even bother praying for help.

It started with the little birthmark on her left leg that had appeared a couple years before it started itching. Mom had tried rubbing alcohol, peroxide, even calamine lotion to get the black, ugly "little map of Italy" she called it to stop itching. I had just started second grade at St. Joan of Arc's when she woke up one morning worried about a lump under her left arm.

"I probably have the flu or something," she told me as we walked to the parish school. She kissed me and handed me my white lunch bag with plums printed on it.

"I'll pick you up after my appointment."

That was the beginning of one doctor's appointment after another till the one where they stuck the lump with a needle and did the biopsy. Malignant melanoma is what the surgeon at the City of Hope said to me and Mrs. Wagner just after they finished removing the lump and several lymph nodes. That's when Mrs. Wagner started

41

staying with us to help.

But the chemo therapy and radiation treatments didn't help. Mom took to staying in bed. On her best days, she could get out of bed just long enough to throw up. On her worst, she couldn't talk and Mrs. Wagner or I would take turns sitting next to her feeding her ice chips. Mom couldn't attend church any longer so Father Christopher would come by on Sunday afternoons and do Mass for Mom. Praying helped as much as the chemo and radiation—not really at all. I even quit making altars and doing Mass because that didn't make Mom feel any better.

At the beginning of September, just a couple months after Mom had been diagnosed, I was adjusting the fan near the window to cool her down. It was a humid day with no breeze coming in from Torrance Beach to help. Mom's skin, already transparent from her wasting, now shined with perspiration. As I turned back toward her to take my seat, she reached out for my hand. I took hers and it was a weightless thing that reminded me of my skeleton costume from last Halloween.

"You okay, Mama?"

Her eyes were caves as dark as the tar around the base of the front yard telephone pole. I didn't understand where the gray-green had gone. She looked me over from the top of my head to my chin, as if she were trying to remember who I was or maybe memorize who I was. At least that's what it felt like.

"Gemmy," she whispered. I didn't want her to talk because it seemed to hurt her. She also now breathed so fast that the dent at the base of her neck pulsed almost as if I could see her heartbeat.

"Don't be afraid. I'm not."

I didn't know what to say. All I knew is I wanted to hug her but couldn't because she was so frail and weak. As if she knew what I was thinking, she squeezed my hand as tight as she could.

"You will always be my good boy. God has special plans for you."

She let go of my hand and reached out with her weak index finger and touched my chest. It felt as if a butterfly had landed there.

"I'm with you here forever," she managed to whisper.

She dropped her hand back to her side and began to breathe more slowly. I recognized by now that her painkiller was taking effect. I lifted her arm and placed it under the blanket. For a few seconds, I watched her face as she slept. Her skin was almost transparent as it stretched over her once beautiful cheek bones. The skin of her eyelids was cluttered with webs of tiny veins. Her mouth was drawn tight and she made a soft suckling sound. I couldn't stand it anymore so I ran out of the room. I guess tears were streaming down my face because the air stung as I threw open the front door. My stomach was in knots. The next day, they took Mom to Torrance Memorial. When I watched them wheel her down the porch and place her in the ambulance, the voice spoke: *This is it. You're never going to see her again.* I ran to the back of the ambulance but the driver pushed me aside as he closed the door. Mrs. Wagner patted my shoulder from behind.

That Friday Sister Delores called me into the coat room. I didn't know what I had done but I flinched and held out my wrists.

"No, no, Gem. You're not in trouble."

Then she did something unexpected and odd. She pulled me to her and hugged me. I looked up at that face, usually like a hawk in horned-rims, and saw an expression like a sad mom. Maybe even tears in her eyes?

"Get your books into your book bag. You're dismissed for the day."

Confused, I ran back into class and pulled my books from under my desk chair. Everyone stared at me sure that I was really going to get it. But I shrugged and shook my head. Back inside the coat room, I crammed the books into my green vinyl book bag. The zipper broke and tore into the side of my book bag. I looked up at Sister Delores, convinced I was about to get in trouble. But she just shook her head and patted my back.

"You get yourself home and don't dawdle."

I nodded and ran out of the coat room. I was trying to figure out what 'dawdle' meant and concluded that like everything else, it must have been a sin so I wouldn't do it even if I knew what it meant. Once again, I figured my soul was safe from hell for now.

Mrs. Wagner wasn't out front in her black Corvair to pick me up so I walked home from school. I was glad that I got to leave school early and start my weekend, but I didn't know why. That didn't matter and I began to skip and drag my fingers along the front yard fences I passed. When I finally turned the corner onto our street, I saw several cars parked in front of the house. Was Mrs. Wagner having a Tupperware party again? I recognized Mr. Farrington's Volkswagen Bug and Mrs. Nielsen's Camaro. Was the choir having practice at our house? My chest suddenly felt tight.

Your Mom is gone away like your dad now, the voice said. *You're like an orphan and nobody's gonna want you.*

I didn't know what to think about that so I ran toward home. As I got to the walkway, Mrs. Wagner stepped out the front door and walked toward me. Her eyes were red and she bit her lower lip. She stopped and stood between the two junipers on either side of the front path.

"Gem, you need to come inside and sit for a second."

It seemed the entire choir stood inside the living room. Everyone stared at me as I followed Mrs. Wagner into the kitchen. Mrs. Wagner pulled out one of the gold, vinyl kitchen chairs and patted it for me to sit. She grabbed my arms and held them in her thick fingers.

"Gem, your Mother has gone to heaven."

Mrs. Wagner might as well have pushed me over. My head felt like an expanding balloon and I thought I was going to throw up. And how did the voice know she was gone?

"Why?" was all I could squeeze from my pinched throat.

Mrs. Wagner bit her lower lip and I could see tears build on her eyelids.

"She just couldn't make it, Gem. The disease was too much for her. She died."

My chest and stomach felt like someone was bending me backwards. Fog seemed to fill my head up now.

"Gem, it's okay if you cry."

I almost did, but then I stopped.

She's in heaven where everyone's supposed to be, so why cry? The voice said.

"So I'm like an orphan, then?"

I wasn't sure. I knew from the movies that a kid without a mom and dad was an orphan. But my dad was still alive and I almost asked about him until Mrs. Wagner pulled me to her. Her skin smelled like stale apples.

"We'll find a way to take care of you. Don't you worry."

But I was very worried. Dad was taken away and I missed him. Everything went crazy after that. Mom was gone now, too, and I felt a million awful things. I was scared of what was going to happen to me, too. But then something occurred to me and I asked Mrs. Wagner.

"So Mommy's in heaven now, like an angel?"

"Yes."

"She's now sort of like a guardian angel, then?"

"Yes, I suppose that's right, Gem."

"So she's with me all the time and can see what I'm doing?"

"I'm not sure that's part of the catechism, Gem, but it sounds about right."

Mrs. Wagner stayed with me for the next couple of weeks. Every morning, I would wake up and for the first few minutes I would forget that Mom had died. I would smell breakfast cooking, and for a second, I expected that when I turned the corner I would see Mom in the kitchen smashing the boiled egg onto the buttered toast for my favorite breakfast. But I'd walk in and see Mrs. Wagner in her pink robe frying bacon and then I'd remember. Every time I would start to think about how my Mom colored with me, or tucked me into bed, or anything else, the voice would say the same thing: *She's in heaven where she's supposed to be, so why cry?* Just like the way I would get mad when I'd ask Mom about Dad, now I got mad every time the voice would say this. But I would be careful with not being bad because Mom could see everything I was doing. I even started to be careful about bad thoughts because I figured she would know those, too. But the voice was different from my thoughts and I wondered if Mom could hear the voice, too.

The voice was going to say something else soon.

Mrs. Wagner picked up my breakfast plate the day after Mom's funeral and underneath I found two small pieces of clear plastic about the size and shape of Pez candies. Attached to the top of each piece was a clear, ruby-red thing shaped like an aspirin. They reminded me of the red tablets the dentist sometimes had me chew to check for cavities. I picked them up.

"What are these? Did something break?"

Mrs. Wagner flipped a dishtowel onto her shoulder and came back to the table. She squinted as I held them up. Then her eyes opened wide.

"You don't know what those are?" she asked.

"Nope."

"For sure?"

"Nuh-uh."

"They're special seeds. You go plant them in the backyard and water them. And make sure to water them every day, Gem."

I grabbed up the seeds and rushed to the backyard. The best

45

part of our house was the backyard. It wasn't just some crabgrass and rusty laundry poles. A low cinderblock wall topped by a chain-link fence ran along one side of our backyard. This separated our yard from the sump. The sump was a giant ditch that was a full square block. During winter rainstorms, it filled with the gutter run-off and rain since our streets had no storm drains. The effect was a murky, dark pond where reeds, leathery bushes, and all forms of weeds grew. Ducks, frogs, crickets, garter snakes, and mice occupied it. It was a place of mystery—someone said a kid disappeared in it back in 1951—and a comfort to me. Crows were always cawing, sounding just like Indian war cries in the movies.

One cawed just as I rolled the seeds between my fingers while I decided where I should plant them. The wall along the sump wasn't good because it received too much shade. The seeds would need sun so I settled on a corner near the faded, burgundy-red stained fence at the front of the yard. It was the same spot we set the light blue, hard plastic kiddy pool we bought at White Front every summer. So many times I could remember splashing in those pools and then raising my cold, wet face to the sun. No place was quite as special as my backyard with the mysterious sump.

I planted them, but I didn't know what could possibly grow. I watered the spot for the next few days. Even though I couldn't see anything growing, I was getting excited to see what these things might be. The next Saturday morning, I found out, but not before Mrs. Wagner sat down on the couch to talk with me.

Her thick thighs made the sides of her gray skirt bulge. I sat down next to her, but felt as though I was balancing on a slide. She really made the couch cushion sink.

"Gem, I have something important to tell you."

She looked as serious as she looked when she told me about Mom. My stomach tightened.

"I have to go back east to help my daughter with her family. I can't take care of you anymore."

I shrugged. I didn't know what that meant.

"Gem, some nice people from Los Angeles County are going to help you."

"They're gonna come stay here with me?"

You know what she means, the voice said.

"No. They're going to take you to a nice place with other kids like you. You'll have a nice time."

46

She means an orphanage.

My stomach tightened so much at the word that chills shot through my body. I just couldn't go live in an orphanage. I almost couldn't breathe.

"An orphanage? Why can't somebody come and live with me here at home? "

"That's not the way it works, Gem. I'm afraid you're going to have to go to the county foster care home."

Mrs. Wagner pulled a pink hanky from her skirt pocket and blew her nose. She sounded like she was starting to cry.

"That's an orphanage? Why? Daddy's still alive. I'm not an orphan."

"*He* can't take care of you, Gem."

"But why not?"

"He just can't. You understand, don't you?"

I had no idea what she meant. But I nodded because once again, there was something I was supposed to understand.

"Just where is he?"

Mrs. Wagner's mouth pinched like she was mad at me. She shook her head.

"Out in the desert in the California Men's--."

That was the first time I ever heard where Dad was.

"'Men's' what? Are you sure I couldn't go live there with him?"

"Now you know you can't do that, don't you?"

I didn't. But I figured by the way she said it, I was supposed to know.

"Yep."

"Let's not talk about that anymore then, hmm?"

I nodded. I folded my hands in my lap and made my thumbs wrestle with each other.

"Gem?"

"What about Grandma O'Connell? My other grandma and grandpas are in heaven, but she's still alive."

"She's in a convalescent hospital in Minnesota."

"She's sick too? Everybody's sick."

"No—she's just very old and frail."

"What about Mr. Farrington?"

"Too many kids of his own, and he's just lost his job."

"Mrs. Nielsen?"

"Nope."

47

"No one else in the whole choir can take care of me?"

"No, Gem."

"Can't I go with you, Mrs. Wagner? I mean, you're my godmother and all. Doesn't that mean you're supposed to take care of me?"

"No, Gem, that's not what it means. I would take you with me in a second, if I could. But it just can't be. You understand."

Again I thought there was something I should know already so I nodded to make her feel better. Mrs. Wagner pulled the hanky from her skirt pocket and blew her nose again.

"Gem, why don't you go and see what grew from those special seeds."

Something grew! I forgot all about the county orphanage as I ran for the back door. When I got to where I had planted the seeds, I stopped in shock. There, growing like Jack's beanstalk, was a huge bush. As I stepped closer to it, I saw what grew from it: bubblegum!

"A bubblegum tree!" Mrs. Wagner said. "How about that?"

I couldn't believe it. I saw Bazooka gum, balls of cherry and grape gum, even ropes of Bubb's Daddy gum wrapped in blue-striped plastic. All the bright colors and different shapes of gum, even a packet of Juicy Fruit and Doublemint, all of it on the tree, grown from those weird seeds. It was like some sort of crazy Christmas tree, and it was all for me.

Then I noticed something else: the leaves on the tree looked just like the bushes that grew in front of the breezeway between the garage and the kitchen. But the breezeway bushes weren't bubblegum trees. Now I was confused, but still excited about the gum. That was until I saw the tape. Clear pieces of Scotch tape held each piece of the gum to the tree branches. I wanted to believe in the tree, I really did. But the tape gave it all away. I toyed with the tape holding one of the Bubb's Daddy packages. Mom came into my mind, and then I pictured Dad out in the desert somewhere dressed like a sheik. Then the image of a movie orphanage popped into my head. I dropped my hand to my side and looked up and down the bubblegum tree. It seemed like there was nothing a kid could believe in anymore.

Don't let her know you understand this is fake, the voice said.

"Gem, why don't you go ahead and pluck the gum from the tree?"

"Wow, Mrs. Wagner. I just never saw a bubblegum tree before."

Just then, a crow flew over our heads and landed on a tall bush in the sump. It seemed to be eyeing the bubblegum tree. 'Caw!' it screamed at us. The sound of the crow made me cry. I realized I wouldn't be hearing them much longer. I turned away as Mrs. Wagner stepped up from behind.

She ran toward the crow and he flew off. She stopped at the short cinder block wall and leaned forward to look through the chain-link fence. She had seen the sump every day she had been with me, and had even wondered when the city of Torrance was going to put in storm drains so that the neighborhood's gutters would no longer drain into the sump. I didn't think she cared about it, or the dragonflies that skimmed its foamy surface during the day, or the frogs that croaked from its weedy edges at night. I plucked the gum but kept a curious eye on her.

"The frogs make a racket at night, but all the trees and bushes growing around the water remind me of Wisconsin. There was a swimming hole near where I grew up."

I had rolled the bottom of my T-shirt to hold the gum I plucked, and the load felt heavy as I walked up to Mrs. Wagner's side.

"You didn't finish plucking all the gum."

"I just wanted to look at the sump for a sec."

Mrs. Wagner turned and her mouth tightened.

"You go pluck the rest of the gum now. I'll help you."

She walked back to the bubblegum tree and I followed her. She rolled her apron up and filled it with gum. I never had seen so much different gum in one place – it was almost like Halloween.

"Gosh, Mrs. Wagner. Bubblegum trees sure grow a lot of gum!"

She laughed and hugged me from behind. The last time Mrs. Wagner would hug me would be just a week away, right before Halloween.

I stood at the cinder block wall of the sump. I closed my eyes and breathed in the earthy, almost sulfur smell. I held a paper grocery bag tightly in my arms. Everything that was important to me was in that bag: my sixty-four box of crayons and drawing pad; the magic tricks book from The Haunted Mansion my dad had helped me pick out on my only visit to Disneyland; a wiffle ball from my last game with my dad; a photo of me as a baby in my mom's arms; a bunch of school spelling and math tests with A's. I glanced down and had the urge to try to dig up my lost time capsule coffee can. Two years before, I had filled the coffee can with everything that I thought would be important for a six–year-old. I had climbed the sump fence, and dug a hole just on the other side of the cinder block wall. I was careful to choose high ground that never flooded when the rains came. I stuck the can in the hole. I tied together two plastic rulers with an old shoe lace in an 'x' form and set them on top of the hole. I had just been able to make out the edges of the rulers under dead leaves and muck. A crow cawed and then Mrs. Wagner honked the horn. My daydream was over.

"I guess I'll never see you again," I said to the sump. Before any tears erupted, I turned and ran toward the car.

5.

It took an hour to drive from Torrance to Hollywood due to traffic. I had spotted the Hollywood sign high in the hills from the San Diego Freeway as we drove north. Mrs. Wagner and I had been playing the name-the-make-and-model game my dad taught me when we drove to Disneyland. I knew lots of cars.

"Volkswagen Beetle!" I yelled.

"Chevy Impala!" she answered back and pointed.

"Cadillac Coup de Ville!" I yelled.

"Okay, Gem. I give—you win!"

Once we exited the Hollywood Freeway and drove down Melrose, I noticed the white water tower with the word 'Paramount' standing out in bright blue.

"Am I going to live in Hollywood?"

Mrs. Wagner nodded. She pursed her lips and I thought I was about to get it.

"Only because Maryvale has no room right now. They referred us to this place."

She grabbed my hand with her right hand as she gripped the wheel tighter with her left. She squeezed so tight that it felt like my fingers were turning into balloons.

"You promise me that you won't get into any trouble. There are a lot of sinful people here in Hollywood."

"Okay, but Mrs. Wagner?"

"What, Gem?

"Would you let go of my hand. It's starting to hurt."

"The Brady Bunch!" I hollered a few minutes later.

"What on earth are you—"

51

"The blue and white Paramount mountain always ends 'The Brady Bunch.' That's the same mountain on that water tower. I knew I recognized it."

I wondered if the Bradys lived at Paramount. They were funny but they weren't like my favorite show, 'The Partridge Family.' I kept my eyes on the water tower and it grew bigger and bigger as we drove on. It had what looked like a little walkway around the bottom of the tank and I wondered what Hollywood looked like from there. I decided I would find out some day.

The Paramount water tower disappeared as we turned up the last street but I realized the studio stood only a block or so away. When we pulled up in front of the big, old house, it looked like a mansion with eight windows and a porch surrounded by columns with a balcony above it. It reminded me of Elvis's house on the cover of the Graceland album. Everybody on TV lived in big, two story houses so somehow, it made me feel special that I was going to live in one. A metal and brick fence surrounded the house and it reminded me of the fence around the sump. My stomach tightened and my throat slammed shut. I thought I was going to cry. *Why cry? Nobody cares anymore,'* the voice said. As Mrs. Wagner put the car in park and shut off the engine, I read the metal sign hung on the front of the brick and wrought-iron gate: 'Hollygrove'.

"Here we are, Gem," Mrs. Wagner said.

But I couldn't move my legs. I imagined the sump, the dragonflies skimming the water, the crows in the bushes, and it was as if I were numb. I looked down at my chewed fingernails and picked the skin around my index fingernail. Mrs. Wagner poked my shoulder.

"Didn't you hear me? We're here."

I nodded. I sighed and slid out of the front seat.

We sat in wooden chairs in the middle of a front room dominated by a large staircase with iron rails and dirty, burgundy carpet. A woman sat at a desk. Mrs. Wagner played with her light blue, clear rosary beads and I sat next to her. But I really wasn't paying much attention because I was drawing a picture of Samantha from the TV show 'Bewitched'. Last night, she was in England as one of King Henry the Eighth's wives, and I wanted to see if I could make up another story about her in England. My box of crayons – an off-brand I got in my Christmas stocking, not Crayola – sat on the chair next to my paper bags of clothes and things. The woman behind the desk said we would have to wait a while in this lobby, so Mrs. Wagner said I could color. My sketchpad was spread open on my lap.

Just as I was coloring in Samantha's dress with light moon shapes on a black background, I heard tennis shoes slapping on the tile floor. I looked up and saw three kids run past. The woman behind the desk stood up and clapped her hands once.

"Back to the dormitory, now!" she yelled.

Her hooked nose and crinkled face made her look just like the Wicked Witch of the West. I glanced at the kids to see if she scared them as much as she scared me with her scratchy, high-pitched voice. They didn't seem afraid. I realized that they were much older than I – probably as old as twelve or thirteen. One of them pointed at me, and the other two laughed before they clomped up the stairs.

The front door of the house creaked open and a woman with black curly hair stepped up to the desk. I could only see her from behind in her dark blue skirt and black coat. Her voice sounded like she was out of breath. She paused and set her briefcase down as she raised her sunglasses.

"I'm Maureen Johnson. I'm here for Gem O'Connell."

The woman behind the desk pointed past Maureen toward me. Maureen turned and I now noticed she was black with Tootsie Roll-brown eyes. They seemed to sparkle at me. Her curly hair bounced like black springs on her shoulders as she walked over to greet me. She reminded me of Diahann Carroll, the actress who played 'Julia' on TV at the time. She was very pretty and my heart sped up when she greeted me.

"Hi, Gem. I'm Maureen, your social worker."

Maureen held her hand out to me. She wrapped her long fingers with red polished nails around my hand. It was the softest hand I ever felt. Mrs. Wagner held out her hand.

"I'm Mary Wagner, Gem's godmother."

"Hello, Mrs. Wagner. I remember you from the courtroom the other day," Maureen said.

"I didn't realize you were there."

"Yes. We get our case assignments after the custodial hearings are finished. I'm the lucky one assigned to Gem."

"Maureen. Does this mean I'm gonna live with you?"

Her eyes sparkled a little less when I asked that. Was there something I should already know?

"No, Gem. You'll be living here. But I'm going to see that you get placed into a nice home as soon as possible. Do you know what a foster parent is?"

I shook my head and sat back down. I guessed we were done waiting so I shut my crayon box and went to close my sketchpad.

"Oh, can I take a look?" Maureen asked.

Mrs. Wagner hadn't even asked to do that the whole time she stayed with me. I don't know why, but I felt happy when Maureen asked. I handed her the sketchpad. As she flipped through, she smiled.

"I knew from your school records about your high grades. But nothing mentions your artistic talent. You know, you could grow up to be an artist someday."

It was not only the first time an adult asked to look at my drawings, it was also the first time anyone ever said I could be an artist. I really liked Maureen.

"Your first name's so interesting," Maureen said. "Where does it come from?"

I sighed and folded my arms.

"It's a really boring, stupid story."

"We have a minute. Tell me."

"Mom used to do astrology before she met Dad. When I was born in June -- that's the month for the sign 'Gemini'-- she named me that. Dad was only okay with it because of the astronaut program. The priest got mad, though."

"The priest?" Maureen asked.

"Mom told me he wouldn't baptize me unless she changed my name. She told him it was just like the name of the boy in the movie "To Kill a Mockingbird", only spelled different. He still wouldn't baptize me unless I had a middle name from the Bible, so Mom and Dad called me 'Gemini Andrew', and then called me 'Gem' the whole time I was growing up."

"Gem, now that Maureen is here, I've got to get going," Mrs. Wagner said. She stood up, straightened her skirt, and dropped her rosary into her little gray purse.

Before I could say anything, Mrs. Wagner wrapped her arms around me and pulled me close to her. Her body seemed to push through her dress and pull me into her, as if we were both made of dough. I felt her chest shake and I was afraid to look at her face. I began to feel warm and a little sweaty and then she let me go.

54

"I'll be praying for you, always. Be a good boy, and I'll send Valentine's and birthday cards just like always, okay?"

In all the time she spent with me, I never saw her face look so sad. A lump pushed into my throat.

If she was so sad to say goodbye, why is she leaving you at this place? The voice said.

The lump in my throat eased up. Mrs. Wagner stepped away from me and she backed toward the door. She pushed against the front door and paused.

"Be a good boy, and remember, the Lord is always watching you."

The doors creaked open and Mrs. Wagner was gone. After a second, Maureen handed my sketchpad back to me.

"I'm going to take good care of my little artist."

Her words made me feel good. I thought then that maybe I would be an artist some day. But first someone else would look at my drawings and ruin some of them.

"What're you doing that for?" Bobby Anderson asked me as he pushed his glasses with the masking-taped frames back onto his nose. I wondered if his flat nose caused his glasses to slip.

"Don'tcha' know anything? Us younger ones always go out to foster families. Better keep 'em."

He bounced back onto his bed, causing it to groan with a metallic squeak. I considered what he said for a second, and then remembered what Maureen told me earlier. So I rolled out the paper grocery bag I just wrinkled up and began to fold it. Bobby's bed squeaked again and again as he bounced his butt up and down.

"What kinda' p.j.'s you got? Mine's got the Roadrunner and Wile E. Coyote all over them. See?"

He held out his arm and I noticed the cartoon characters on his sleeve, and the Nestle's-Quik brown color of his arm. As he turned his arm to give me a good look at the Roadrunner, I saw the light skin of his palm. Because I had never been really close up to a black person, I couldn't take my eyes off the pretty pink-brown color. From what I had seen on TV up to that time, I understood something was supposed to be wrong about his skin color. But it was just pretty to me, and Bobby was nice. I decided to show him my p.j.'s so I pulled them out from the drawer of the dresser separating our two beds.

"Scooby Doo! Wow!" he said.

"Where's the bathroom? I gotta go change."

Bobby stopped bouncing and shook his head, making his tight, black curls sparkle in the dim light.

"Bathroom is only for brushing your teeth, or taking a bath, or making poops. You can't just go against the rules and change there. I know all the rules here, case you don't, and I can teach them to you, if you want."

"Where am I supposed to change?"

He held his palms up and shrugged.

"Right here, I guess," he said.

I looked toward the opposite side of the bedroom at the row of five twin beds with their metal pipe headboards. The other boys in the room, all about the same age as Bobby and I, were already tucked in. Their bodies made sand dunes of the orange bedspreads. The beds on either side of Bobby and me were empty except for the gray-striped mattresses stained brownish-yellow. That's probably what made the room smell like a dirty sock.

"I'll go under my covers if you are afraid to change in front of me," Bobby offered.

"It's okay."

I pulled off my shirt and then my pants. Bobby covered his eyes with his hands. Once I put on my pajamas and got under the covers, the bed felt springy but warm.

"Do you need to sleep with the light on? They do allow that in the rules. Because of the red brick walls, this room stays really dark."

"I don't need the light."

Bobby reached over and clicked off the lamp on the dresser.

"You draw a lot? I saw your crayons and stuff," Bobby now whispered.

"Yeah."

"You don't pee the bed, do you?" he asked.

"No."

"Good. I don't either and if you did, it smells real bad. The rules say if you do pee your bed, then you have to wash your own sheets."

"I don't wanna hear about any more rules today, okay, Bobby?"

Bobby managed to stay quiet for thirty seconds.

"Stay away from the older boys. They call us the guppies and they do mean things. That's why my glasses got broke."

"Thanks, Bobby."

Music started playing from somewhere near Bobby. Something even worse started to happen.

"R-E-S-P-E-C-T. That is what you mean to me..."

Bobby was singing along with the music. And he didn't sound too good.

"You got a radio?" I asked.

He stopped singing and I heard the 'click' of a radio dial.

"Yeah. I got a real transistor radio. Used to be my momma's before she went to heaven. Wanna see?"

Bobby switched the light back on and he held the radio out to me. It was a little bigger than a pack of cigarettes and looked girly because it was pink. I toyed with its vinyl strap as I held it.

"Isn't it against the rules for you to play it at bedtime?" I asked.

"Don't tell. Everybody in here knows it's the only way I can go to sleep. The station plays the music Momma liked. It's called Motown."

I handed it back to him.

"I won't tell. Just don't sing, okay?"

"I won't then."

He clicked off the light. His bed squeaked as he slid back under the covers.

'Reflections of, the way life used to be...' I heard now coming from the radio. The low volume coupled with the lady's pretty voice made me start to feel sleepy. Just as I started to drift off, my eyes opened.

Don't you need to pray? The voice reminded me.

Now it was my turn to make a little noise. I crossed myself. I asked the Lord to watch over me during my stay here at the orphanage and to help Maureen find me a foster home soon. Whatever His plan was for me, I was just going to go along. That's what I understood from catechism, at any rate. So He sent Dad away and let Mom die; He must have had a very special plan for me. But just in case God was too busy, I thought I should ask Mom to look out for me, too.

"Oh, yeah, Mommy, please watch over me, and keep the older boys away. I miss you bad. In the name of the Father, and of the Son, and of the Holy Spirit."

I rolled over and could still hear the song from Bobby's radio. 'Reflections of, the love you took from me...'

"Well look at this, Guppies!" a kid's voice woke me up the next morning. I opened my eyes and saw two skinny, short boys standing on either side of a kid who looked both tall and fat. The word 'stocky' would apply. He must have been thirteen or fourteen. As my eyes cleared, I noticed the blue T-shirt he wore stretched over his fat belly. It didn't quite cover it at the bottom. Somehow I felt bad for him. He reached out his chubby hand and grabbed mine before I had a chance to offer it.

"Welcome, Guppy. I'm Eugene. Look at this."

He dropped my hand and picked up my sketchpad. He slowly flipped pages.

"That's some good coloring. Wow."

He flipped through a few more pages and nodded. He pointed at one and smiled.

"That looks like Samantha from 'Bewitched'. You are a very good artist."

I felt good that he liked my work.

"Can I show you another one I really like?" I asked.

Eugene nodded. He turned the sketchpad toward me but held on to it while I flipped to another page.

"Look at this one. I even made up a story about it."

Eugene smiled like an old lady. He nodded and patted my head. I thought he was pretty nice. He held on to my sketchpad as he reached up and set my pillow against the headboard. He patted it for me to sit against it. I sat up.

"You sad you're here? Most kids are when they get here."

I was sad. I nodded.

"Scared a little maybe, too?" he asked softly like a mother. "I was when I first got here. But it gets better."

"Sort of. I'm not sure yet."

He patted my head and shoulder.

"Don't you worry. I'm here to help anytime. Aren't I, Guppies?"

"Yeessss..." the other boys in their beds echoed like a chorus.

Eugene smiled at me. He was about the nicest kid I had ever met. He patted my head again. He turned around, still holding my sketchpad.

"Wait a second, let's celebrate the new guppy. What's you name?"

"Gem O'Connell."

" 'Gem' ???!!! Oh, that's a pretty name."

With that, his Farmer John-sausage fingers yanked a couple of my drawings from the sketchpad. He let the pad drop and I dove across the bed and pulled it to safety. But the boy kept his piggy nose and beady eyes focused on the drawings in his hands.

"Welcome, new guppy, Ruby!"

Like I hadn't heard that one before. Or a hundred other stupid teases about my first name. I just smiled. Eugene smiled back.

Then he started stretching my pages between his hands. He shredded and tore them into small pieces. He tossed the pieces into the air and they fell like crayon-covered snowflakes. I couldn't tell which drawings he tore up, and I was mad enough to hit him. That's when I noticed just how big he was. He wasn't just fat; he seemed to be a foot taller and two feet wider than me. He grabbed my blankets near my chest and pulled me up to his face. He snarled like a bulldog.

"I'm the boss around here. Remember that, Ruby."

I was so scared he was about to hit me that I closed my eyes. Suddenly I dropped to the bed. When I opened my eyes, the mountain of a boy rumbled out the bedroom door. Two boys jumped up from their beds and sped out the open door. Bobby drew back his covers.

"Is he gone?" he asked.

"Yeah. Why'd he do that?"

"That's Eugene Aragon, the meanest kid here. You made him mad. You're doomed!"

"I didn't do anything."

"He's the boss around here, so don't make him mad anymore. He's always around, too, because he stopped going to foster homes a long time ago."

I looked down at my sketchpad and its binding was twisted from where he held it. I turned to the torn-out part and saw that the 'Bewitched' story I made up about Samantha saving the 'Titanic' was missing two of its pages. They lay on the floor in shreds. But that wasn't the worst of it.

As I looked over the mess of paper, I noticed my crayons spilled all over the floor. They were crushed and broken and some were even ground into the grooves of the wood floor. Getting down on my hands and knees, I pried the shards of crayon from the floor. My eyes begin to water. Bobby kneeled down next to me and helped pick up the fragments. Some of them were in such bad shape that they looked like used firecrackers. I felt something odd that I had never felt before that moment – I could just crush Eugene Aragon's head, and then kick him all over. I was angrier than I ever had been in my life, furious, truly.

A month after I arrived to Hollygrove, it was the day before Halloween. I loved Halloween. We always went to Hall's Five and Ten on Lomita Boulevard. The glass windows above the red brick store front displayed scenes with stuffed scarecrows, witches on brooms, headstones, and of course, pumpkins. Everything a child could think of as spooky was on display in the windows. And once you stepped inside, just past the bins of penny candy, two aisles were stocked floor-to-ceiling with boxes of costumes. Whether it was Casper, a skeleton, Superman, a tiger, or anything else you wanted, there was a box costume with the plastic mask staring out from the top. It's funny how most of the time trick-or-treating, I would end up wearing the mask on my head and then pulling it down just when I knocked on someone's door. The mask always made my face sweaty and hot. Even after Mom got sick last year, Mrs. Wagner still took me to Hall's to pick out my costume.

At Hollygrove, though, it was already the day before Halloween and no one had even mentioned taking us to a store for a costume. Bobby and I were putting away our math and reading books. I looked at the wall above my bed and the pumpkins I had drawn with the orange and yellow crayons the first day of October made me sad. Bobby had an orange construction paper pumpkin and a black cat with a long, curved tail hanging above his bed. I sighed and sat.

"We don't even get costumes or anything?" I asked.

"Nope. It's against the rules I guess. But we're gonna make 'em pretty soon." He pushed his horned-rim glasses back up on his nose.

"What's that mean?"

"We'll have assembly in the dining hall and that's when we get to make our costumes."

"But I really wanted to be Scooby Doo this year. I can't make that."

Bobby shrugged.

"That's what happens when you're an orphan," he said.

"I'm not an orphan—I still got a dad."

"That's what you always say." Bobby said.

"I do because it's true. He lives in the desert and some day I'm going to find him. He might even come get me first, who knows."

Bobby pinched his lips together for a second. I thought he might be starting to get sad. But he nodded and shrugged. He switched

60

on his radio. 'Walk on by…just walk on by…' the woman's voice sang.

I tapped Bobby's shoulder. He turned down his music.

"Yeah?"

"If you could have any costume, what would you be?" I asked.

Bobby chewed the inside of his lip and looked sideways toward the ceiling. He folded his arms and rolled his eyes.

"Promise you won't tell nobody."

"Yep-okay."

"Angelique from 'Dark Shadows'."

"A girl?"

"Anything I want to be so it doesn't matter, right? Besides, she's so pretty and a witch, too."

It was my turn to shrug. Bobby turned his radio back up.

A little while later, I figured out why it didn't matter about my wanting to be Scooby Doo or Bobby wanting to be a girl witch. We were all lined up behind big tables in the dining hall. Each table had piles of black, green, orange, and white construction paper, bottles of LePage's mucilage with the shark fin-shaped tips, rolls of Scotch tape, strips of elastic, and rounded kiddy scissors. Mrs. Jeffers ran Hollygrove and was also the main teacher. She wore her hair in an old lady bun and glared at you through her gold wire glasses if you missed an answer. She hollered:

"Aye!" No one knew why she said 'aye' instead of 'yes' and why she hollered it in such a high pitch. It did get our attention that was for sure.

"We're going to make different masks this year. No ghosts!"

I got a little hopeful until she held up the three masks. She tugged the elastic band and pulled one over her head.

"Aye!" she said. "A pumpkin!"

Some of the littler kids screamed with joy. She pulled the pumpkin mask off and pulled on the next one.

"Aye! A skeleton!"

That one looked more like a bad paper doll to me. The little kids clapped and laughed. She pulled on the final one, made of green and black construction paper.

"Aye. And a witch!"

It looked nothing like a witch. Bobby and I looked at each other and shrugged.

"Guess I'm gonna be a witch, then," he said.

That was fine for Bobby who must have only been six. For me, being eight, they all looked like stupid construction paper masks you'd make in kindergarten. I thought maybe I could do something to make the pumpkin mask at least look like the Headless Horseman in 'Scooby Doo'. I started to get a little more interested until Mrs. Jeffers spoke again.

"Once you have your masks made, we'll line up on the playground and do the annual parade. Then we'll come back in here for some punch and cookies."

Some of the little kids again clapped and hollered with excitement. But one little kid toward the back with a runny nose and buck teeth raised his hand.

"Yes, Trent?"

"Do we getta go trick-or-treating after punch and cookies?"

Mrs. Jeffers tucked a strand of hair that had come loose when she pulled off the skeleton mask back onto her bun. She shook her head.

"No volunteers this year to help so no trick-or-treating this year."

The whole room seemed to sigh at once. I felt like someone had punched me in the belly.

You better get used to this. No one cares about making sure you have anything, even tricks-or-treats, the voice said.

Construction paper masks were one thing, a stupid parade another, but no trick-or-treating. That was it. I got up and kicked my chair. Bobby flinched and pushed his glasses back up on his nose. I didn't mean to scare him it's just that on top of missing my mom, I wasn't going to have a good Halloween, either. I ran out to the play yard where the older kids were playing horse at the rusty basketball hoop. I noticed for the first time there wasn't even a net and that's when I realized the voice might be right: nobody really cares about me or anybody else here.

"I feeeel goooo d!" Bobby sang a few weeks later. He jumped up and down on his bed, holding his mom's transistor radio to his ear. Each time he jumped, he blocked the morning sunlight coming through the window.

"You're gonna get it if you keep jumping on the bed," I said.

I was trying to draw a picture of the Eiffel Tower but when he'd block the sun, I'd have a tough time seeing the black crayon on the paper. This was another episode of 'Bewitched' that I had made up. His singing was making me crazy, too.

"Bobby! Stop it!"

"Okay, grouch."

He stopped jumping, turned down the radio, and sat on the edge of his bed.

"How come you always draw pictures of 'Bewitched' anyhow? Magic powers are just on TV. They ain't for reals."

He swung the radio like a pendulum from its strap he had slipped over his wrist.

"I know that. But sometimes I just like to make believe they are, and so I draw pictures of Samantha and everyone."

"What would you do if you had magic powers?" he asked.

"For one thing, turn Eugene Aragon into a toilet or something. I hate him."

"Yeah…" Bobby said wistfully. "Then everybody'd just poop and pee on him."

We both laughed at the idea.

"What about you?" I asked.

"I'd just make my Momma alive and have her come get me. That's all I'd do."

"She's in heaven. Even Samantha doesn't have that much power," I said. "How'd your mom die?"

Bobby shook his head.

"Can't talk about it 'cause it's against the rules since she died from drugs and it makes me cry. What about you?"

I understood what Bobby meant. I missed my mom so bad and I couldn't stop dreaming about her, either. My throat started to ache.

"Cancer."

"Oh," Bobby said quietly and nodded.

The first Thanksgiving at Hollygrove was better than the Halloween parade and even better than the ones I had at home. Those were usually just Mom and Dad and one time, Grandma. They were always the same: Mom got up early to put the turkey in; Dad watched a college football game after I watched the Macy's Thanksgiving Parade; then we'd eat at three in the afternoon. And every year, by eight-thirty that night, we were eating turkey sandwiches. It was always pretty boring. This first one at Hollygrove came with a surprise.

All of our meals at Hollygrove took place in the dining hall. The bell rang at seven thirty in the morning, then again at noon, and finally at five o'clock for dinner. We would gather and form a line from the open, wooden doors to the kitchen. We'd slide orange plastic trays down a metal counter and be served. Sometimes we could ask for more of one thing or less of another as long as we took each main part of the meal. Then we would carry our trays into the dining hall and take a seat at any of the long, yellow Formica picnic tables with the built-in yellow Formica benches. But on Thanksgiving, things were very different.

Mrs. Jeffers met us all at the doors. They were closed this time, which was unusual. She was dressed special for Thanksgiving. Instead of a plain dress with roses or cherries on it, she wore a white blouse with lace across the front and a brownish-orange skirt. Her hair was done up in its usual bun but she had a little crown of yellow, brown, and red maple leaves around it. I was pretty sure she was going to tell us that there was no food for Thanksgiving. Instead, as Bobby and I walked up, she waved the boys to one side and the girls to the opposite side. That's when I noticed two men with cameras with large flashbulbs and a woman with a notepad. They reminded me of Clark Kent, Jimmy Olsen, and Lois Lane but what were they doing here?

"Aye! Form lines now, boys separate from the girls."

More kids walked up and shook their heads in confusion. The older ones folded their arms and rolled their eyes. It seemed they might know what was going on since they had been at Hollygrove for so long.

"Aye. Now quiet and listen. We have some special friends from television who have come to help serve us Thanksgiving once again."

"Charlie Brown?" one of the little ones hollered. "Snoopy!" another hollered and clapped his hands. Bobby looked at me and rolled his eyes. We both thought those kids were stupid.

"Settle down, settle down. When I open the doors, you are to stay in the lines you're in, girls first, and make your way into the kitchen for your trays as usual. And be sure to thank each person you see."

"All right already," one of the older kids said.

"These nice people here are going to be taking some pictures so you be sure to let them alone while they do that."

Mrs. Jeffers tucked her blouse into her skirt and touched her hair once more as if she was going to meet a boyfriend or something. She pulled open the doors. I could see just past the line of girls that the ceiling was lined with festoons of crepe paper leaves and what looked like paper turkeys with honeycombed, orange paper tails. As the girls made their way into the kitchen area, I could hear some of them scream and squeal amidst soft 'thank-yous.' My stomach started to flutter when I thought about who might be inside. Could it be Jeannie? Or Samantha?

"Aye. All right, boys, you may enter the kitchen. Keep in a single file line."

Before I got my turn in the kitchen, the smells of roast turkey, and melted butter, and something like baking bread made my stomach growl. At least we were going to have real food instead of blobs of instant stuff. When Bobby and I stepped up to the counter, he nudged me with his elbow.

"It's Julia, it's Julia!"

I looked through the glass above the counter and there she was, even more beautiful than she was on television. Diahann Carroll. Even though she wasn't dressed like a nurse but wore an orange blouse, there was no doubt it was her. For that minute, I didn't care that she wasn't Jeannie or Samantha when she smiled and nodded at us. She raised a platter of turkey toward us and asked which meat we preferred. I suddenly wished I were sick so she could take care of me. Right then, one of the photographers stepped between Bobby and me and took a couple pictures. Diahann smiled, her white teeth gleaming. Once the photographer finished, she looked back down at Bobby.

"I like white," Bobby said.

She set down the platter and picked up a pair of metal tongs. Her hands looked like chocolate, velvet candles and I almost couldn't speak.

"And you?" her voice sent a shiver down my spine. I was sure something was very wrong with me.

"Umm, I like both kinds."

"Is TV fun to be on?" Bobby asked with his nervous, fast quiver.

"It is and maybe someday, if you work hard, you'll get to be on a show, too."

Bobby nodded.

"I'm gonna be an actress someday."

"You mean an actor. Good for you."

Bobby looked down and nodded. I could tell he was embarrassed. He thanked her for his serving of meat and slid his tray down to the next area. I couldn't take my eyes off her face.

"You need to move along now so I can serve the other kids," she said.

It felt as if I just woke up from a dream and when I realized I

65

had been staring, I blushed. I slid my tray down next to Bobby. He was already getting a big portion of mashed potatoes and stuffing heaped on his plate by George Takei, the man who plays "Sulu" on Star Trek.

"And I love the tribbles and how Scotty always gets the Enterprise going again," Bobby talked non-stop.

"Oh my," George said. "Mashed potatoes and stuffing for you, young man?"

I nodded. I couldn't say much to Sulu because he reminded me of watching 'Star Trek' with my dad and I suddenly missed Dad so much. I smiled and just said 'please' and 'thank you.' I didn't see Samantha or Jeannie anywhere so I was glad to follow Bobby out the kitchen door to the main dining room. Kids were laughing and talking. We were allowed to say grace by ourselves or not at all. I crossed myself and began quietly:

"Bless us, oh Lord, and these, thy gifts—"

Bobby poked me.

"Why you always gotta pray before we eat? There's no preacher around so who cares? Food'll get cold, you know."

I finished grace and crossed myself. I believed that God and now Mom could see me so I wasn't going to sin.

The first bite of the mashed potatoes and gravy warmed my mouth with buttery flavor. The potatoes tasted different than the watery ones we usually had. The gravy was less salty and tasted more like turkey. The bite of turkey was juicy and good, too. I turned and looked around the whole dining hall and there was no sign of Samantha and Jeannie. I sighed and Bobby rocked back and forth, swinging his legs and smiling. Once all the kids were seated, Diahann and George came out to the dining hall. George picked up a platter with gravy and Diahann started pouring milk from an aluminum pitcher. One photographer followed George, and the other followed Diahann.

"This food is good," Bobby said.

I looked up from my plate just as the two photographers and lady with the notepad walked up to someone standing next to Mrs. Jeffers. After the cameras flashed, the photographers stepped aside. I recognized the actor.

Ed Asner, who played Lou Grant in the "The Mary Tyler Moore Show," stood by the wall with an aluminum pitcher of water. Mrs. Jeffers. stood right next to him telling him some sort of story.

When she gestured with her right hand, she bumped the pitcher and he steadied it and checked to see if it had spilled. But Mrs. Jeffers just giggled like one of the little girls. She reached up and touched her hair and kept gabbing away. Ed Asner looked around the room and he caught my eye. He pointed at the pitcher and at me but I shook my head. He nodded and the smile left his face. Mrs. Jeffers just kept talking and he looked at the ground and nodded. I was pretty sure then that Mrs. Jeffers had a crush on Ed Asner.

I gripped the crayon tight between my thumb and index finger and carefully began to draw in the crossbars all over the Eiffel Tower. I was full of turkey and stuffing and almost wanted to take a nap. Just as I was about to draw in the crossbars of the second section, the sunlight cut out. It was Bobby again and just as I looked up, he hollered.

"Ouch! Stop it!"

Eugene Aragon had hold of Bobby's radio and held it up to his eyes, ignoring the fact that Bobby's arm was still inside the strap. The same two pimply-faced boys stood on either side of him.

"Look at this pretty thing. Wow, I sure could use a transistor radio. What do you think, Ruby?"

I ignored him and kept coloring. I kept my eye on Bobby just in case he needed help. Eugene tugged at the strap but Bobby tugged back with his wrist.

"That's my momma's! That's my momma's! That's against the rules!"

Eugene gripped the top of Bobby's head with his right hand and flung him back onto his bed like he was spiking a volleyball. The radio strap snapped.

"Now it's mine!"

He turned around and ran out of the room, with the two other idiots laughing behind him.

"Momma! Momma!" Bobby lay on his back crying.

That made me mad and suddenly, I ran after Aragon and the other two boys. I didn't care that they were all four or five years older than me. Just as I neared them, they ducked into the bathroom. I followed them.

Inside the bathroom, Aragon stood there, his chest and belly panting from his run down the hall. His face looked like a mad bull.

"What's it to you, Ruby?"

"That's Bobby's mom's radio. Give it back to him."

The two boys on either side of Aragon started to laugh. One of them jumped behind me and slammed the door.

"Who you think you are? Super Chicken?" Aragon said.

"Just give it back. That's all."

I felt my throat start to shake. My stomach twisted. I didn't know what I was doing there.

He picks on smaller kids because his dad probably beat him. The voice said in my head.

"Just 'cause your Dad beat you up, doesn't mean you gotta pick on everybody else."

I don't really know why I said it out loud, but Aragon's face became white all of a sudden.

"What?" he growled.

"Nothin' Just give back the radio."

Before I could think of another thing to say, I felt the force of Aragon's fist in my belly. Air left me and suddenly I was on the floor.

"Get a hold of him, guys. He gets the ultimate!"

As soon as the other two boys grabbed my wrists, the black feeling of hate I felt for him before gripped me again. I fought against their grip, and the more I fought, the tighter they held. If I could get loose, I would really hurt Aragon. All at once, they flipped me onto my stomach.

"The ultimate!" Aragon screamed, and with that, I felt the twisting burn of my underwear going up my butt. Aragon pulled and twisted tighter and tighter.

"Ultimate Melvin! Ultimate Melvin!"

It burned. My testicles felt like they were wedging back inside my body. It hurt so bad I thought they were pulling me in two.

Over the laughter, I heard the bathroom door burst open. The twisting pull of my underwear instantly stopped, and they released my hands.

"What do you think you're doing?" I heard one of the male dorm managers say. He had Aragon by the back of his neck and I could see the tips of Aragon's Adidas just off the floor.

"You crazy or something?"

As he shook Aragon, Bobby's radio fell from Aragon's hand and crashed to the floor. The square battery burst from its side, and little blue and white bits of plastic spilled from the same hole.

"That yours?" the dorm manager asked me.

I shook my head.

"It's Bobby Anderson's"

"These clowns are gonna pay for that. You okay?"

Other than my jockeys wedged in my butt, I didn't hurt any longer.

"I'm okay."

"You-clown face. Pick that up!"

One of the boys picked up Bobby's radio and its guts.

"Give it to him.'

He handed me the radio.

"Tell Bobby he'll get a new one. These three bozos will be delivering it personally."

With that, the dorm manager let go of Aragon's neck, making Aragon's big feet slap hard against the floor. He shoved Aragon and the other two boys out the bathroom door. I looked at the broken radio in my hand. I hated Aragon.

When I brought it back to Bobby, he just stared at it. He opened his hand and I set the radio into his palm. He stared at the radio. I held out my hand and showed him the bits of broken plastic. He nodded for those, too. Cupping his right hand under his left, he turned and set the radio and its bits onto his bed. He pulled back his pillow and set the radio and parts under it carefully as if they were baby chicks. He finished by setting his pillow right on top. I wanted to say that it might feel lumpy under his head, but I kept my mouth shut. He lay down on his bed, nuzzled the pillow with his cheek for a second, and rolled onto his side. He left his back toward me.

"Bobby, I'm sorry it got broke. I tried to get it back from them."

He didn't make a sound.

"They have to get you a new one for breaking it."

I think I saw his shoulders shake a little. He spent the whole day lying in bed, and he didn't talk for a couple more days after. Even when they gave him the replacement radio, one of those modern bowling ball-shaped ones, he didn't say anything.

The first time he talked again was a few days later and he came running into the dorm smiling and excited.

"Gem, Gem, Gem! The best news!"

"What?"

"Eugene Aragon got sent to Juvenile Hall! He can't hurt us no more."

"What'd he do?"

69

"He broke a kid's arm down on the first floor yesterday. They packed him up and got rid of him today!"

There are a million Aragons. No one cares about orphans so orphans don't care about anybody, either, the voice said.

I didn't say that to Bobby because I knew how happy he was that Aragon was sent away. It didn't matter to him much longer, though, because a week later, Bobby was on his way to a foster home. He was packing his paper bags so carefully the morning he was getting ready to go. He picked up the replacement transistor radio and handed it to me.

"Why you giving me this?"

"It's an early Christmas present. I didn't really like it because it wasn't ever my momma's."

He rolled the tops of the paper trash bags so that they looked like lunch bags. He looked around the room and then under the bed. When he stood up, he pushed his glasses back onto his nose, which for some reason, made me almost want to cry. I distracted myself with the transistor radio.

"Guess that's all my stuff."

He sat down on the edge of his bed. He pulled the two paper bags toward his chest and held them tight.

"Guess you getta make Christmas decorations today. I'm gonna miss that. I'd probably do a snow girl with some glitter."

I couldn't look up from the radio. A lump was growing in my throat. I just nodded.

Bobby clapped his hands together and stood up. He jabbed my shoulder with his finger. That made me look up.

"You remember all the rules I taught you, right?"

"Yep."

"Okay, well, you gotta make sure you follow 'em."

He turned and grabbed up the grocery bags. He walked to the dorm door and turned, pushing his glasses up on his nose.

"Merry Christmas, Gem. You're my best friend."

When he closed the door behind him, I squeezed the radio so hard that my hand turned white. My heart pounded and I thought I was going to faint. I sat on the edge of my bed and all I could think about was my mom.

"Aye" Mrs. Jeffers said to us in the dining hall a few weeks later. She stood in front of the giant pull-down screen where they sometimes showed Disney animal or science movies. Red and green tinsel garland hung from the ceiling and one of the tables was pushed against the wall. A cut-glass punch bowl stood in the middle of platters of cookies, fudge, and divinity. We had already filled up our paper plates with goodies from the table. I took a sip of the red Hawaiian Punch and tasted little bits of pineapple, too. I secretly hoped that Mrs. Jeffers was going to say that since it was Christmas Eve, Santa hadn't forgotten us and would be bringing us all a load of presents. It wouldn't have made me believe in him again, but it would have been a nice surprise. Instead, she held up a book.

"Who remembers reading this book last year?"

I remembered reading it at St. Joan of Arc's school last year. I shot up my hand. It was my favorite book up to that point—'Charlie and the Chocolate Factory' by Roald Dahl. Willy Wonka was weird and a little scary but turned out to be a good guy after all. Most everybody who was seven or eight like me had their hands raised. Mrs. Jeffers set the book back down. She picked up a couple of film cans.

"Aye, then, most of you will like this special treat. The nice people at Paramount Studios just up the street loaned us a copy of the movie they made from this book. They call it 'Willy Wonka and the Chocolate Factory.'

The dining hall erupted with clapping and cheers. I didn't join in because right away I had a problem: the book is about Charlie and what he gets for being an honest boy. Willy Wonka was integral to the story, but the book was about Charlie, not Willy Wonka. As usual, Mrs. Jeffers didn't ask us about what we thought.

"Let's watch, then," she said.

She walked to the back of the dining hall as most of the kids chattered with excitement. If Bobby had been around, I'm sure he would have been talking away, too. I just folded my arms and waited for them to turn on the projector. As soon as the candy store clerk began singing 'The Candy Man', I knew I wasn't going to like it. The only musical I ever liked was 'Wizard of Oz' but other than that, it was always so odd to me that people were talking and then broke into song. Even though I liked it when Charlie found the golden ticket, as soon as he sang about it, I covered my ears.

But the worst was when Willy Wonka finally showed up: Gene Wilder. With his young and nice, sort of dad-plump face, he looked nothing like the skinny, old, almost witchy Willy Wonka illustrations in the book. And then he sang 'Pure imagination' and I almost ran out of

71

the dining hall. Because I was so bored with all the songs, and none of the characters looked like I imagined they would, I kept going back to the goodies table and refilling. I ate more than Augustus Gloop in the movie.

Later, as I lay in my bed, with Bobby's bed empty next to me and his striped mattress rolled up like a cinnamon roll, I could hear the stereo in the workers' lounge playing Nat King Cole's 'Caroling, Caroling'. My mom's face flashed into my mind all of sudden, again and again as I recalled how much she liked Nat King Cole. My head began to feel light and I felt like I needed to get up and run. But where was I going to run? My heart began to pound, too, and my back broke out in sweat, as I imagined running up El Centro Avenue in the middle of the night with only the yellow street lights guiding me. Who was going to care if I ran down El Centro, anyway? '...*Christmas bells are ringing...*' Nat sang on and it felt as if my head and chest were deflating. Mom's face, then Nat, then Mom, and all of a sudden, I felt like I was going to throw up.

I jumped up from my bed and made it down the hall to the boys' bathroom just in time to puke. Instead of my mom, all I could see was the opening of 'Willy Wonka and the Chocolate Factory' with cocoa beans grinding into a fudgy swirl. All the cookies, fudge, and divinity came up and all I really wanted was to have Mom there to rub my back as I vomited. Tears streamed down my face from the vomiting, but once they started, I couldn't stop them. I cried and threw up for what seemed like hours that first Christmas Eve at Hollygrove.

They woke us up the next morning and marched us all, still in our pajamas, to the dining hall. As the doors opened, we saw the dining tables each decorated by a small Christmas tree. I could smell breakfast sausage and maple syrup as we sat down at the tables. My stomach ached from the night before so I just sat and started to play with the red paper napkin and butter knife at my place. The little kids at the table behind me suddenly hollered and I looked up to see Gene Wilder, dressed in his own pajamas and robe, step out from the kitchen door with a platter full of pancakes. One of the photographers from Thanksgiving followed him.

"Merry Christmas!" he hollered. The photographer snapped a couple of photos.

"Merry Christmas, Willy Wonka!" some kids hollered back. They clapped and screamed.

I sat back and sighed. Those kids didn't know a thing about the book. Plus, he looked so much smaller than he did in the movie. I didn't really care that Willy Wonka brought in our breakfast, either. Mrs. Jeffers stepped out of the kitchen and she wore a light yellow, quilted robe over a pink and white night gown that peeked out from the bottom of her robe. She carried a platter of sausages and a platter with bottles of Log Cabin syrup.

"Aye! Merry Christmas! Let's all enjoy some music, too."

The little brown speakers above the rolled-up screen started playing 'Silent Night'. The little kids clapped as Gene Wilder served pancakes and Mrs. Jeffers followed up and served the sausages and syrup.

Once we finished breakfast, they led us to the front, main hall of Hollygrove. Mrs. Jeffers stood in front of the oak double doors. She pulled up the collar of her robe and adjusted it and then tucked a strand of loose hair back over her ear. Was Ed Asner in there again? I wondered.

"Aye! There's someone special in there with helpers, too."

"Santa?" one of the little girls hollered behind me.

"You'll find out in a moment. Each of you remember your age, now, because you'll need to let them know."

The song 'We Wish You a Merry Christmas' started playing behind the door. A man cleared his throat.

"Aye, two lines please—boys and girls in each. Youngest up front."

Three little boys who must have been about half my age ran up and stood in front of me. Two of them elbowed each other and whispered something in Spanish. Five little girls, two of them with corn rows, and another with glasses who reminded me of Bobby, stepped in front. Mrs. Jeffers looked both lines over one more time and nodded. She pulled open the two doors. The little kids in front let out a collective "ooohhhhh!"

Inside, at the foot of the front staff staircase, stood the tallest and shiniest Christmas tree I ever saw. It was covered with various kinds of metal and glass ornaments. Between the strands of regular-sized Christmas bulbs you could see midget lights blink with red, green, orange, and blue. The tinsel made the whole thing look as if the tree was frozen. But the tree wasn't the best part: on either side of the tree lay stacks of presents in four different sizes, wrapped in red, green, blue, and candy-cane striped foil paper. I don't think any child had ever seen so many presents.

"Ho-ho-ho! Merry Christmas!" a skinny Santa suddenly jumped out from behind the tree. I could see his black hair under his white wig and later found out that he was a department store Santa who worked at the May Company on Wilshire and Fairfax. He fooled the little kids and since I no longer believed in him, it didn't matter that he looked too young to be Santa.

"Who's been good this year?" he asked.

All the littlest kids ran up screaming. Santa jumped back and Mrs. Jeffers stepped in front of him.

"Aye! Santa probably thinks you're all naughty now. You make a line and come up to Santa one at a time. "

Just as Mrs. Jeffers finished speaking, Mrs. Claus and a lady elf joined him on either side. As each child approached, they were handed a present from one of the four stacks. Mrs. Claus looked as young as Santa and was also a worker at May Company. The lady elf bent over to pick up a gift for a little girl, and some of the older boys whispered something about it. When she turned back around, I noticed she was really pretty. When I got my chance to step up to Santa, I couldn't take my eyes off her face.

"Merry Christmas, sonny!" Santa said.

I just nodded and stared at the lady elf. She shook her head and chuckled and handed me the present. As I turned and walked away, I thought I could smell some sort of flowery perfume. Some lady elf, I thought.

I sat on one of the stairs and tore open the present. Inside was the coolest thing: a Major Matt Mason and an Apollo capsule. I would have liked a 'Starship Enterprise' for a space toy, but it still was a great present. All these dumb little kids jumping around and screaming with joy about their Tonka dump trucks or Malibu Barbies were soon going to realize that Christmas was really only for kids with moms and dads who loved them. They'd be all alone in their dorms with nothing but these toys soon.

"We wish you a merry Christmas, we wish you a merry Christmas…" Santa, Mrs. Claus and the lady elf started to sing once all the presents were passed out. Mrs. Jeffers joined in and waved her hands in the air to get everybody to sing. I stayed quiet on the stairs and turned the Major Matt Mason capsule around to examine it from all sides.

6.

Gem paused and took a sip of his Starbucks. He lay back on the couch, his shoes now off, and one of his legs daggling over the arm of the sofa. He folded his arms and exhaled.

"Wow, eight years old and already a critic," Dr. Friedman said. "I love Gene Wilder."

"I would have loved to have been his agent."

Dr. Friedman stood. Her arms made a triangle as she stretched them over her head. Her breath squeezed out of her as she exhaled and lowered her arms slowly.

"You need to try some stretching and breathing for that anxiety of yours," she said. "It would do you some good."

Gem sat back up. He tapped the coffee table with his fingertips.

"I don't go in for any new age, magic crap."

"I didn't say go buy two yards of saffron silk and shave your head. I'm just suggesting another tool for you. I'm going to teach you some breathing exercises when we're all through with this jaunty walk down memory lane."

"Okay, so aside from the strictly passable prose, what do you get from all this so far?" he asked her.

Dr. Friedman stepped back to her chair and picked up her iPad. After a few passes of her fingers and some quick typing, she held up the iPad.

"I can't read it," Gem said.

She nodded. She enlarged the screen with her thumb and index finger and turned the iPad back toward him.

"Better?"

The iPad screen read: *Patient exhibited early childhood detachment syndrome as a result of the loss of his mother and ultimate abandonment. Developed possible father idealization complex.*

"We're going to talk about those things for a while. Especially your mother's death. She clearly taught you how to love, but her loss would have fed into your attachment issues later."

Dr. Friedman and Gem spent the next three hours discussing these observations. They only paused for a lunch break. They slipped out to Fatburger on San Vicente and returned for the rest of the session. By four thirty, Gem looked visibly tired. He sat up while Dr. Friedman made some final notes on her iPad.

"Well?" he said, shrugging his shoulders and raising his palms.

Dr. Friedman nodded, turned the iPad back around and wrote something else. She held the screen up again.

Gem is crazy.

"Oh, you're a laugh riot."

Gem pointed at her framed magazine covers.

"Is this your idea of 'Humor Therapy'?"

"Hang on a second," she said. She typed a few more words and held up the screen again:

This is all old news. Patient's time is up and needs to come back to continue tomorrow.

"You were right. This is intense therapy. Day one and absolutely nothing new," Gem said.

"Give it time. There's a lot more to read here." She pointed at the manuscript. Gem pulled on his Asics running shoes and stood.

"Now don't go skipping to the end," he said.

"I'll try to control myself. Tomorrow, then."

Gem and Kelly had dinner on the west side then caught a screening of Nina Simone's bio documentary at the Nuart theatre. Kelly had said that Nina was a fierce and sad warrior. Gem agreed. He wondered what thoughts and urges haunted her sad mind and it increased his confidence. If someone worse off than he still managed to flourish, he had no business feeling sorry for himself or getting caught up in his lousy childhood story.

He showed up at Dr. Friedman's the next morning. She wore a pink and orange work-out suit.

"Going for a jog?"

"No—my suits are in the cleaners. Sit down and let's get started."

She stepped back and slid into her chair slowly. Gem noticed.

"Your back hurt or something?"

She shook her head.

"No. These pants make my ass look huge and I didn't want to scare you off with a giant, pink moon first thing."

"Thanks—that was thoughtful."

Dr. Friedman slipped off her jogging shoes and let them drop to the floor. She grabbed up the manuscript and handed it to Gem.

"You all set?"

Gem nodded. He began to read.

7.

Hollygrove Home for Children was made famous by an early ward--Marilyn Monroe. There was a hallway on the first floor of the main building that had an array of pictures. Starting with Mrs. Stephens and Mrs. Gibson who had begun rescuing kids—"street urchins"—a hundred years before, it included pictures of Marilyn. I didn't understand why everybody at Hollygrove made such a fuss about her. She grew up to be rich and famous but she also got into lots of trouble with booze and pills. No one really knows if she killed herself or not. Why was that such an inspiring story of success? I was staring at one of the early pictures of her one day. I looked past her brown hair and noticed the Paramount tower in the background.

Looking at the photo, I got the idea for the first time to leave Hollygrove. Not to run away, but just to see if I could finally get to the tower and climb to the top. I had wanted to do that from the first time I saw the tower when Mrs. Wagner dropped me off here. She had called once a week or so after dropping me off, but it seemed after she moved, she forgot about me. After a few months, I began to forget about her, too. It was odd but I started thinking less and less about my mom, the sump, and everything about my life before. Maureen checked on me all the time, which I liked because she was so pretty. The voice always reminded me that she was just doing her job and I wasn't the only child in her care. The only person I was sure must have cared about me was my dad. I hadn't yet figured out how to contact him. Lately, other than the boring school work I had to do, and figuring out how to dodge the older kids, I pretty much did whatever came to mind. So the old Paramount tower was calling.

It had been raining since Christmas and we finally got a sunny day in the middle of March. Ever since I looked at that photo, I had been strategizing about how I would get to the tower and climb it. The hardest part was determining how I was going to escape Hollygrove's grounds. Then something surprising happened. On that sunny March morning, we finally we're allowed to go out to the play area. Some of the older boys ran straight for the cracked asphalt and rusty basketball hoop with no net. One of them was dribbling a basketball as they ran to take a shot.

I had the urge to steal the ball and demonstrate my great lay up, but instead, I noticed the corner of the chain-link fence just beyond the court that was overgrown with ivy. I remembered the bushes and weeds that grew around the fence of the sump and how they sometimes separated the corners of the fence so they could be pried apart. I wondered if ivy could do the same thing and if it did, that would be my way out. I sneaked past the boys who were thumping the basketball and hitting the rusty rim with soft thuds. Usually, if they saw a guppy nearby, it would be some sort of arm twist or a headlock and punch. But since they were so intent on their basketball game, they didn't notice me and I made it into the ivy.

It was like a jungle when I stepped into it. It grew out about seven feet in all directions and had a sharp, wet metal aroma. It took me a few steps to reach the fence. I realized I was about four feet over from the corner so made my way toward it. I heard the basketball dribbling pause and one of the boys behind me yell: "Hey!" I froze. A second later, the ivy leaves to my left made an odd rustling sound and I saw the basketball roll to a stop. I braced myself for a yank and a punch.

"It's right here—got it!" someone yelled. The ball was plucked from the ivy and in a second, the bouncing and dribbling started again. I exhaled and relaxed my stomach. I continued to grope against the stringy, slick tendrils. I reached the corner of the fence and just as I thought, the ivy had grown and separated the two sides of the fence at the corner. I yanked away the ivy and the thick stems made my hands sticky with cool sap. But once I cleared away the leaves and stems, I could work my fingers around a rusted support bar that joined the fence sections to the corner pole. I tugged.

The rusty metal gave but let out a loud squeak. I was sure the older boys heard and I stopped. The ball kept dribbling and the shouting continued so I was safe. Tightening my grip now, I pulled harder and the lower clamp gave way. The vertical support bar, weak with rust and the weight of the ivy stems, bent under my pressure. I bent the metal hard as I could while folding the chain-link over itself. I kept working it until I created a teepee-shaped opening. I crawled through and felt the sidewalk scrape dull against the knees of my corduroys. I stood and looked at the busy street. I looked back at the opening and saw that the ivy growing on the yard side would keep it camouflaged.

I brushed off my pants. They were covered with dust but also some spider webs and one dead, dried spider. Before I could step off the curb and cross to the other side of El Centro, a red Ford Pinto wagon whizzed past me. I hustled across the street and looked back toward the Hollygrove fence to be sure no one had seen me. I was safe. Someone was pounding nails in the distance and I guessed it might be something being built at Paramount. Gregory Avenue was just a half block ahead of me and when I ran to the corner and looked left, I could see the Paramount tower peeking up above two palm trees. To the left of the tower, a beige building with a brown door and writing above it stood right at the sidewalk. I ran toward it, dodging around raised sidewalk sections bulging from tree roots. Moments later, slightly out of breath, I stood on Gower Street looking across at the brown door.

I stared at the door as cars passed back and forth. Above it I could now read: 'Casting Administration'. The door opened and out stepped a lady in a beige skirt and dark blue blouse. She put on a pair of sunglasses. Someone held the door for her and I tried to make out what the room looked like but couldn't. A couple seconds later, a man in a dark suit stepped out the door. They both walked down the three steps to the sidewalk. They talked and laughed. I watched as they walked up Gower to a dark blue Lincoln Mark IV. Once they drove off, I waited to see if anybody else came out the door but no one did. I figured it was now or never so just as the last car passed by, I jaywalked across the street.

The three cement steps that led up to the door were each worn down in the middle. Brown iron railings that curled at the ends looked scraped and dented. Lots of people must have held those over the years, I thought. The door itself looked worn and cracked on its edges, too. I looked back down Gregory Avenue lined with cars and palm trees. I could just see the edge of the Hollygrove fence. Somehow, that fence gave me the courage to walk up the stairs and open the door. I pushed down the latch of the iron handle and the door clicked and gave way.

I walked into a hallway. Dark brown wallpaper with faded floral patterns absorbed the dim, overhead lights. I heard typing and people muttering and laughing. As my eyes adjusted from the sunlight, I saw a handwritten sign that read "Little Prince sign in" and an arrow pointing left. I tried a door on the right side of the hall but it was locked. My options were either run back outside or follow the sign. I walked down the hall past more wooden doors. I noticed nameplates on them so figured I shouldn't just walk in to any of them. Pretty soon, I stood at the open doorway of a large room. Boys and girls my age and younger were sitting in chairs all along the three walls with women who must have been their mothers. A long counter with doors beyond it completed the fourth side of the room. Clip boards sat next to cards with names on them. I had no idea what any of it meant. I thought about continuing down the hall but before I could, someone hollered to me. I looked toward the counter.

"Your mom sign you in yet?" a woman in horned rims with dark hair pulled back into a ponytail said to me. She took a sip of her coffee and waited for me to answer. I shook my head.

"Well get her up here."

"Up here?" I asked.

"To sign you in." She tapped a clipboard with her index finger.

"She's in the bathroom."

"Fine, kid. Why don't you go wait down the hall there and when she comes out, you both head back here. Got it?"

"Yep. Okay."

I looked back toward the open door and hallway and hesitated.

"Go right down the hall and make another right and the bathrooms are there," a lady with a nice smile in a bright yellow blouse and a Mrs. Brady haircut said to me. A little boy a couple years younger than me looked up from ditto pages he was reading. He glanced at the lady in yellow, and then went back to his reading. I nodded and walked away.

The brown wallpaper ended as I turned down the smaller hallway. Beige, dirty walls with dim fluorescent lights led to the bathrooms. Just past the men's room stood another door. It had a metal handle that read 'fire escape'. Someone had left it pried open. I walked toward it and paused when I heard voices coming from the women's bathroom. Someone laughed and a woman's voice sounded angry. Realizing I couldn't pause there for too long, I rushed for the

81

fire escape and pushed through it.

Sunlight burned my eyes for a second as they adjusted. But pretty soon, I realized I stood on a cement walkway with grass on either side. It ended at the curb of what looked like a regular street. That street led off left and right and had another street perpendicular to it. Beige and white buildings with wooden windows stood on either side of the streets in all directions. Further down were the tall buildings with rounded roofs that I recognized from movies to be sound stages. Cars were parked in all sorts of places, but I didn't see a lot of people. I started down the street hoping to see cowboys in costume, or astronauts, or even vampires. No one was around. It just looked like a couple of big city blocks. Nothing special looked to be going on and I felt a little disappointed. Where were all the movie stars and directors with their megaphones? But I wasn't there to meet Joan Crawford or Bette Davis.

I kept walking down the street and as I approached one of the tall buildings, I noticed that its doors were open like a barn. Metal rafters peeked through and men in work clothes were climbing across the steel beams. Figuring I might get caught, I ducked into a short alley and I was lucky: straight down that alley were the giant feet of the water tower. My eyes followed the woven steel legs up to one platform, and then about fifty feet above that was the water tank itself. It gleamed white and reminded me of a blimp on its side, except for the round roof on top. The roof reminded me of the castle tower in 'Dracula'. I could see the center platform and the catwalk that connected to a ladder down one of the support legs. I ran toward the ladder.

I stood at the support leg, breathless from nervous energy, and realized there was a problem: the ladder was fifty feet or more over my head. I guess it was to keep people like me from just climbing up. Another thing made me a little nervous: the platform that wrapped around the bottom of the tank must have been about a hundred feet from the ground. Could I really make it after all?

You'll break your neck, the voice said. But like other times lately, I ignored the voice and instead puzzled over how I could hoist myself to the bottom of the ladder. I touched the thick metal collar that surrounded the leg and it was warm from the sun. If it was anything like a tree trunk, I could handle that since I was a champ at climbing trees. But it was smooth all around with nothing to grip. With no other option, I wrapped my arms around the metal and then raised my legs into a squat so that the bottoms of my feet now made contact with the metal. I'm sure I looked like a monkey and I didn't know if I would have the strength to climb the fifty feet or so of the column. But I couldn't give up now. I pulled my arms tight and pushed with my feet. My arms burned with pain. Grunting, I pulled myself up.

I had advanced maybe two feet when my muscles started to give out. I went limp and fell back to the ground on my butt.

"What the hell?" I heard a man's voice from behind.

I jumped up and turned to see a guy in jeans and a work shirt carrying a ladder and some sort of big light bulb. His shirt was stained with sweat.

"Kid, you gotta get—"

I didn't wait to hear what he said. Now that I was discovered, I ditched him fast. I pumped my arms and ran down another alley between two of the sound stages. People were walking back and forth and I dodged between them.

"Hey!" I heard a woman's voice. But everyone and everything flashed past my eyes as I kept running. I dodged around bushes and then a red Chevy truck. I paused between two storage sheds and tried to catch my breath. My lungs burned from the smoggy air. Heavy men's footfalls pounded toward me.

"Don't you move, kid! You are in trouble."

My feet had minds of their own at that second. It's as if they took off and I followed, chest heaving and heart pounding. Again, a blur of beige and dark figures shot past my eyes. I turned down an alley, looking over my left shoulder, and it seemed the footfalls behind had stopped. I paused again to catch my breath and turned. But my heart sank: a grey cinder block wall faced me. It was probably ten feet tall. Behind me the footfalls caught up and I turned to see who had been chasing me: two heavy older men who had to be at least fifty. They stopped and I could see their chests were heaving.

"Kid, you're under arrest and don't you move."

They weren't cops, they were only security guards. But they could detain me and turn me over to the police. I couldn't be arrested because that would mean juvenile hall. I turned toward the wall and stuck my fingertips into the joints where the cinder blocks met. Eight-year-old hands are just the right size to do that. I pulled myself up and reached for the next blocks two feet higher. The rough edges of the cinder blocks scraped my fingertips but I didn't care.

"What the hell!" one of the men yelled from behind. I heard

them rush to the wall but by the time they reached me, I was only about two feet from the top. I don't know how I did it but I made it to the top, pulled myself up, and now sat on the wall. One of the security officers jumped to try to grab my ankle but couldn't reach. The other one tried to get a grip on the cinder block gaps but his fingers were too big. My chest was heaving and I was finally able to catch my breath as I watched the two Keystone Cops realize they wouldn't be able to catch me. Finally, one of them took off his hat and I could see his thin red hair was matted from sweat. He looked up at me and almost growled through his red face.

"You get the hell outta here, kid, and if I ever see ya' again..."

He made a fist with his right hand and punched his left palm. The other security guard pulled off his cap and swiped away sweat from his forehead with his brown uniform sleeve.

"Yeah!" he grumbled.

Those fat butts couldn't lay a hand on you without going to jail, the voice said. That made me laugh and for the first time, I repeated something the voice said:

"I'm real scared of you two *fat butts!*"

With that, I turned toward the other side of the wall, pushed off from the top and jumped. In a second, icy spikes of pain shot up my ankles and legs. I collapsed to the ground. Crabgrass blades pushed into my cheek as I writhed in pain. I was sure I broke my legs but in less than a minute, the paid subsided. I sat up and rubbed my shins and looked around. When I saw where I was, I suddenly wished I were on the other side of the wall with the Keystone Cops beating me up.

I was surrounded by granite headstones and flat markers in the ground. Was this a movie set or a real graveyard? My eyes followed the lumpy ground and for maybe half a mile, all I could see were graves. I turned around and considered the wall again. Maybe I should just climb back over and surrender. But I turned back around fast when I heard something rustle in the leaves. A pigeon hopped around one of the head stones, pecked at something on the ground, then flew off. My skin broke out in goosebumps. All I could think about was the opening of "Creature Features" when a dead man opens his coffin, lifts himself out of it, and walks stiffly off the screen. It was daylight but that didn't make the graves any less spooky.

I saw no option but to start walking fast around the headstones. My feet sank and my right ankle twisted a couple time as I made my way trying to avoid lumps in the grass, and flowers that dotted the graves. The entire time, I was waiting for a hand to pop out and grab my leg like I had seen on 'Dark Shadows.' My heart pounded in my chest once again. The sounds of cars honking and tires hitting pavement started to come up in the distance so I knew this graveyard wasn't going to go on forever. Just ahead of me on the left, in a corner off by itself, was a tilted, rounded head stone. No other graves were near it and it made me pause. Something drew me toward it—I think mostly because it was off by itself in a corner.

I stepped up to the head stone and carved into grimy, gray granite were the words: 'Sophie Pimpson. Mother. 1898 – 1942'. It was so odd that there weren't any other graves for several feet in all directions. You would have thought she must have been someone special being off by herself but if that were true, why didn't she have a big tomb, obelisk, or statue like so many of the other graves nearby? *Nobody remembers her like no one's going to remember you,* the voice said.

I ignored the voice and my eyes locked on one thing: the word 'Mother'. Sophie had been somebody's mother, that much was clear. But that ended when she died almost thirty years ago. Judging by the looks of the neglected headstone and grave, no one had visited her for years.

We all end up lost and forgotten like this. You will, too.

But as if to contradict the voice, I heard my mom say again: *'God has special plans for you.'* Those words meant nothing right then because I hadn't thought about my own mom's voice in a long time. I hadn't thought about how she stayed right next to me whenever I was sick, or how she always kissed my cuts and bruises to make them get better. This ugly, forgotten headstone might as well have been for my mom. Its face was bumpy and rough against my fingers, and cold. I traced the letters M, then O, and by the time I started on the T, I felt my throat close and my head grow dizzy. As if I were frozen and stuck to the head stone, it seemed like it was swallowing me up. I had never been so scared and so sad. 'God has special plans for you' my mom's voice said once, and then again.

I looked around to see if anybody noticed I was crying. Nobody was around and nobody would have cared, anyway. Should I just run away? Where was I going to go at eight years old? I cried harder now.

"Look here, boy!" a voice said from behind.

I jumped up and wiped my face. The two fat security cops stood with their hands on their hips.

85

"You're in a lot of trouble," the one with red hair said. Whatever else he said didn't really matter because all I could think about was how alone I was. The other security guard grabbed my neck from behind and the three of us walked back to the studio. Pretty soon a real cop showed up and I told him I was from Hollygrove. I rode in the front seat of the police car the few blocks back to Hollygrove, which was pretty neat. I pretended I was Jim Reed from 'Adam 12'. A call came in from dispatch.

"Oh, can I answer that? I watch 'Adam 12' so I know what to say."

"No."

I shrugged and sat back. We pulled up in front of Hollygrove and a bunch of the kids ran to the side yard fence to look at us. I felt pretty special right then. It didn't last for long.

"Aye, that was very dangerous what you did," Mrs. Jeffers said the next day. She sat behind a big oak desk with carved, smiling angel faces and wings in each corner. They had also called Maureen who sat to my left. I just looked down at my scuffed Thom McCann high top sneakers with holes near the big toes.

"I'm sorry. But we can't have our wards leaving Hollygrove any time they please," Mrs. Jeffers said. "Let alone trespassing on private property."

I didn't care that much what she said because I was a hero to all the kids. At dinner the night before and into TV time, I told the story of almost climbing the Paramount Tower. Kids just 'oohed' and 'ahhed' at each part of the story. They got scared when I told them about the graveyard (I didn't tell them about crying) and wanted to know if I saw any ghosts. All of them were excited to hear about my police car ride and I told them the officer even let me take the dispatch calls. When I saw their faces light up over that fib, it's when I realized that telling stories about myself made kids think I really was special. They might even have liked me more. So whatever Mrs. Jeffers was saying, I just sat there remembering how cool I was.

"Gem, do you understand what Mrs. Jeffers is telling you?" Maureen asked.

I nodded. Maureen pulled a file out of her leather bag. She handed it to Mrs. Jeffers.

"There's finally an opening at Maryvale, Mrs. Jeffers," Maureen said. "I think Gem will get the supervision and discipline he needs there."

I recalled that Maryvale was the place Mrs. Wagner originally wanted me to live. I assumed this was good news. Since I was a ward of the court, it didn't really matter where I lived. That was another way I felt special—being a ward of the court. Not many children got to say that—just kids at orphanages. All part of God's special plan for me, I knew.

A couple weeks after I tried to climb the Paramount tower, I was packing up my paper grocery bags for the move to Maryvale.

"I just knew you would break some of the rules."

I turned around and saw Bobby. He stood at the doorway with his arms folded in that bossy way of his. A duffle bag sat at his feet. He pushed his glasses back up on his nose. When he did that, I noticed that one of his arms had a dark bruise.

"You're back!" was all I could think of to say.

"Yeah. It didn't work so good for me with that family."

"Where are your paper bags?"

"Don't need those anymore. I got this from the foster family."

He walked over and threw the duffle bag on the bed next to mine. He wore a pink T-shirt with a cartoon version of 'I Dream of Jeannie'. It was sort of a girly thing but it was nice. He opened the duffle bag and pulled out his radio that Aragon broke a long time back. It was taped up with Scotch and masking tape and it didn't look like it would ever work. He placed it carefully on the nightstand. I pointed to another bruise on this arm.

"You break your arm or something? Why so many bruises?"

He shook his head. He kept unpacking but then stopped. He looked around briefly and closed the door. He plopped onto the bed.

"'Cause you always been my best friend, I'm gonna tell you something nobody else knows."

Now I was curious. I pushed aside my grocery bags of stuff and sat facing him. He stroked his right hand with his left hand and then did the same in reverse. Nervous, I guess. He suddenly stood up and patted the sides of his thighs.

"Everything was okay at the foster family till they caught me."

"What did you do?"

Bobby dropped his eyes. He crossed his legs and pulled on the knees of his JC Penney jeans like they were the edge of a skirt or something. He leaned over and picked up the taped radio. He ran his fingertip along one of the tape edges.

"Well?" I said.

"Member how I used to always wanna dress like 'Bewitched' or 'I Dream of Jeannie' for Halloween?"

I nodded. He picked at the tape on the radio and wouldn't look up.

"So at the foster family, their daughter had the prettiest outfits. If I ever got left alone, I would go in and look at them. I knew it was against the rules to be in her bedroom."

"So. What's the big deal?"

Bobby jumped up and set the radio back on the nightstand. He turned his back toward me and raised his shirt. He had brownish welts and dark bruises all over. He dropped his shirt and turned back around.

"One day last week, I couldn't help it. I put on one of her dresses with pink daisies and ruffly collar. She also had a light blue crocheted poncho so I put that on, too."

"Why'd you do that?"

He shrugged.

"Then I was jumping up and down on her bed and turning around so that the poncho twirled around me like an umbrella. I could see it in the mirror and it made me happy. Then foster dad Edward walked in."

Bobby's voice started to quiver. When tears rolled down his eyes, I didn't know what to do. I patted his shoulder.

"So he beat you up?" I said.

Bobby nodded.

"And sent you back here?"

He nodded again.

"But you know it's okay because a boy shouldn't wanna wear a dress," Bobby almost whispered.

Bobby turned around and collapsed on the bed. He cried into his pillow. I stayed with him until he calmed down. About a half hour later, it was lunch time. He sat up and wiped his face.

"I'm hungry," he said. "Wanna go eat?"

Someone knocked on the door.

"Who's that knockin'?" Bobby looked at me. I shrugged

"Can I come in?" I recognized Maureen's voice behind the door.

"Yes," I answered.

When she walked in, Bobby smiled. He looked over her cream-colored blouse and emerald green skirt. Maureen nodded at him. She tapped the manila envelope with her shiny, apple-red fingertip.

"You all packed and ready?" she asked.

Bobby stood up and brushed the wrinkles out of his plaid shirt. He pushed his glasses up on his nose.

"You're the best roommate I ever had. So you going to a foster family?"

"No. I got into some trouble here and now I gotta go live at Maryvale orphanage."

"What rule did you break?"

"A big one. I even left Hollygrove for a couple hours."

"All by yourself?"

I nodded.

"Why'd you do that?"

I shrugged.

"I always knew you'd break a big rule someday. Where's Maryvale, anyway?"

I shrugged and looked at Maureen.

"Rosemead," she said.

"That far away from here?" Bobby asked.

"Pretty far," she answered. "We need to get going to beat the traffic."

I grabbed up my bags and this time, I was leaving Bobby. I didn't need to remind him to follow the rules. I didn't really know what to say. I had forgotten about him when he left months back so it wasn't like he was my best friend any longer. I had to say goodbye so much I got used to it.

"So, bye, Bobby. Have a Happy Easter."

Bobby nodded. He picked up the taped radio and ran his fingertips along its edges.

"Hope the Easter bunny brings you some pretty robin eggs," he said.

I turned with my bags and followed Maureen to the car. Shortly after, we drove onto the Hollywood Freeway and the tall buildings of downtown Los Angeles stood high and reflecting the early afternoon sun. We drove under decks of freeways and around tall buildings. I felt so small. Once we drove past the edge of the city, I noticed that we were on the 10 Freeway heading east.

"How far we gotta go?" I asked.

"A little over ten miles. Rosemead is about fifteen or twenty minutes away I'd figure. You know, my house is another seven or eight miles past."

"So you can come and see me more often maybe," I said.

"We'll see," she answered.

We eventually drove up a long driveway surrounded by lawns and arrived to a red brick rectangular structure. It was topped by an arch of weathered bronze with a cross at its center. The word 'Maryvale' was spelled out in bronze letters below the arch. Maureen stopped the car for a second.

"It sure is beautiful, isn't it?" she said.

I nodded.

"I wonder why no one is playing catch or touch football with all these lawns," I said.

Maureen chuckled and drove on. Palm trees that looked like columns popped up along the driveway and soon we pulled left in front of a two-story, red brick building that resembled a church. A carved image of the Virgin Mary in white stone lay above the oak front doors. Somehow I suddenly felt like I was going to church and I didn't like the feeling. Praying had begun to feel more and more like a waste of time.

We walked through the oak doors a few minutes later. My sneakers squeaked on the tile floor with its blue and red shiny glaze. The light of a wrought iron chandelier with artificial candles cast yellow light over a long, oak counter. As we stepped up to it, Maureen pulled a file from her briefcase. A nun stood up to greet us.

"Hello, I'm sister Agatha," she said. She smiled but the corners of her mouth turned downward. As she and Maureen talked, I regarded her face. The black frames of her glasses reflected the light from the chandelier so her eyes were more like mirrors. Her habit veil was unusual. It looked as if square welding goggles had been pushed up under the black material. The veil flattened the top of her head in such way that it reminded me of Frankenstein's monster's head. The only other thing I noticed was her white collar that made a long triangle almost to her belly button. All of it was strange to me.

"So, yes, we're very happy that you had a spot open up," Maureen said.

"I'm sure Gem will be well provided for here," Sister Agatha replied. "Let me ring Brother Harold, our director."

Maureen and I stepped over to a dark wooden bench up against the wall near a set of narrow stairs. I noticed the thick, swirling white plaster and I touched it. Though it was rough, I liked the patterns. A painting of Jesus with his exposed heart, surrounded by a crown of thorns, hung on the opposite wall. That sort of depiction of Jesus always made me feel creepy since it seemed as though I were seeing Jesus' guts. The creepy feeling faded quickly when I heard the loud clomp of someone coming down stairs.

Pretty soon, I saw the sharp tips of cowboy boots as they thudded down the tile stairs. Loose jeans tucked into the tops of the boots followed, and then came a slight belly pushing out a tucked beige shirt. I wondered if John Wayne was visiting the orphanage. I could smell a men's aftershave that was sort of a blend of a metal ice cube tray and a rose—Brut Cologne I would later find out. When the man stepped down the final stair, I saw it wasn't John Wayne. The man wore horned-rim glasses and a ten-gallon cowboy hat. He looked toward Maureen and me and smiled. He was more handsome than John Wayne and it was almost as if his teeth sparkled. I liked him. He reached out his hand and I noticed his fingernails needed to be clipped.

"You must be Gem," he said. I expected a Texas accent but his deep voice had no accent at all. I took his hand.

"Yes, hi."

"I'm Brother Harold. Welcome to Maryvale."

Sister Agatha joined us. She stood as if she were about to salute Brother Harold.

"Brother, this is Maureen, Gem's social worker."

Maureen reached out her hand and Brother Harold just nodded. Brother Harold put his hand on my back and it reminded me of my dad.

"Sister Agatha here will take you around and get you situated. We're sure happy the Lord brought you to us."

Sister Agatha put her arm around my shoulder and began to lead me away. I paused and looked back at Maureen.

"You're fine, Gem. I'm going to talk with Brother Harold a bit and get everything settled, okay?"

That Brother Harold is odd, the voice said. I shook my head.

"You alright, Gem?" Sister Agatha asked.

"Yeah."

"'Yes', Gem."

"Huh?"

"We say 'yes', not 'yeah'. And you say 'excuse me', not 'huh',"

And that began a whole year's worth of correcting, of all kinds.

"Aaaahhhhhhhhh!!!" the little blond boy screamed awake in the bunk above me. It was my second night at Maryvale in the young boys' dorm D. The gray steel tubes of the bunk bed creaked and squeaked as the boy fell back to sleep. He didn't seem to wake any of the other nine boys. I stared up at the striped mattress that pushed slightly through the support tubes supporting his bunk. Just as I started to fall back to sleep, I saw what looked like the light of a lighthouse scan across the room. Someone had cracked the door of the dorm and was shining a flashlight around in arcs. It gave me goosebumps and I lay still.

Once the door closed, I was wide awake. I had to find out what was going on. I got up and the linoleum floor tiles pressed coldly against the bottoms of my feet. As I made my way to the door, I glanced at the other bunk beds but nobody stirred. I looked over my shoulder once more to be sure no one was awake. I turned the heavy brass knob and pulled the door open.

The soft light from the hall sconces made me squint as I stuck my head out the door. Nobody was to the left, but when I looked right, I saw Brother Harold. He wore a shiny, navy robe over red-striped pajamas. Following just behind him was an older boy, probably twelve or thirteen, in a t-shirt and grey sweats. The boy carried a large, silver flashlight. He followed close behind Brother Harold as they paused at the next dorm door. Brother Harold pushed the door open and the boy stuck the flashlight in the room. After about thirty seconds, Brother Harold pulled the door shut. I watched as they made their way down the long haul, opening each dorm door, moving the flashlight about, and then closing the door. Once they looked into the last dorm door, Brother Harold nodded toward the boy and took the flashlight. Brother Harold and the boy walked down the end of the hall and disappeared.

"He's a Buckaroo!" the little blond boy who I now knew was Teddy said the next morning as we ate breakfast. "When you get to be older, Brother Harold makes you a Buckaroo sometimes."

"OK, but what do you get to do?" I asked. I took a bite of hot Malt-O-Meal cereal. The brown sugar and wheat grit rolled around on my tongue.

"All kinda' stuff," Teddy went on. "Get to stay up late and watch the late show. Sometimes even go to Santa Anita and watch the horses. Just all kinda' stuff."

"Hey Teddy, why you here? What happened to your mom and dad?"

Teddy shook his head. He took a bite of his cereal.

"You don' talk about that?" I asked. I knew he wouldn't. Most kids never did. But I wasn't really curious about it.

"Nope."

"Oh, 'cause you know, I'm just here till my dad gets back."

Teddy dropped his spoon. He looked up at me. His eyes sparkled with wonder as if it were Christmas morning.

"Really?" he asked.

Don't tell him where your dad really is. He won't like you very much.

"Yeah 'cause, see, my dad put me here because he's away on business trips all the time."

"Why doesn't your mom take care of you, then?" Teddy asked. He folded his arms and raised his blond eye brows.

"They got a divorce. Mom went away and married a famous prince in Europe."

Teddy shook his head. His mouth twisted so tight with doubt that it made his little chin dimple.

"You ever watch 'The Beverly Hillbillies'? "

Teddy nodded. But he went back to his bowl of Malt-O-Meal and slurped up the last spoonful.

"Well whenever they're in the backyard by the cement pond, you can see a house off in the background. That's my house!"

"Nope. That's just pretend."

"No it isn't. That's where I live and my dad is a big, important businessman. He's so rich and he even knows J. Paul Getty."

Teddy dropped his spoon into his bowl. He wiped his mouth with the back of his yellow-striped, long sleeve shirt.

"If you lie like that, you won't go to heaven." Teddy slid off the polished walnut bench and pushed away from the heavy wood table edge.

"I'm gonna go watch 'Scooby Doo'." He walked away.

He's just jealous because his mom and dad are probably dead.

The voice was right. And I liked the way it felt to pretend that I was from a rich family with a mom and dad. Everybody was rich on TV, lived in two story houses or mansions, and everybody was happy. So why couldn't I just pretend I was, too? A few days later, I got another idea. While the other kids were watching 'The Waltons', I snuck out of the TV room with the TV Guide. I had been flipping through it and ran across an ad for Wella Balsam shampoo. The model was so beautiful.

Back in my room, I used a pair of school scissors and carefully cut a small rectangle just around the model's face. My plan was to make it the same size as a school picture wallet photo. The rectangle was slightly off so I trimmed little bits from the edges until the picture was the right size. I pulled out the vinyl wallet they gave me at Hollygrove last Christmas. The plastic photo inserts were all empty except for a Pirate's License I had cut and filled out from a box of Jean LaFoote's Cinnamon Crunch. Carefully, I slid the photo of the model just behind my Pirate's License. That way, you could see the photo when I flipped the insert page and it wouldn't be too flimsy and fall apart.

I placed the wallet in my back pocket and pretended I was in the TV room with Teddy and the other kids. I rehearsed standing in front of the TV and waving my hands.

"Does anybody want to see the new picture my older sister just sent me?" I said.

I imagined all their faces lighting up.

"Yeah—the one who's the model?" I pretended Teddy asked.

I nodded. I pulled my wallet out and opened it up. One of the other boys would point at it I was sure.

"That's your sister?"

I would nod.

"Yeah. She's away in Hollywood doing more modeling stuff till dad takes us back to the mansion."

I finished rehearsing and I held the wallet out for a minute longer and enjoyed my handiwork. I tucked the wallet back into my pocket. I was ready for the real thing and headed back to the TV room. 'The Waltons' theme song was playing so I knew it was over. Now was my chance to do just what I practiced. I jumped up in front of the TV.

"Who wants to see the new picture of my sister?"

Two older boys who were playing checkers in the back shook their heads and gestured for me to shut up and sit down. Three girls about my age looked up from their tea party then looked back down, giggling for some reason. But Teddy and two younger boys came running up. One of the little guys had his hand down his pants and was scratching his butt. I held up my wallet a little higher so he couldn't touch it with his butt fingers.

"Your sister is like a movie star," the other little boy said. Teddy was carefully looking at the picture. His eyebrows knitted with suspicion.

"So she's in all those shampoo commercials?" he asked.

94

"Yes," I said. My chest swelled with pride.

"Hmm," Teddy said. "Then why don't she ever come and see you here if she's so famous?"

"She doesn't have time for me right now."

"Yeah, Teddy, shut up," the little one with the butt fingers said. "She don't got time like that. She's so pretty."

"Ohhhh, yeah," was all the other little boy managed to say.

"Well I just don't believe in a sister who doesn't come to see her brother, that's all."

"The Buckaroos are back from the race track!" one of the boys playing checkers said.

Everybody ran to the doorway and looked out. I sighed and tucked my wallet back into my pocket. So much for my moment of glory. What I didn't realize was how famous the Wella Balsam lady was becoming and how much trouble that picture was going to get me in. But it didn't matter right then. I stood with the other boys and watched as Brother Harold led the five Buckaroos through the front door.

The thing about the Buckaroos was everybody wanted to be one because they got so many privileges, like going to the race track with Brother Harold. They got to get their food first in the dining hall, and if a Buckaroo wanted to watch Bugs Bunny instead of Scooby Doo, everyone had to let him. Since they were all twelve or older and bigger than everybody else, who was going to stand up to them, anyway? What was unusual, though, was how quiet and disciplined they were around Brother Harold. I also didn't understand until much later why there were no girl Buckaroos.

When Brother Harold paused to hang his cowboy hat near the front door, they all paused, too. I could see that one of them had a white bag of leftover popcorn, and another had a giant box of Good and Plenty. Brother Harold nodded at them. He unbuttoned the cuffs of his long-sleeve white western shirt with blue shoulders as he walked upstairs. The Buckaroos followed each other in a line toward the dining hall. Just like a bunch of zombies from a Creature Features afternoon movie on Channel 13. It didn't matter to me, though. Race Track, popcorn, Good and Plenty. I wanted to be a Buckaroo just like all the other younger boys.

At Maryvale, all wards had chores. 'Responsibilities', Sister Agnes once said. Just like later when I eventually lived in foster homes, I had chores at Maryvale. To me, it just felt like I was a source of free labor. Somehow I also got it in my head that if I didn't do the chores perfectly, or keep getting straight A's in my classes, then I would be kicked out of Maryvale. That thought made my stomach tighten and head go light. I didn't know if I would ever find my dad, but I was sure that if I got kicked out of Maryvale, I would end up in juvenile hall and later, jail. That's where I thought kids who got kicked out of orphanages ended up—they had to live somewhere. That made sense to me. So I was afraid to not get straight A's and do my chores perfectly. The particular chore I was assigned was emptying all the trashcans on the first floor, including the offices, and then washing them on Saturdays.

I was scrubbing away at the gray lobby trashcan one particular Saturday. A new kid who was just being checked in had thrown up in it so I really had to use a lot of Comet to get the smell out. As I emptied the barfy water that smelled more like bleach than anything else, someone pulled my wallet from my pocket. I turned too quick and lost my grip on the trashcan. The water poured out and across my sneakers.

"Hey!"

Before I screamed or reached for the wallet, I stopped. It was a Buckaroo named Bradley. He was the biggest Buckaroo of all, a head taller than I. His black-brown eyes were looking at the photo. His mouth, surrounded by thin, black peach fuzz and dotted with zits that looked like red chocolate chips, tightened into a smile.

"So all the little punks say this is your sister?"

He held the wallet open to the TV Guide picture. I looked down and nodded.

"Yes."

"She's hot."

I shrugged. I wasn't sure what he meant.

"Why doesn't she come and take you away from here then?"

"Well she could if she wasn't so busy. She's at our family house in Beverly Hills."

Bradley shook his head and started to laugh. He threw the wallet at my chest and I caught it with a wet hand. I dried it off quickly.

"Liars go to hell, didn't you ever hear that?"

I nodded and tucked my wallet back in my pocket. I grabbed up the edge of the trash can.

"You're busted. Just wait."

He turned around and ran his long, bony fingers with their stubby nails through his black hair. His shoulders flexed under his green-striped shirt and they looked like logs.

"You smell like puke, too!" he said over his shoulder as he laughed and walked off.

I didn't really care what he meant by all that as long as I had my wallet back. He was right that my sneakers smelled like vomit and Comet. I took them off and scrubbed them with Comet and rinsed them. When I slid my feet back into them, they felt soggy and cold but at least they didn't stink. Right then, I wondered if my mom was looking down and knowing that I was making up stories like this. I paused to see if there were any signs that she was around. After a couple minutes, nothing happened so I went back to scrubbing the other first floor trash cans and forgot about it all.

But that didn't mean I wasn't thinking about other stuff. One of the hardest things for me was being left alone so much to think. Mom and Dad used to do a lot of thinking for me and told me what to do and so I did it. Now, though, except for rules about school, or meal times, or bed time, no one was around to tell me much of anything. For me, that meant I thought a lot about scary things. Monsters like Bigfoot, or Jeremiah from 'Dark Shadows', sometimes scared me when I thought about them at night, but that's not what I'm referring to. I would recall my mom dying, or if I would ever see my dad again, and that made my stomach twist. Pretty soon, I would be feeling nervous like I needed to throw up. Being alone as a kid made me feel like throwing up often. Nobody knew that and who would care if they did, anyway? So it was pretty easy for me to forget about Buckaroo Bradley and his threat. That was until two days later.

"Brother Harold will see you now," Sister Agnes said.

She stood outside the oak door with carved panels of crowns of thorns around hearts. Sister Agnes grabbed the brass knob stained by soil from years of use and turned it. As I stepped past her, I felt a slight pat on my right shoulder. Somehow that made things worse because I really didn't know what I had done.

Brother Harold sat behind a huge desk. It was rare to see him without his cowboy hat. With his dark brown hair slicked back, he looked like William Holden. Why he didn't become a movie star instead of a priest was anybody's guess. He nodded for me to sit in the chair across from him. I sat, more like sunk, into the oxblood leather chair. Brother Harold looked three feet taller now. Nervous, I picked at the dark cherry, carved arms of the chair.

"O'Connell," Brother Harold said. "Are you aware of why I called you to my office?"

I shook my head. Just over his right shoulder was a picture of Pope Paul in his white robe and beanie. Brother Harold cleared his throat and I looked back at him. He folded his long fingers such that he made a triangle with his index fingers and thumbs. I noticed a class ring with a cat's eye sapphire on his right ring finger as he raised his finger triangle to rest on the bottom of his chin, just touching the deep cleft.

"My I please see your wallet?" He held out his hand.

I sighed. So this is what Buckaroo Bradley meant by my being busted. I stood up and pulled out my wallet. I handed it to Brother Harold and sat again, feeling even smaller than I did before.

Brother Harold opened the wallet and turned right to the Wella Balsam photo. He held it up to me.

"Who is this?"

"My sis—"

Brother Harold's eyebrows rose into tight arches. He looked angry.

"I don't know. Just some lady."

Brother Harold reached into the plastic photo folder and pulled out the picture. He looked it over for a moment.

"Actually, this is an actress named Farrah Fawcett who is becoming very famous."

That I didn't know. Now I felt even more stupid.

"Oh," was all I could say.

"I understand that you have been telling the other wards that she is your sister."

I nodded. My face grew hot.

"Also, that you really live in a mansion in Beverly Hills."

I started to sweat. I nodded.

Brother Harold inhaled sharply. He tore up the picture of Farrah Fawcett and handed the pieces back to me.

"Go place those in the trash can by the door and come back and sit."

I dropped the pieces into the trash. I had the fleeting hope that I could rescue them on Saturday when I dumped the trash, but realized that if Brother Harold knew about my stories, then everybody else probably did, too. There would be no point to carrying her picture in my wallet any longer.

"Lying is a grave sin, do you understand that?"

98

I nodded. I wasn't sure making up stories about yourself was the same as lying to get out of trouble but I nodded.

"O'Connell, I understand that you have had a very difficult life so far. All of the wards have. But you have to understand that lying isn't the way to make your life better. Being truthful always, even about who you are and what you come from, is the only way to live the life the Lord expects of you."

It was the first time in a long time a grown-up cared about me enough to talk to me in that way. I wanted to understand more. I decided to ask a question.

"What does the Lord expect of me?"

Brother Harold's blue-green eyes sparkled and he smiled. He shook his head.

"Each of us has to find that out for ourselves."

Another nothing answer. How was I supposed to understand anything?

"So no more lying, understood?"

"Yes, Brother Harold."

Right then, since we were sort of close, I decided to ask another question.

"Can I become a Buckaroo?"

Brother Harold's eyes tightened and his lips curled down. It was as if he was Mr. Hyde all of a sudden. He unfolded his hands and lay them palms down on his desk as he leaned back in his chair.

"That is not an acceptable term for the older boys."

I didn't understand. I shrugged.

"Everybody seems to call them that," I answered.

"The older boys earn special privileges doing the Lord's work for me."

"Yeah—oops—yes, that's what I want to do."

Brother Harold stood up and walked around the desk. He grabbed my arm and pulled me to a standing position. He turned my shoulders towards the door and pointed.

"No more lying. We'll talk again when you're a couple years older about your request."

He led me to the door, opened it, and prodded me to go. Confused, I walked back to my dorm.

8.

Dr. Friedman's iPad alarm with its temple bell ringtone made Gem pause. He closed the manuscript. Gem leaned back and crossed his hands behind his head.

"You know you could re-set that thing to something more apt to your profession," he said.

"No. I had it set to 'Let's Go Crazy' because I love Prince so much. I got some phone calls and emails about it."

Gem grinned and nodded.

"So we're done with this romp through my Dickensian orphanage era for the day, then?"

Dr. Friedman was chuckling quietly.

"What?" Gem asked.

"Farrah Fawcett—you must have crapped your pants when she became a Charlie's Angel the next year after your fib."

"That's real supportive and therapeutic."

"Sorry—the self-aggrandizing deceptions are symptomatic of the privation you found humiliating."

"I liked it better when you were laughing. What a shitshow that whole time was."

"Anymore you want to add?"

"No. But I had forgotten about that perv Brother Harold."

"You never mentioned before that you had been sexually abused. We should discuss that."

"I wasn't. I never got to be a Buckaroo because I started fostering out pretty regularly. So I never got any action

100

from Brother Harold."

"Whatever happened to him?"

Gem stood up and stretched. His left knee cracked and popped as he stood. He glanced at Dr. Friedman whose eyebrows arched at the sound.

"You're my shrink not Richard Simmons so don't get started."

Dr. Friedman raised her hands palms upward and shook her head. She then formed a small circle with her right thumb and index finger and rotated the circle against her lips.

"Tick a lock, tick a lock," she said.

"A bunch of the Buckaroos brought it all up to the L.A. Times and they were part of that big settlement the church paid. Brother Harold it turns out had been transferred to Peru or Chile, somewhere down south."

"I have treated a few guys over the years who had been through molestation. It's hard to treat and it's one of those areas that there just isn't enough good science to understand it fully. But there is nothing worse, nothing, than an adult in charge of kids sexually harming them."

"That's what I would have thought, too. But there are some things that are worse."

Dr. Friedman's iPad alarm went off a second time. Gem shrugged and raised his palms to the air.

"What was the last alarm—the two-minute warning or something?"

Dr. Friedman punched off the alarm and tossed her iPad into her purse.

"I just can't get the thing right sometimes. Now that last comment of yours—want to explain?"

"The two minute alarm?"

"Really?"

Gem stepped toward the door and grabbed the knob. His head felt tight from the stress of the memories.

"We'll get to that. Just not now, okay?"

Dr. Friedman stood and untucked her pink running suit that had made its way into some uncomfortable folds.

"That's fine. Next appointment is due in about twenty, anyway. Farrah Fawcett, you slay me!"

The next morning, Gem stopped at Starbucks on Wilshire and Arnaz, a few blocks down from Dr. Friedman's office. He picked up two café lattes. When he stepped into Dr. Friedman's office, she tapped away at her iPad screen. She gestured for him to sit and nodded without looking up. Gem stepped over and waved one of the café lattes under her nose. Now she looked up.

"I had to stop at the cleaners this morning so I didn't have time to grab one," she said. "Kelly *is* a lucky woman."

Gem rolled his eyes.

"Yeah, right."

"Sit already," Dr. Friedman said. She tapped her iPad a few more times then set it aside.

"Okay, so this voice in your head," she began.

Gem took a sip of his café latte and burned his lip. He grimaced.

"Yeah, what about it? Am I schizo?"

"Ha."

Dr. Friedman took a sip of her café latte.

"Ah-shit!"

"I know—it's hotter than usual, isn't it? And that's after a few blocks in my car," Gem said.

"I might be able to taste my dinner later. No taste buds right now. So, anyway, the voice. Did you realize you had discovered your conscience and mind at that point?"

"I hadn't thought it through, pardon the pun."

"So you were at ease with that new awareness?"

"Yep. I trusted that it was seeing things the way they were, whether I liked it or not."

"With your anxiety disorder, it's surprising that you were at ease with it."

Dr. Friedman picked up the iPad and made a quick note. She nodded at him.

"Okay, let's get started. I just wanted to check in with you about the voice."

She handed Gem the manuscript. She pulled the lid off her Starbucks and waved her hand over it.

9.

Maureen continued to reassure me that she was working on a foster home, but it took time. I guess she started to feel bad, so just before Easter, she got permission to take me to her house to watch 'The Wizard of Oz' on TV. She lived only a few miles east of Maryvale so we arrived quickly.

"And I have permission to let you spend the night tonight, too, so that's why I told you to bring your p.j.'s and toothbrush," she said as we drove along in her black Corvair. The sun was blaring in on us, making it hot inside the car, even though we had the windows down.

"It's not too much farther, and if you keep going on the 10 Freeway, you know where you end up?"

I shook my head. I didn't care.

"The Mojave Desert."

"Do you live near the desert?"

Maureen's face lit up for a second because it was the first thing I said on our drive.

"Well, sort of. It's an hour and a half or so."

So from Maureen's house, I determined, I could probably get to the desert. That's where Dad was. I kept quiet the rest of the drive. The dry air from the open windows made me think of the dry air my dad must breathe all the time. In some strange way, that made me feel closer to him. I was going to get to him, one way or another. Eight years old, with no money, right then I could sure use Samantha's powers. But it didn't matter. I was going to get to him.

Maureen made Hershey's fudge that night, and invited her fiancé Bruce over to watch the movie. I was surprised at first to see that Bruce was white but then I figured that if I could have a black best friend like Bobby, why couldn't Maureen have a white husband? I didn't really understand why all that mattered as long as people loved each other. And since Maureen was now officially taken, which disappointed me, I decided I was going to have my own beautiful, black wife some day.

Maureen's fudge didn't set up correctly so we ended up having to eat it with spoons. We sat on the couch with the lights off. Maureen sat between Bruce and me. I slurped up a thick, gritty rope of fudge as the Wicked Witch of the West sent the flying monkeys ahead to get Dorothy and the others.

'...I sent a little insect ahead to take the fight out of them...' the Wicked Witch said. I stopped slurping the rope of fudge.

"What's she mean by that, anyway?" I asked.

"What?" Maureen answered.

"She sent 'an insect ahead'. I've been watching every year my whole life, and I never know what she means by that."

Maureen shrugged. "Bruce?"

"I didn't hear her say it," he said. "Must not be important to the story. Maybe they cut a scene."

By the time we got to the end of the movie and the Wicked Witch melted into the floor (I covered my eyes – that part always scared me), my mouth was sticky with fudge and my teeth gritty from sugar.

'...There's no place like home...' Dorothy said and I started to feel like I was going to cry. There was something I knew about Dorothy.

"She died from taking sleeping pills, didn't she?" I asked.

Maureen stood up and shut off the TV. She turned toward me.

"Where did you ever hear that?"

"I don't remember. But now when I see her at the end of the movie, I always think of her being dead from sleeping pills."

"That's awful, Gem. I'm sorry you think about that."

What I didn't tell Maureen was that it made me think of my mom, too. I didn't know why it reminded me of her but I guess it was because they were both dead, or in heaven as I still believed.

"Gem, let's get you a blanket and pillow and get you set up on the couch here for the night. Right after I say goodnight to Bruce."

"Goodnight. Huh? I don't get to spend the night, too?" Bruce asked.

"Yeah," I chimed in. "Maybe we could all stay up late and watch Seymour and a scary movie."

"Not tonight. We're all filled up."

After Bruce left and we set up the couch, Maureen went to bed. I thought about Dorothy again, and Mom. What made me feel less sad was knowing that I was going to go find my dad in the morning.

The early morning light was orange and blue, and I could hear Maureen snoring in her bedroom. I quietly dressed but did not put on my shoes. I tiptoed to the front door in my socks. When I got outside, I sat on the steps that led to her apartment from the ground floor. The little pebbles stuck in the steps pushed through my jeans and poked at my butt. As soon as my shoes were tied, I stood up and ran down the stairs.

Maureen had told me that the desert was east of her house, and I knew the sun rose in the east. So I ran down Maureen's street, and then another side street until the morning sun hit my face with stinging warmth. I knew I was walking east.

Because I was too young to wear a watch, I really couldn't say how long I walked. Questions swirled through my mind. What would my dad look like now? I hadn't seen him for a couple years. Would he recognize me? I couldn't wait to play catch so he could see how good of a third baseman I was. I got more excited as I walked. The sun had risen higher, and I was getting hungry. I never got anywhere near the desert, though, because just in front of Woolworth's on some city main street, a police car pulled up to me with its siren blaring. I stopped as a policeman jumped out of the car.

"Your name Gem O'Connell?" he asked.

"Am I gonna get it?"

"No."

"Then that's my name."

"You gotta come with me, son."

"You gonna handcuff me?"

"No, you're not under arrest."

Just then, two old ladies opened the glass door at the Woolworth's and leaned against it. They looked at me with suspicion. I suddenly thought if I were handcuffed, they would maybe think I was special.

"Why can't you handcuff me?"

The policeman pushed his hat up to the top of his head and he reminded me of Officer Malloy on 'Adam 12'. He smiled and walked over to me and grabbed my shoulder.

"Let's go."

"Gem, you're okay, you're okay!" Maureen hollered and threw her arms around me as we stepped into the West Covina Police Department lobby. I didn't know what the matter was, and I thought it was funny that she was in her pajamas and robe. I had never seen her hair messed up and with no makeup on her face. She was still so pretty though.

"Why'd you do that?" she asked.

"That was a very dangerous thing to do, running away," the policeman said.

"I wasn't running away."

"What were you doing, then?" Maureen asked.

The policeman folded his arms and I thought I would get in more trouble if I didn't tell them.

"I just wanted to find my dad."

"Huh?" the policeman said.

"Officer, before we finish the report and all, can I speak to Gem a second?" Maureen said.

"Yes. Meet me at the front desk when you're done."

The policeman walked away. Maureen led me to a lime-colored plastic chair. Its shape reminded me of a pear.

"Sit down, Gem."

Maureen slid into the chair next to me. Her checkered flannel robe made the plastic chair squeak.

"Gem, you're a little young for this." She sighed. "But I think it's time I tell you something."

I shrugged, but I was sure glad that this time I wasn't supposed to already know.

"Your Dad isn't just living in the desert, all right?"

" 'Kay."

"He's in the California Men's Colony."

"You mean like one of those hippy communes like Manson?"

"No, Gem. The California Men's Colony is a prison. He did some very bad things."

"What'd he do?"

He played doctor with those little girls... the voice said in my head.

"It doesn't matter. When you're grown up, we can talk about it. Till then, you need to understand: you can never go to your dad, and he will never be able to take care of you. Okay?"

I shrugged. For now, I guess I had to remember I was just a little kid. But someday, I would go find him, jail or no jail. Maybe I could even help him bust out. Or maybe he would bust out and come for me. It made me feel so alone again.

Deep down, and the voice reminded me often, I knew I didn't really matter to anybody. I wasn't even sure my criminal of a dad would care once I found him, either. I hoped he would. When I would go to a foster home I liked it, unless the foster mom stuck a hot iron against my back or a foster brother tried something nasty. But those things didn't happen very often and Maureen was always there to take care of it if they did. I could tell a lot of foster parents took care of me just because it made them feel good about themselves, like they would go to heaven for taking care of me. Even Maureen was just doing her job—she couldn't have really cared that much about me.

I thought about doing it lots of times before, but for some reason now felt like the right time to give it a try. I pinched the handle of the plastic magnifying glass--the prize I took from a box of Crackerjacks a sucker at school asked me to keep an eye on——and held it up over the sidewalk. The grains of cement looked as big as boulders. But what I was going after, the vibrating trail of black ants, turned into a line of plump monsters. I trained the sharp point of sun on the back end of one of the ants, and it revved up its six feet. It reminded me of the 'Roadrunner' taking off, but not for long. Pretty soon, its back end blew up like a water balloon.

It smelled like burned asparagus. The whole line of ants swirled and ran in all directions away from the crispy critter one.

You just killed a living thing and made it feel pain. You're afraid of pain, too. How could you do that?

The voice was right and I already felt something new: maybe I did deserve to be alone if I could hurt something on purpose. I looked once more at the poor ant. Another idea came to me: God probably didn't have a special plan for me after all. I was alone. And worse, as a child without a real family, I was no better than that poor ant. A nothing ward of the court with no family. Not sure what to do, but feeling so sad, I blew the dead ant's body into the grass. I heard a car's engine that sounded like a coffee percolator just then. I looked over my shoulder and saw the sky blue Pinto hatchback coming down Morning Glory Avenue. What would I explain to my foster mom, Jennifer?

When the Pinto's engine chugged to a stop in the driveway, I slid the magnifying glass into the pocket of my moss-green corduroys. I was nervous she might have seen what I was doing so I kept an eye on the driver's side door as it creaked open.

In the three-and-a-half years since Mom died and I became a foster kid, I had learned how to read adults' faces for signs. Frowns could mean they're mad or frustrated or ready to kill me. If they wrinkled their eyebrows up, I was really done for and I was going to have to pack my grocery bags and leave. So I figured out the right things to say or do at the right time, and if their faces relaxed --they didn't even have to smile—-I was staying put and okay for awhile. That's why her face would tell me everything, and if I needed to lie, I was ready. I couldn't tell her the truth about what I was doing, because that would get me sent away for sure. And if she asked me why, I really couldn't explain why I wanted to try it and worse, how awful it made me feel after. The most important thing was not to get in trouble and get sent back to Maryvale and Brother Harold. The only thing that kept the teenage boys from beating the crap out of me whenever they felt like it was that I was so good in any sport and they all wanted me on their side. I got picked first for everything even though I was only eleven and a half now and not real tall. Brother Harold still wouldn't let me be a Buckaroo and that meant I remained a guppy at Maryvale.

I walked toward the car door. My legs made my corduroy pants wheeze and it could have been from muscle or fat since I wasn't getting to play any team sports at foster homes. No sports meant no exercise and I still liked anything from Hostess.

'...Who needs wings to fly?...' The song started in my head. I can't explain the song at all. It started just after my ninth birthday at Maryvale. One night I woke up from a nightmare about my dad – his face looked like the Devil's in my old religion book – and I couldn't get back to sleep. Every creak or moan in the dormitory made my skin tingle with goosebumps. Then, all of a sudden, this song popped into my head. It kept going and going and pretty soon, I fell asleep. After that, anytime I felt scared, the song came into my mind.

'...Who needs wings to fly?...' I only knew those five words, and couldn't remember then what the song was or how I knew it. I only knew that whenever I was scared, the song popped into my head and kept repeating. The same five words, always a grown-up man's voice singing them. The voice in my head said once: '...You'll find out when you're ready...'

'...Who needs wings to fly?...'

"Whatcha doing?" Jennifer said.

Her big green eyes and freckled nose folded into a smile when she asked the question, and I knew I was okay. The song stopped, too.

"Nothin'."

Jennifer stepped to the back of the car and I followed her as she opened the hatch. She leaned forward to grab three paper bags of groceries and I could see shiny spots of sweat where the ends of her red, shag hair met her neck.

"Do you want help with the groceries?" I asked.

"You're always so good. And just for that, I'll give you the surprise I got you when we get inside."

"Okay."

I wasn't all that excited about a surprise -- whenever she went to the store, she always brought me back something boring like a Hardy Boys book or a plastic kaleidoscope. *She feels sorry for you, but that's still kind.* The voice was probably right: I knew that Jennifer and her husband, Ted, were waiting to hear about adopting a baby. I was probably just practice for that. I was just a big practice baby to them.

I walked through the front door and past Ted who sat Indian-style on the floor with his back against the bottom of the orange and brown, Naugahyde couch. You would have thought he was asleep, but I knew what he was doing: meditating. Ted and Jennifer had learned Transcendental Meditation just before I arrived. One of them was always mentioning their 'mantra' or that if I wasn't good, my 'karma' would catch up to me in another life. As he muttered his mantra, I stepped past him into the kitchen. I set the grocery bag on the brown Formica kitchen table. Jennifer stooped over and was staring at a spot on the avocado-colored wall. She licked her pointer finger and rubbed. The thin straps of her rose-colored halter-top dug into her shoulders. She shook her head and said with a whisper:

"We just painted. How could there already be a grease splatter?"

I shrugged. I had no idea.

"Oh, yeah. Let me get your surprise, but—"

She lifted her finger to her closed mouth so that I wouldn't disturb Ted's meditation. I nodded as Jennifer rustled through the paper bags. She turned around and held something behind her back.

"Before I give this to you, I want you to know something. This is a reward for all your good grades."

A loud snore erupted from the living room. Jennifer looked at me and rolled her eyes.

"Ted, wake up!" Jennifer hollered. "It doesn't do any good if you fall asleep!" Jennifer said. "Anyway, Gem. Here."

She handed me a brand new box of sixty-four Crayola crayons. This was a surprise I could use; it was a perfect surprise. I didn't know what to say. I turned the box over to look at the built-in sharpener, a yellow cone inside a hole. Popping the edges of the box top, I flipped the lid and looked at the tips of the crayons. Four smaller boxes divided the crayons into rows of eight tips of an array of colors. They were perfect like rocket points. I stuck my nose into the box and inhaled: wax and raisins.

"Smelling them?" Jennifer asked.

I almost couldn't even nod because the smell made me anxious to use them. I ran toward the kitchen door but Jennifer stopped me.

"Look what else I got."

She held up a bag of Nestlé's Semisweet Chocolate Chips.

"'Creature Features' is on tonight and guess what they're showing?"

I just wanted to get to my room.

"Don't know."

"'Frankenstein'. You can stay up with me and we'll whip up the cookies."

I nodded and as I turned to leave, Jennifer stopped me again.

"Here's a box of Crackerjacks, too."

Crackerjacks too! I reached for them but Jennifer held them up.

"Promise you won't dig into the other five boxes to get the prizes, though."

"Okay, I promise."

Jennifer handed me the box and I grabbed it and ran toward the bedroom.

"I didn't even get in my twenty minutes," Ted said from behind.

"Ted!" I heard Jennifer yell. "Crap, that cat got a bird again!"

I closed the bedroom door. Even though it was my room for awhile, it was half finished being painted yellow for the baby. I opened the crayon box and smelled the crayons once more. Ripping open the Crackerjacks, I dug past the sticky, rough kernels of caramel popcorn and pulled out the flat prize wrapped in red and white paper. My heart sped up: it was the right shape and size to be a paint kit with a flat paper brush and colors. Tearing it open, I saw what it was: a book of tattoos. I was disappointed.

I sat down at a three-drawer desk and pulled open one of its bright yellow drawers with the teddy bear stickers on its front. Those teddy bears were the dumbest decals I ever saw. I hated the yellow color Jennifer was painting the room, too. But what I felt about the color didn't mean anything. I would be gone by the time they got their baby. That's why I never unpacked my brown grocery bags and one cardboard box that I had added since Maryvale. They held everything I owned. I left them on the closet shelf and went into them only when I had to. The desk drawer held my belongings that were most important to me: my map to the movie stars' homes with Mrs. Partridge's house marked on it; my drawing supplies; my baseball cards; and my Crackerjack prizes. I dropped the tattoo booklet into the bottom of the drawer with the rest of the prizes I had collected. When I pulled out the Academy sketchpad with the charcoal drawing of a hand and pencil on the red cover, and its black binding still twisted from Eugene Aragon's fat fingers, I stopped thinking about the teddy bear stickers.

I opened the sketchpad halfway, past all my old 'Bewitched' drawings I did back at Hollygrove. I didn't believe in magic any longer—it was just stupid kid stuff. Two pages had drawings I had done of my dad. Actually, they were drawings of who I wished my dad was. One was an astronaut, complete with a helmet. Another was a fireman next to a bright red truck. Then there was the doctor with the stethoscope. I even did one of him hitting the Oakland A's winning home run in the 1972 World Series. Now that I knew he did some bad things, I felt embarrassed looking at the drawings. I started to bunch up the pages to tear them out and throw them away but I stopped. I couldn't do it.

I flipped to the drawing of the 'Partridge Family' bus. Its sides were covered with mosaics of different sized and colored rectangles, each outlined in black crayon. The Partridges seemed so real, like a real family. Not from old times like the Waltons. I liked that show a lot, too. But the Partridges had exciting adventures and all the kids mattered when they played their music. The bus was so neat to me that I had the official lunch pail. I looked over the drawing. That one I did quite well. I flipped to a blank page and my stomach tickled with butterflies of anticipation. What secret did the blank page have that I was about to discover? I popped open the cover of the crayon box and pulled out the burgundy crayon. Its unused tip came to a perfect point. I gritted my teeth -- it always hurt to have to mess up the crayon tips -- then pressed the crayon to the paper and began to draw. In a couple moments, the outline of a lady's pantsuit began to take shape. I switched to the peach crayon and drew in the arms and face. Grabbing up the lemon yellow crayon, I lightly stroked the head and made blonde hair.

"Keith, I need you to help Lori with her campaign for class president," I said, doing the voice for Shirley Jones. I made up my own episode of the show, doing everybody's voices, drawing by drawing.

"Okay," Jennifer said later that night. "Try this."

She held out her finger and a grainy, pale beige blob of cookie dough hung off the tip. I leaned back and shook my head.

"Just get some yourself, then. But you gotta taste it."

I dunked my finger into the bowl and scooped up a blob of the gooey batter. When I licked it off, brown and white sugar mixed with Imperial margarine and egg to make fluffy sweetness in my mouth.

"Not so bad, huh?"

"It's okay."

"I'll put the flour in now and we'll try it again. You're gonna like it even better."

I already liked the dough enough, in the same way I liked Jennifer: enough. She was real nice compared to other foster moms. We spent a lot of late nights together because Ted worked the graveyard shift at Dunkirk Pneumatics. *She's lonely at night,* the voice told me. I guess I made a good substitute for Ted. Ted wasn't all that interested in me except for when we talked baseball. For the whole time I was there, Jennifer and Ted were both pretty good to me. Other foster parents hit me, or locked me in a room, or just ignored me. Some even made up nasty nicknames—always based on my first name and ones I had heard so many times before like 'Doobie Ruby', ' Sissy Sapphire' or ' Jerkon Zircon'. One time, this really strange foster mom took whatever money she got that was supposed to be for my food and spent it on clothes for herself at Zody's. So when you compared Ted and Jennifer to those kinds of foster parents, they were very good.

"Ooh, 'Creature Features' is starting," Jennifer said.

She reached for the volume knob on the dinky black and white TV, but she stopped when she realized she had flour on her fingers.

"Gem, get the volume."

I turned up the TV and a cracking roll of thunder came from the black screen as it warmed up. The thunder sound raised goosebumps on my arms and I looked at Jennifer to see if she could tell I was scared and squinting. As the picture faded up, I saw it through my narrowed eyes: the coffin sitting by the window. The four candles flickered around it, and another flash of lightning and crack of thunder rumbled. Now I closed my eyes and listened for the creak of the coffin hinges. I put my hands up to cover my eyes, but as soon as I heard the creepy, raspy laugh, it was no use: I could see the figure in my mind. The tall corpse in a Sunday suit climbing stiffly out of the coffin, shuffling and twisting, its face nothing but a shadow. But even worse, the walking dead man reminds me, the coffin reminds me, the candles remind me, of Mom.

'...You're soaking in it...' Madge the Manicurist said and I dropped my hands when I realized a commercial had started. I looked at Jennifer but she was now busy adding the chocolate chips to the batter.

"This is when the dough tastes best. But don't fill up on it because you won't want any cookies later," she said as she plucked up another wad of the cookie dough.

We baked cookies while we watched 'Frankenstein.' My hands shot up to my eyes several times through the movie. The scariest part for me was when the Monster threw the little girl into the lake. But even though the movie had scary parts, none of it was as scary as the beginning of 'Creature Features'.

When I went to bed that night, I left the light on in the room. I hated those stupid teddy bears on the wallpaper, but it made me feel better to look at them. Anything was better than thinking about the corpse rising out of the coffin. Each time I thought about him, my whole body shivered like I just touched a filling with Wrigley's gum foil. Pulling the blankets up tightly to my neck, I tried to stare at the teddy bears.

"Frankenstein wasn't scary at all," Marty said the next Monday.

He stood in line behind the chain-link backstop, waiting for his turn at kick ball. I watched as Wheezing Marty—everybody called him that because of his asthma--reached up with one of his skinny arms that looked like Popsicle sticks and fooled with the little chain around his neck. The thing on the end of the chain fascinated me: a white plastic asthma inhaler. Wheezing Marty told me his mom made him wear it around his neck for safety.

The black top sent up heat like a pancake griddle that day. My face felt hot and sweat made the tips of Wheezing Marty's short, sandy hair stick to his forehead. My lungs burned from the smog that made the sky brown and orange like fall leaves and made Wheezing Marty hold onto the inhaler.

"I shouldn't be out for P.E. at all when it's smoggy," Wheezing Marty said. "But Mom said it was okay as long as I keep my inhaler with me."

But I wasn't really paying attention to what Wheezing Marty was saying. I felt embarrassed about being afraid of 'Frankenstein'. And not only was he not afraid of Frankenstein, he also had a mom who made sure he had his inhaler.

"So you really aren't afraid of 'Frankenstein'?" I asked. But I really wanted to ask how it felt to still have a mom who cared about him. The feeling of not mattering and being a ward of the court made me go quiet.

"Nope. Hey, I'm up."

Wheezing Marty ran to home plate, but just as Glenn Umemoto wound up to pitch the kickball, Wheezing Marty stepped away from the plate. He ran up behind the backstop and took off his inhaler, setting it on the wooden bench.

"Don't want this to hit me in the face when I go to kick. Would ya' watch it for me, Gem?"

I nodded. I thought about opening it up and breathing from it just to see what it felt like, but I didn't want his germs near my mouth. I felt stupid that I was scared of 'Frankenstein', and then I felt like nothing. Even Wheezing Marty was better than me because he had a mom who cared about him.

Glenn pitched the yellow kickball that was stained with black top skid marks and it bounced toward Wheezing Marty. He caught it.

"Too high," Wheezing Marty said, tossing the ball back to Glenn. "Pitch it again."

This time, Glenn rolled the ball back toward Wheezing Marty, and it thudded and hopped. Marty rushed the ball and slammed it with the tip of his black sneaker. The ball arced into the air, heading for right field. Wheezing Marty took off for first base, his arms pumping from under his short-sleeve shirt.

Roxanne Liston ran like a blonde comet to catch the ball but it fell in front of her, bounced once and then a second time, right over her head. Wheezing Marty raced to second base and as he rounded it, he stopped. He grabbed his chest. His shoulders heaved a couple times and his face turned red. He ran toward the backstop.

"He needs his breather!" Glenn Umemoto screamed.

Wheezing Marty ran past Glenn and made it to the wooden bench. I saw that his face was pink and wet, and his eyes were big, blue scared marbles. I got scared for a second.

"Gem, where's my --?" he choked.

I shrugged. Wheezing Marty wasn't better than me at that moment.

"Go tell Miss Steen!" Glenn Umemoto hollered. "He's gonna die!"

Wheezing Marty's chest rose and fell as fast as a dog's. Each breath he took sounded like a cat scratching on a window screen. Wheezing Marty looked at me and I held my hands up in the air. I acted as if I was looking for the inhaler under the bench.

"What's going on?" Miss Steen said as she ran up.

My stomach twisted into a knot. *Miss Steen knows you're involved.* If the voice was right like always, then I figured Miss Steen hated me.

"Marty lost his breather!" Glenn Umemoto yelled.

"Marty, sit down," she commanded. "Where did you leave it?"

Wheezing Marty pointed to the bench.

"Everyone, start looking!"

The entire class looked like hound dogs as they crawled and searched under and around the bench. I pretended to help, too. When the Phillips twins came around the side of the bench where I was, I realized Miss Steen couldn't see past their tall bodies. I pulled the inhaler out of my pocket and dropped it. I stepped past the Phillips twins and went to Wheezing Marty's side. I shook my head and shrugged at Wheezing Marty.

"Here it is!" the Phillips twins screamed in unison.

Miss Steen snatched up Wheezing Marty's inhaler with her claw-like hands and held it while Marty took two deep breaths. Marty nodded and Miss Steen pushed her short, blonde hair back over her ears.

"You understand what almost happened, Marty? Why did you take it off? Let's get to the nurse's office."

As Miss Steen and Marty stepped past me, they stopped. She looked at me for just a second, her narrow blue eyes becoming cobalt slits.

"Gem, you don't know anything about this, do you?"

"Marty asked me to watch his thingamabob. After he kicked and started running back here, it wasn't on the bench anymore. That's all I know."

Miss Steen lifted her hands off Marty's shoulders, wove her fingers together and cracked her knuckles.

"I asked Gem to watch my inhaler, Miss Steen," Marty said. He had begun to catch his breath and breathe normally again. "I guess it fell off the bench and he didn't know it."

Miss Steen's lips, which looked like strips of thin, gray wax, squeezed together in a sort of smile, turned down at the corners. It made me wonder if she just took some Kaopectate. But I knew she didn't like me and it was no surprise to me that she suspected me. She was right. I made brave, Wheezing Marty gasp for a little while. It made me feel better to know that he was scared like me.

"Our problem is this, Mrs. Thompson," Miss Steen said the next Wednesday afternoon to Jennifer. Miss Steen slid a manila file across her desk and opened it.

"Gem is my highest scoring student in all subjects – except vocal music, of course."

Jennifer nodded. I sat at my desk and thought about how weird it was to have Jennifer in my classroom. Sunlight made orange and black stripes as it passed through the blinds. I had never seen light like this before because I never had been at school as late as four-thirty.

"Gem," Miss Steen said. "Would you mind erasing the blackboard for me while I talk to your -- Mrs. Thompson?"

"Yes, Miss Steen. Should I wipe it with wet paper towels, too?"

"No. Just erase it, please."

Miss Steen hushed her voice, but not enough so that I couldn't hear what she said.

"Just the other day, one of our students --an asthmatic-- lost his inhaler temporarily. Gem was asked to keep an eye on it but it disappeared."

"So," Jennifer responded.

The powder and metal smell of chalk dust filled my nose as I erased the board. Rubbing hard, I tried to make the brushing sound loud enough to fool Miss Steen into thinking I couldn't hear what they talked about. SWISH, SWISH, SWISH the eraser sounded.

"Gem and three other students --all girls-- ran ahead of the

116

class after P.E. a few weeks back. When I returned to the classroom, someone had written 'the noon aide is a nymphomaniac' on the blackboard. Now it wasn't neat enough to be Gem's handwriting, and no one would admit who wrote it. None of those girls could know what that means."

"It's nineteen-seventy-three, Miss Steen. Kids know a lot more than you think."

I heard the word 'nymphomaniac' on 'One Life to Live', a soap opera I had started watching after 'Joker's Wild' the previous summer. I never looked up the word in the dictionary but it seemed to be something bad to call a lady.

SWISH, SWISH.

"Then there was the lunch bag burning incident. Gem found it and helped the noon aide put it out. But he was there again. Oh, and Cherilyn Snell's chair was pulled out from under her as she started to sit and she bounced to the floor. Gem said he was just resting his legs on her chair bottom when it slid."

I did the chair thing to Cherilyn after she told me I was weird for being a child without a mother. I had nothing to do with the lunch bag fire.

SWISH, SWISH.

"If he was causing all these problems, why are his grades so good?" Jennifer asked.

"Troubled children can be very capable academically. Many are even gifted like Gem."

SWISH. SWISH.

"Miss Steen, if he gets into trouble here, he's going to have to go back to Maryvale. Unless you can prove something, I think you're wrong to bring it up to us."

My stomach twisted when Jennifer said I would have to go back. I really hated Maryvale. Over the swishing eraser, I heard the CRACK. I looked over just as Miss Steen relaxed her knuckles.

"Mrs. Thompson, I really just wanted to talk with you in order to find out if Gem was having behavior problems at home."

"No, he isn't. I think he trusts my husband and me."

"I'm sure he does. But I've got a whole classroom to think about and—"

A chair scraped the floor as Jennifer stood up.

"I'm finished talking to you. Gem, let's go."

I dropped the erasers on the chalkboard tray and followed

behind Jennifer.

"I'll let you know of anything further," Miss Steen hollered though the classroom door. "See you tomorrow morning, Gem."

The rotted meat smell of old potato peelings made me feel like I was going to throw up as I carried the paper trash bag out to the garbage can. A light morning breeze blew the smell away from me as I lifted the aluminum can lid and dropped the bag. I ran to the kitchen door so I could get back to 'Scooby Doo' when a rustling sound made me pause. I followed the sound off the patio and around the side of the house where the peach tree grew. A black and white cat was shifting its head like a shark and when the cat turned toward me, I could see the spread wings of a mocking bird flapping in its mouth. The bird looked too big for the cat and when the cat saw me, he dropped the bird. His green-gold eyes stared at me.

The bird fluttered to take off, but fell over on its side. The cat leaped toward the bird. The bird hopped onto a low branch of the tree. Sylvester, the cartoon cat, that's who the cat looked like. He crouched so low his belly seemed to rub against the dry dirt around the tree. His neck extended so far from his body the cat looked like a turtle popping out from its shell. I squatted to watch the creeping cat and the frantic bird.

The cat skirted up the trunk. With its feathers and tail spinning, the bird hopped to a higher branch. Sylvester clawed up the trunk again, and this time, thumped the bird with his paw. The bird fell and Sylvester jumped on it. As the cat tore and ripped into the bird, I felt my heart pound in my chest and my palms sweat. I wanted to help the bird. I couldn't move, and I watched as the bird's wings fluttered once, twice, and then stopped. It seemed its body let the air out like a balloon going flat. It didn't move anymore. The cat lifted its head, stretched out its paws, and let out a sound between a moan and a growl. I stepped back because I didn't want to see the cat eat the bird. But it didn't. Instead, the killer cat slunk over to the redwood fence. The cat jumped up and sat on top of the fence, dabbing and slurping at its paws with its bubblegum-colored tongue. My eyes were moist and I almost started to cry. Why didn't the cat eat the bird? Why would it just kill the poor thing?

When I walked up to the bird, I heard the cat skitter down the fence. I leaned over the bird and touched its left wing, where the bone of the wing met the bird's chest. The feathers were soft. Its orange

118

and yellow beak, caught in a scream, stood open under its gold eyes that were blank as a notebook page. I wondered if it hurt as it was dying. Something was so odd about the dead bird, and something was so interesting, and something was so horrible, too.

On the Tuesday morning before Halloween, I started to fold the permission slip and place it into my math book. I stopped and lifted the copied note, the ditto as Miss Steen called it. It wasn't the words 'human reproduction' that interested me; it was the smell of the paper. Somehow, when the purple ink hit the white paper, it always smelled like Bluebird school glue. The bird, I remembered as I sniffed the paper. What's it look like now? I put the note into my math book and went out into the yard.

As I stepped around the corner of the house, I saw the same black and white cat napping in the shadow of the peach tree. I stopped because the odor of the dead bird hit my nose with its rotten mushroom and burnt sugar smell. Sylvester didn't care because he lay right next to the mess of a bird. At first I thought that maybe the cat had come back to eat the bird, but the feathery blob looked like it was in the same twisted position. Why did the cat kill it, then? I wondered again. To gloat? To enjoy its kill? For no reason at all?

I decided to chase the cat away. I jumped for the cat, just missing the bird as my belly slid across the pile of dry peach tree leaves.

'Rrrrrowwww' the cat screeched as I caught hold of its back paw. As I pinched the cat's paw between my fingers, the cat tore at my hand with his other claws. The sharp jab of the cat's claw made me let go. The cat shot to the corner of the yard, flattened its ears and hissed. Blood trickled from the scratches on my hand. But I knew I won--the cat was scared. Maybe it would think twice before attacking a bird in this yard again.

I clicked open the yellow plastic latch on my 'Partridge Family' bus lunch box and pulled out the turquoise paper napkin Jennifer packed with my lunch. Spitting on it, I dabbed at my hand. The bleeding stopped. I brushed away some dust from my nose and forehead. I brushed the leaves and dirt from my shirt. Time for school, and the birds and the bees.

"Those are the main occurrences in human reproduction," Miss Steen said later. A drawing of a circle and a polliwog, or a human egg and a sperm, as Miss Steen called them, showed bright and big on the wall above the chalkboard. For the first time that I could remember,

119

the only sound in the classroom was the overhead projector fan. It whirred softly until Miss Steen switched it off. Now the classroom was silent.

"Are there any questions?" Miss Steen asked.

Annie, one of the Phillips twins, raised her hand.

"Is a Kotex the same as the feminine napkin thingy?" she asked. Her face went pink.

"Yes. But we're not going to talk about that in any detail together. Does anyone else have any questions?"

No one raised a hand. Miss Steen cracked her knuckles.

"For the next hour, then, the boys are to report to the cafeteria for a short film and assembly. The girls will stay here and when the girls from Mr. Bowers' class arrive, we'll watch a film also. Boys, line up outside single file and wait for Mr. Bowers to take you to assembly."

As we lined up outside, I got excited because I didn't know we were going to get to see a movie. Cafeteria assemblies always meant a movie of some kind.

"I wonder what the girls are gonna see?" Scotty Butler said from behind.

I turned as Scotty ran up and watched as his belly bounced under his light pink shirt he wore buttoned all the way to his neck. Even though I couldn't make friends for very long because I was always moving, I liked Scotty because he did funny things. Once he told a kid named Kevin to call Miss Steen by her first name. When Kevin did that, the whole classroom gasped. Miss Steen just looked at him through the slits of hers eyes and said: 'Detention after school— one hour.' I looked over at Scotty and he was holding a freckled hand over his mouth so that he didn't laugh. I wanted to laugh, too.

Scotty wanted to be a movie star. He gave me one of his most special things: the map to the movie stars' homes. Scotty brought a bunch of them to share one day, and ended up giving me one. He even showed me where Mrs. Partridge lived in real life. 'You can ride a bus right past her front yard,' Scotty had said. And on top of all this, Scotty was funny.

"...those are the main occurrences in human reproduction ..." Scotty said in a funny, high voice, twisting his freckled nose and squinting his big, green eyes to look like Miss Steen.

"You're gonna get in trouble if she ever sees you do that," I said.

"Miss Steen doesn't scare me. She ain't anything like Mrs.

Pratt."

Scotty twisted his shoulders and raised his chin, making his face tight and stretching his mouth like a fish. He raised his right hand and wagged his pointer finger.

"...We don't behave that way at Lincoln Elementary..." Scotty said like a lady with a cowboy accent. "...To the Principal's office..."

I laughed and Scotty bent in half, giggling.

"Do Mrs. Garvey again," I said.

Now Scotty raised both shoulders and dropped his chin, turning his mouth into a frown. He kept his mouth tight.

"...Let us say the Pledge of Allegiance..."

Now my lips vibrated like a boat motor when I laughed this time. Scotty laughed and scratched the top of his head.

"All right you two," Mr. Bowers' deep voice interrupted us. "Maybe you should stay back here with the other giggly girls."

The rest of the line of boys laughed at us. "Dorks!" someone yelled. "Yeah. Goons!" someone else said. Scotty turned red, folded his arms and looked at the ground. I patted his shoulder and got in line behind him.

"Quiet down," Mr. Bowers said. "Let's get to the assembly."

"And that is what will happen as you grow from a boy, into a man..." the movie narrator said. The music turned up and the film rattled out of the projector. The lights came up and Mr. Bowers stood in front of the screen. No one made a sound. Pots and pans clinked and clanked behind the swinging aluminum doors where the cafeteria aides were busy making lunch. Baking sugar cookies mixed with a barbecued meat aroma.

I looked at Scotty Butler who just stared at his lap. All the boys seated at the cafeteria tables seemed to just be looking down at their laps. I wondered if they were thinking what I was thinking: I'm going to grow hair down *there*? The idea bothered me and I hoped maybe I would get run over by a car before it happened. And girls -- how could I ever look at girls and feel new things for them, like the movie said?

"Any questions, boys?" Mr. Bowers asked. He reached up and took off his thick glasses, rubbing them with his red tie.

John Randles, who was a foot taller than everyone else, raised his hand.

"If that's what happens to us, what happens when the girls go through pottery?"

Mr. Bowers put his glasses back on and ran a hand through his hair. He seemed kind of shy as he stood up there.

"The word is 'puberty'. You need to ask your mother that question. Anybody else?"

Wheezing Marty took a deep breath from his inhaler before raising his hand.

"If you get one of those erectors in the middle of math and you gotta go up to the board for a percentage problem, what do you do?"

Mr. Bowers let out a deep sigh.

" 'Erection.' The word is 'erection'. Just take your math book with you, hold it in front of yourself till you get to the board, and keep your back to the class. When you're done at the board, put the book back in front and walk back to your desk."

The lunch recess bell rang and all the boys jumped up to go.

"Hold it!" Mr. Bowers said. "You're not dismissed yet. Are there any other questions?"

No hands went up. The lunch aides swung the doors of the cafeteria open and locked the stops down. Students lined up outside the right door.

"Okay, gentlemen. Remember what you've learned."

Scotty and I sat and ate our lunches in silence. I felt a little funny as I took my bologna and cheese sandwich from my 'Partridge Family' lunch box. Did Scotty feel different, sort of silly, with his 'Star Trek' lunch box? If we were going to be young men soon, growing hair in odd places and talking with deep voices, weren't TV show lunch boxes too babyish? I looked around and saw that the sixth grade boys and girls stood in groups separate from each other. No one played four square or tetherball together like they usually did. It was as if everyone had secrets and things to hide about themselves now. Even the silence between Scotty and me made me feel like that.

As I rolled the bologna, cheese, and mayonnaise around in my mouth, Roxanne Liston, the Phillips twins, and Patia Johnson walked past us. They were walking real close but it didn't look like they were talking to each other, either. When Annie Phillips looked over her shoulder and wrinkled her nose at me, I remembered her Kotex question. Now I knew what was in the light purple box with the flowers on it that Jennifer kept under the bathroom vanity.

"Annie Phillips sure is dumb," I said.

Scotty nodded, dropped his turkey sandwich into his lunch box, and wiped his mouth. He stood up and starting swaying his shoulders back and forth.

"Miss Steen," he said with a girly voice. "Is a Kotex the same as the feminine napkin thingy?"

I blew sandwich crumbs out of my mouth as I laughed.

"What a retard," Scotty said as he sat back down.

"What a ... Kotex head!" I added.

Now we couldn't stop laughing.

"Hey, Scotty, I dare you to go call Annie that."

"No way. I'll get in trouble?"

"It's not a dirty word. It's just a fact of life."

Scotty took one more bite of his turkey sandwich, seemed to think about it a second longer, then stood up nodding.

"Okay. But don't steal my chocolate mini doughnuts."

Scotty ran toward the group of girls. The girls froze, crossed their arms, and stared at Scotty. I dropped my head and looked sideways. I couldn't believe he was really doing it and I didn't want the girls to think I was part of it.

"Hey, ugly weirdo, get away from us," I heard Roxanne Liston yell.

"You know what you are, Annie?" Scotty yelled.

"Shut up, weirdo!" Annie's sister, Abbie Phillips, said.

"You're a Kotex head!"

My whole body started to shake. It was so funny.

"Shut up!" Annie yelled back.

"Kotex Head! Kotex Head!" Scotty taunted her.

"You're in big trouble! We're telling!" Patia Johnson yelled.

"You're all gonna have to wear 'em. You're all Kotex Heads!"

"Shut up!" they yelled together.

"Kotex Heads! Kotex Heads!"

Scotty hurried back to the bench, his face red from running and laughing. I laughed out loud now because I couldn't hold it back.

"You're gonna get in trouble, too, orphan boy!" Abbie said, pointing at me. As Scotty bent over to catch his breath, I watched as the girls ran to the noon aide.

"Uh-oh," he said.

"I'm not an orphan, Kotex head!" I shouted at her back.

Scotty looked up as the noon aide nodded her head with its gray ponytail and looked at them, her eyes hidden behind black sunglasses. She turned toward Scotty and me and her arms pumped as she ran toward us. Her silver whistle swung like a pendulum from her neck with each stomp of her feet as her pointed, white tennis shoes slapped the blacktop.

"You two, to the Principal's office, now."

As soon as we stepped into the office a few minutes later, we were separated. The office roiled with commotion: ringing phones, Ethel the office secretary hurrying between her desk and the counter, and teachers stepping in and out of the backside of the office. All the activity made me nervous.

I lost track of time as I waited. I saw Scotty leave with a teacher's aide. Miss Steen stepped into the office, looked at me and curled her lip like she smelled sour milk. She went into the Principal's office. The noon aide clomped in, holding Annie Phillips by the hand. *Get ready for something bad,* the voice said as I watched them go into the Principal's office.

"Mrs. Thompson will be here shortly," Ethel said through her prune lips covered with bright red lipstick. "When she arrives, you'll be meeting with the Principal and Miss Steen."

'...Who needs wings to fly?...'

Not the song! It started repeating in my head.

'...Who needs wings to fly?...Who needs wings to fly?...'

"You okay, Gem?" Jennifer said a few minutes later. She startled me and stopped the stupid song.

She opened her hand-made leather purse that had been tooled with pink tulips and her initials, tucked in her sunglasses, and pulled out a Baggie. Inside were cinnamon graham crackers. She held it out to me.

"You forgot your snack today."

"Can I have one now? I didn't get to finish my lunch."

"Yep. I hope this is important – they interrupted my afternoon meditation."

I bit into the graham cracker as Jennifer stepped up to the counter. The embroidered daisies on the back pockets of her jeans sparkled in the greenish, fluorescent light.

"I'm Mrs. Thompson," she said. She sounded angry, but she wasn't mean to me just a minute ago.

After Ethel told Mrs. Garvey, our principal, that Jennifer had arrived, she brought Jennifer and me into her office. I stepped in behind Jennifer and I could smell it right away: Miss Steen's peach perfume. 'I'm dead' I thought. She sat in a chair next to Mrs. Garvey. Jennifer walked up to Mrs. Garvey's desk. Mrs. Garvey nodded toward a chair across her desk. Jennifer sat. I didn't know what to do.

"Please sit here, Gem," Mrs. Garvey said, pointing to the other chair. I had never noticed how deep her voice was till then.

Mrs. Garvey's eyebrows made me think of coloring book lines as they wiggled while she looked at a manila folder. Bi-focals magnified her brown eyes. She nodded and her pile of hair bounced like it was brown and gray cotton candy. Her head and face bobbed up and down.

"We have a serious problem, Mrs. Thompson."

Mrs. Garvey shut the folder and held it between her hands as if she were going to pray. Jennifer jerked her head to the right when Miss Steen cracked her knuckles. I wanted to say 'See, isn't that a creepy thing to do?' but I wasn't about to say anything.

"You'll get arthritis from that," Jennifer said.

Mrs. Garvey raised her chin so that she looked down though her glasses at the file. She puckered her lips into a circle that made me think of a blackberry Life Saver.

"Gem's behavior problems can no longer be tolerated," she said, still reading from the folder. "This latest incident involved him encouraging a classmate to call a group of girls 'Kotex Heads'. This would be bad under any circumstances, but with the students having just gone through the sensitive subject of human reproduction, this was unseemly."

"That's it?" Jennifer said.

"Beg your pardon?" Mrs. Garvey answered. Her chin dropped so that now she looked over her glasses toward us.

"So a couple of girls were called a silly name. The boys must have been just as uncomfortable as the girls with the whole thing. They let off a little steam."

I thought of the hair that would grow someday and looked down at my lap.

"It's the cumulative total of all of his behavior that's at the core here," Miss Steen added.

"His grades are excellent, remarkably so," Mrs. Garvey said. "But they must be considered separately from his behavior. It seems we have no choice. Gem is expelled."

"You can't do this!" Jennifer said. "Do you know what that'll mean? He's going to have to go back to Maryvale orphanage. Have a little heart."

"Mrs. Thompson, I assure you," Mrs. Garvey began. She took off her glasses and touched her knuckle to her chin.

"We have considered the matter carefully, but I'm afraid we have to think of the well-being of the entire school. I'm sorry."

Jennifer stood up and opened her purse. She yanked out her sunglasses and pointed them at Miss Steen.

"You. I hope you can live with yourself. The only thing you've taught him is that he doesn't matter again. You're making some bad karma for yourself. Bitch."

Jennifer grabbed my hand and as we stepped out the Principal's door, I heard Mrs. Garvey say: "Well."

"Well," Maureen said later that night as Jennifer, Ted, and I sat at the kitchen table. "It doesn't look good. The principal isn't willing to work anything out and when these situations occur, my hands are tied."

As Maureen moved her baby from her left shoulder to her right, her hair bounced as if it was a row of brown Slinkys. Then her baby's green eyes opened wide as she blew bubbles at me. That made me laugh, and when the bubbles popped, they smelled just like plums.

"Baby girl likes Gem," Maureen said in a baby voice. "Mommy does, too."

Maureen looked at me as she smiled, and I felt like things might be okay. I liked her so much. Ever since she started as my social worker, she spent extra time with me. After the first time watching 'The Wizard of Oz,' no matter whether I was in a foster home or at Maryvale, she would show up to watch it with me. The only time she missed that was when she and Bruce, who was now her husband, had their baby in April. It all made me a little sad. First that she married Bruce: I had a secret hope that maybe I could marry her when I grew up. And then she had a baby and I knew I would never be able to marry her. But it was okay after a while.

"So he has to go, then," Jennifer said. She leaned against Ted and his forehead wrinkled up to meet his wavy hair.

"Yes," Maureen said.

"Sorry, Babe," Ted said as he pulled Jennifer to him and kissed her.

I looked at the gray-blue tattoo on Ted's forearm that read: 'Da Nang '67'. I knew it had something to do with the Viet Nam War, and that when he was there, Ted had learned a little about Buddhism. Jennifer explained once that was why they learned Transcendental Meditation. But that was about all I knew about him because Ted never really talked to me. I never asked anything, either.

A breeze blew through the slats of the open kitchen window, and I could smell the flowers Jennifer called night-blooming jasmine. Right then I felt the nervous feeling in my stomach I got whenever I had to move. Was I going to be stuck at Maryvale, being jumped and beat-up by the Buckaroos, or would I end up in a new foster home? And how would the new foster family treat me? Even though I had been moved around tons of times by now, I still never could get used to any of it. That's why my stomach ached, I think.

"How long before he has to go?" Jennifer asked. Her voice sounded like a frog. I could see her eyes were wet around the edges. She reached out and ran her hand through my hair.

"Two weeks," Maureen answered.

'Who needs wings to fly?...'

The song played through my head as I sat under the peach tree a week later. I got a vacation when Lincoln Elementary wouldn't let me come back, but it wasn't fun. I was in the limbo between foster families and Maryvale. I hated the in-between times. *You're not any more important to anyone than that dead bird.* The voice was right again: that's how I felt. The dead bird's feathers were rolled up around the quills and now looked like straight pins, and its wings were two bony rods with a few feathers still stuck to them. Its eyes were just creepy sockets in its head. A smoky fog hung on everything in the backyard, making me think of the boiling brew they drank on the re-runs of 'The Addams Family'.

Even though the rotting bird still interested me, and I had come out to see it everyday for the past week, I was now bored with it. But it was going to serve another purpose: I hoped it would tempt Sylvester the cat to come poking around again. I sat cross-legged on the ground, with a black Hefty lawn bag spread over the triangle my legs made. What I decided I was going to do was throw the bag over Sylvester, grab up the edges and twist it shut, then throw the bag into the trash can. I would then watch to see how long it would take Sylvester to claw his way out of the trashcan. That would teach him for killing this bird.

I was bored, to say the least. All I did was watch TV. 'Joker's Wild' and 'High Rollers' came on in the morning, and then 'One Life to Live'. Those people always had something going wrong in their lives, just like I did. And most of the actresses were so pretty. I'd shut off the TV around lunch because the stupid Watergate hearing was the only thing on in the afternoons. I'd draw for as long as I could stand the paint smell while Jennifer worked on the baby's room, and then I'd turn the TV back on in time for 'Love American Style' followed by 'The Big Movie' in the late afternoon. Coming out to stare at the dead bird and waiting for Sylvester was my only source of fun that last week at Ted and Jennifer's. I wished I could just play on a little league team again but that was impossible for a foster kid. I was lucky I got to play softball at foster schools.

Jennifer took me to the Carson Mall the Tuesday before my forced vacation to buy some Levi's and Hang Ten shirts, but I didn't really want to spend time with her anymore. She tried to ask me how I felt about leaving, and she seemed to care, but I didn't tell her. *She's just asking to be nice. As soon as you're gone and she gets her baby, she'll never think of you again.* The voice told me something like that every time I found out I was leaving a foster home. Once I heard it, I would withdraw and stop participating in the particular foster family's activities. Even if I liked the mother like Jennifer, I wouldn't have much to do with her. Last Saturday, I even skipped watching 'The Scars of Dracula' on 'Creature Features' and making butterscotch chip, oatmeal cookies. I was able to fall asleep better without thinking about the creepy guy coming out of his coffin in the opening.

"Rrrrrowwww."

Finally, Sylvester! As Sylvester dug his claws into the redwood fence slat and slid down to the ground, I got up on my knees and slipped my fingers into the Hefty bag. The plastic felt smooth. Sylvester sat at the bottom of the fence and watched as I crawled toward him. I jumped at him and my belly skidded on the dirt like I was sliding into home plate. Sylvester coiled his back legs to jump, but I threw the bag over him. Like a pinwheel with needles, Sylvester spun around inside the bag. I pulled the bag's sides together and twist-tied them. I jumped up and ran for the trashcan.

"...sheeeerrrowwww..." Sylvester screamed between low moans.

He gashed and clawed at the sides of the bag. It looked like the bag would be shreds in just seconds but I yanked the lid off just in time and lobbed the black bag into the trashcan. I slammed the warped lid onto it, and could now hear Sylvester's shrieks echo off its aluminum walls.

Just as I jumped back and turned, Sylvester shot out of the trash can, and I heard a tinny clang as the lid hit the ground. But the cat didn't run off like its tail was on fire. Instead, he got to the base of the peach tree and stopped. The black fur eyebrows over his gold eyes stretched into a scowl that pinched his face, and his ears lay flat as a hound dog's. If cats felt hate, then this cat's eyes were filled with it for me. I didn't dare to move. He raised a paw toward me, and let out a growling hiss. Sylvester whipped around and jumped over the redwood fence. I was glad that he didn't attack me and I looked over at the dead bird.

"That was for you," I said.

When Sylvester jumped over the fence and ran off, I realized something: I could do the same thing. Sylvester couldn't do anything when I had him in that bag, and I couldn't do anything to stop from being put back into Maryvale. If he could run away, then so could I. And I knew exactly where I was going to go.

I ran back into the house, and I could hear the voices of the neighborhood ladies in the living room with Jennifer. A Tupperware party was going on. When I got to the bedroom, I pulled open the desk drawer and reached for the movie stars' homes map.

If I were ever going to try to get away from Maryvale and all the foster homes, this would be the time. I opened the map and felt the fuzzy, soft folds of the paper. As I looked over the map, I felt my stomach twist: I remembered a few years back trying to run away to find my dad. But when Maureen told me where he was, I gave up on ever seeing him again. Now I couldn't even remember what my dad looked like. But there was someone else I knew who could maybe take care of me and her house was on this map.

I found the spot that marked Shirley Jones'--Mrs. Partridge's-- house. How was I going to do this? I couldn't take any of my stuff because Jennifer would figure it out. *You need money to get along in the world.* Money! I'd need it for the bus, to eat, for everything. There was only one place I could think of to get some. I shoved the folded map into my back pocket and sneaked to the kitchen.

"...Just like with the salad keeper, you need to burp the lid to get the air out and keep your cheese longer," Jennifer said in the living room. The song 'Popcorn' played quietly from the console stereo.

Her leather purse sat on the counter by the living room door. To get to the purse without being seen, I was going to have to crawl to the counter, and then sneak it down from the other side. Sliding down, I felt the carved octagons in the linoleum floor tiles push into the skin of my knees. I crawled quickly to the cupboard underneath the counter where her purse sat.

"...Okay, I'll take the cheese keeper, but don't try to talk me into cereal bowls!" some lady hollered.

I reached over my head and felt around until I touched the strap of Jennifer's purse. With the strap at my fingertips, I could already see Shirley Jones' smiling face as she let me into her house. She was a rich actress and why wouldn't she want to help a foster child? So went my reasoning. That was all the courage I needed to tug the purse down. I pulled, but the purse got stuck on something. I pulled harder, but it still wouldn't budge. Giving it one last tug, it popped free, but I pulled so hard that I fell backwards onto my butt and the purse hit me in the face as it exploded all of Jennifer's stuff onto the floor. When I looked up from the floor, I saw Jennifer standing in the doorway. Her arms were folded and her forehead crinkled. There was nothing I could think of to say.

"What the hell was that all about?"

I sat up quick.

"I wanted some Trident."

"Bull. What were you doing with my purse?"

"I really wanted gum."

"Why didn't you ask me for it?"

She got me. I shrugged.

Jennifer stepped around the corner and bent over. I thought she was going to pick up the stuff from her purse, but she grabbed up my map of the movie stars' homes from the floor. It must have fallen out of my pocket.

"What's this?"

"A map."

"I see that. Where'd you get it?"

"From a kid at school."

She turned it over in her hands.

"Movie stars' homes? These things aren't for real, you know."

I yanked the map from her.

"Hey, watch it, Gem. That's rude."

"It's rude to say that my map is phony."

I bent back over and swept the rest of her stuff back into her purse. It bothered me so much that she would say that. Even worse than that, what if it was true? I handed her the purse.

"Sorry," I said.

I stepped back toward the kitchen door, but Jennifer stopped me and turned me toward her. The look on her face made me nervous as if she might now think I was a bad kid. That made me sad.

"You still haven't explained what you were doing in my purse."

Now I folded my arms. Since I had to go back to Maryvale in a couple days, I figured if I told the truth, it wouldn't matter anyway.

"I needed some money."

Jennifer nodded. It seemed I was off the hook.

"Why didn't you ask me for some? You know I would have given it to you."

"Even if I wanted it to run away to Mrs. Partridge's—Shirley Jones'?"

"Huh?"

"I needed money for the bus. That's all. Can I go to my room, now?"

"Yep."

I left the kitchen.

"You didn't burp the cake carrier!" someone hollered at the party.

Three nights after I attempted to steal the bus money, I carried one of my paper bags out to Maureen's Datsun. When I went back through the front door, the TV was blaring. I was going to miss that big Magnavox console. I stood for a minute and watched.

'...Here's the story...of a man named Brady...'

'The Brady Bunch' was just starting, but Maureen had shown up a half hour sooner with news. She stood in the kitchen with Jennifer and Ted. As I watched TV, I heard them talking.

"A single woman?" I heard Ted say.

"Can she handle it?" Jennifer added.

"Yes. She has been screened thoroughly and is a very fine person. And we need good foster parents, married or single."

I stepped toward the kitchen door because I figured they were talking about a new foster home. Jennifer was dabbing at her eyes with a napkin and Ted stood with his arm around her.

"Gem, come on in here. You need to hear what I'm telling Jennifer and Ted."

I walked into the kitchen and leaned against the doorjamb.

"I've been able to get you placed with a family in Torrance. They already have three kids so you'll have some new friends right away."

"That part sounds okay," Ted said. Jennifer nodded and dabbed at her eyes.

"That's not too far from us," she blurted out. "You can come and visit if you want."

"Oh, yeah," Maureen added. "You're not afraid of dogs are you?"

I didn't think so. I shook my head.

"Good. Because your new foster mom rescues dogs and places them with new owners. There are always dogs around, and I think they have a couple of their own, too."

"I love dogs," Jennifer said.

"What's the father do?" Ted asked.

"The woman is divorced," Maureen said.

"How can she handle her own kids, let alone dogs and now a foster child?" Jennifer asked.

"She has a live-in housekeeper who helps her manage. We place children with single people as well as with married ones. Anyone who's available to help—things are bad out there."

"You screen everybody, right?" Ted asked.

"Of course. Gem is going to be with a good family near where he grew up. What could be better?"

Maureen patted my back. It seemed she was trying to make me feel better, but all I could think about was if this new family was horrible, I was going to run away. That was it. I was tired of foster families, tired of changing schools, tired of Maryvale, tired of all of it.

"I know this is hard for you, Gem," Maureen said.

I heard her, but right then, I didn't feel anything other than relief. I was very accustomed to changing foster families by now and as long as I didn't have to go back to Maryvale, I was fine. I was sad that Jennifer was so sad, but that was it. I nodded to go along with Maureen, then picked up my other paper bag and started to walk out. I stopped because Maureen started to say something else.

"Torrance is where you grew up, you know. You'll be back home in a way. Maybe you'll be able to remember some happy times."

I shrugged. I guessed I had some happy memories. The sump next to our backyard made me happy whenever I thought about it. My Torrance neighborhood was comprised of three and four bedroom California ranch houses with diamond-shaped window panes and low-slung roofs. Something about all that did feel safe, secure, as if the rest of the world didn't exist; nothing bad could ever happen behind those raised-panel front doors. For me, that proved to be untrue. But still, I had some happy memories.

'...*Who needs wings to fly...*'

132

Oh, why the song now? I just wanted to get the last bag out to Maureen's car and leave. I stepped toward the front door.

"Gem, wait!" Jennifer yelled.

When I turned around, Jennifer and Ted stepped up next to me. I knew what was coming: the hug and the tears. But I didn't want either. I set down the bag. Ted put out his hand and I grabbed it. Ted dropped his elbow and gave me one of those handshakes that looked like arm wrestling.

"You mind yourself. You're a good boy."

Jennifer wrapped her arms around me and I could smell the orange Jafra face cream and flower scent of her Secret Deodorant. My face was warm and I didn't like it. She kissed my cheek and I felt her tears against my skin. I felt myself start to shake but I bit my lip. I wanted her to just let go of me.

"I'm gonna miss my horror night, baking buddy. Please come and visit us again, okay? And remember, what you put out to the universe will come back to you as good or bad karma."

I nodded and pulled away from her. She said all that to be nice, like they all did. But it still made me sad. A lump blossomed in my throat and I felt so alone. *When she gets her baby, she'll forget all about you.* I picked up the paper bag and walked to the trunk of the Datsun.

10.

I clomped down the gold and orange shag carpeting of the stairs. When I got to the middle landing, I stopped and looked up at the swag lamp that hung over the stairs. Since it was the middle of the day, it wasn't on. I liked its onion shape, and the sun that came through the little window at the top of the stairs made the ribbed edges of the gold glass sparkle. This was the first two-story house I ever lived in and it amazed me. I felt like a Partridge or a Brady. I even had my own room in the big house, and it wasn't being painted for a baby.

"Is that you, Gem?" my new foster mom, Dale, asked.

"Yeah."

As I went to step down the last couple steps, the dogs ran toward me from the kitchen, their paws clicking and scratching against the parquet wood floor by the front door. A brown one with floppy ears stood up and held onto my thigh with his top paws. I petted him and his tail went crazy like a helicopter blade. Another little dog with gray and white hair as thick as a sheep's ran around my ankles. A black dog and a German shepherd – the only kind of dog I recognized – barked at me. Dale whistled and they all ran back toward the kitchen.

"You pick up your room?"

"Yeah."

"Why don't you go on out to the garage with Buzz and Gerry while I finish making lunch? They're getting the bikes cleaned up for next weekend."

I stepped down to the front hallway and sighed. In the few days I had been with this family, I already knew I didn't fit in with Buzz and Gerry. They talked about football, the only sport I didn't like. Motorcycles excited them and I just thought they were dirty, loud, and

134

they made me nervous. I thought maybe I could interest one of them in my magnifying glass – not to kill anything ever again, but to look at something – so I put the magnifying glass into the pocket of my brown cords. I pulled open the front door. The yellow and orange bubbles of glass that formed the front door window looked interesting so I ran my hand over them. They were smooth.

"You're letting in a cold breeze," Dale said. "You're gonna give the tuna goosebumps. Would you shut the –"

I closed the door. As I stepped off the stone front stoop, I could hear Gerry and Buzz talking in the garage. Just as I got to the thick, black garage door spring, they stopped talking.

"That you, Sapphire?" Buzz asked.

I heard the thump of Gerry's hand against the back of Buzz's head.

"That's not how you treat a guest," Gerry said.

I stepped around the garage door spring and saw Buzz sitting next to his motorcycle with the dented and scraped red tank that read in rusted letters: 'Yamaha'. His hands were black with grease up to his wrists and I could see a grease smudge on the tips of his blonde, flat top hair. He must have scratched his head while he was working. Gerry stood on the other side of the motorcycle. Her eyes squinted as she examined a greasy part of the motorcycle. Her blonde hair, cut so short it almost didn't look like a ladies haircut, did not have a grease smudge on it. It was flecked with gray.

"Come on in, kid," she said.

Buzz looked at me, and his down-turned mouth with almost no lips cracked into a mean smile. His two fang teeth stuck out ahead of his other front teeth, making them two points on the edge of his bottom lip. They reminded me of Dracula.

"Yeah, maybe you can learn somethin' 'bout bikes," Buzz said.

"Shut up and clean this filter out," Gerry said.

Gerry seemed to always speak tough like that to Buzz. I guess it was because she had been a nurse in the Korean War before she became the nurse supervisor at County-USC Medical Center. She was in charge, and she knew how to deal with tough soldiers in the war and tough doctors in the hospital now. Buzz grabbed the part from Gerry. As he held it over a round pan and began to dab at it with a round brush, I could smell gasoline. I always liked its smell.

"This must be why the fuel line keeps jammin'" Buzz said.

I didn't like the garage with its grimy, black floor, and wooden

135

workbench piled with dirty tools and dusty machines. I didn't like garages or tools much. Then my eyes landed on something else entirely: a poster. I could stand being in the garage forever as long as I could look at the poster that hung just on the other side of the open garage door. My heart sped up and I felt a sort of electric tickle down near my penis as I looked at the poster.

A nude woman with long brown hair held her arms folded over her head, and the locks of her brown, wavy hair covered her breasts. My eyes moved involuntarily down past her chest, to her navel folded like a flat doughnut, then past her navel to where her skin became a creamy white. The edge of the poster cut off the rest of her.

"Hey, looks like someone's got the hots for Raquel!" Buzz laughed. "That a little pup tent you got started?"

I didn't know what he meant, but I was pretty sure it was dirty.

"Clean the friggin' filter and leave the kid alone, Buzz, or I'm going to tear down that poster once and for all and throw it away," Gerry ordered.

"I got that from Dad. You can't tear it down – Mom won't let you."

"Are you kidding? Dale hates that poster almost as much as I do."

As Gerry bent down to look at the chain of the motorcycle, her knees cracked. Buzz snorted with a laugh.

"Nice knees, Gerry. You're doing good as Jim Langer."

"Nothing's wrong with him," Gerry said. "He'll play Monday night."

"Dolphins gotta keep all their best players on the line if they're really gonna take the championship."

I also couldn't believe that a lady could know so much about football like Gerry did. I tapped my magnifying glass and tried to think of something else to interest them. Maybe the caterpillar I saw on the lawn a while ago would interest them.

"It'll be Minnesota and Miami in January," Gerry said. "You'll see."

"Did you guys wanna see a caterpillar with my magnifying glass?" I asked. I thought it was worth the try.

Buzz's face crinkled up.

"No," he practically spit at me.

Gerry looked at the motorcycle part in her hand. She looked at me and smiled.

"Sure, kid. Let's go take a look. Buzz can get these parts cleaned up while we look."

"Jesus, Gerry. Why do I gotta clean them all?" Buzz said.

"Because I said. Now get to it. Come on, Gem."

"I saw one on the edge of the lawn. Come on, I'll show you."

Gerry followed me out of the garage. Just at the end of the concrete driveway, the dichondra front lawn started. Dale, who gave me all the rules of the house, had told me that no one was to walk on the dichondra because it could kill it. I stood at the edge and pointed at the caterpillar that looked like a hairy, black worm. Gerry stepped on the front lawn to get the caterpillar.

"Dale said no one's supposed to step on the lawn!" I said. I sounded like Bobby and all his rules. It made me sad to think about him.

"That's right. But I'm not 'no one'. I weed and feed the lawn so I have privileges."

She plucked up the caterpillar and it wiggled and curled up in her hand. I pulled out the magnifying glass and could now see a light gray stripe running along the side of its body.

"Look at that."

Gerry leaned down and stared at the caterpillar for a few moments.

"Looks like some sort of sensory mark."

"Huh?"

"Something the caterpillar might use to feel the environment. Maybe changes in temperature that would signal a predator."

"I thought you're just a nurse for humans. What do you know about bugs?"

"I like to learn about everything that's alive: humans, animals, bugs, plants. You name it. Where did you get the magnifying glass?"

"Crackerjacks."

"Not a bad prize."

No, but the way I used it on that poor ant was awful, I thought. I felt sad. She handed the magnifying glass back to me and pushed her glasses back up the bridge of her nose. That was the first time I noticed how clear-blue her eyes were. Like Blueberry Otter Pops.

"Back to the bikes."

She started walking back up the driveway, her plump backside bouncing in her jeans. She turned toward me suddenly, with a big grin on her face.

"If she asks, make sure you tell Dale it was me who stepped on the dichondra."

Just as I was about to follow her up the driveway, a bright yellow moving van with a green Mayflower ship painted on its side drove by. It stopped just across 234th Street and down four houses. A light-pitched horn went off as it backed into the driveway of a one-story house. I watched as the moving men hopped out the front cab and opened the back doors of the big truck. After they hooked a ramp to the back of the van, they climbed into it. A minute later, they carried out a blue velvet couch. While the men struggled, I wondered if anyone my own age would be moving in.

"Lunch!" Dale hollered.

I turned and walked up to the middle of the driveway. I paused and looked at Gerry and Dale's house again. On the right side of the pink house with the brown trim, next to the open garage door, I noticed a wooden sign. The edges of the wood sign were burned black like a cigarette had been pressed along its edges. Dale told me Buzz made it in wood shop. Just above the address numbers the sign read: 'The Buhlerts'. I knew that was Dale and the kids' last name, but Gerry's last name was 'Braley'. Was she an aunt? Wouldn't that make her Dale's sister? And why didn't Buzz call her 'Aunt Gerry' then, instead of just by her first name? I would have to work on figuring it out. I walked the rest of the way up to the front door.

As I made my way down the wood parquet floor, I could hear the other two Buhlert kids in the kitchen: Audrey, two years older than me, and Janis, named after Janis Joplin when she was born in nineteen sixty-eight. When I reached the kitchen, I saw them sitting at the imitation marble table with its aluminum edges. The kitchen's walls were bright yellow like a lemon, and along with the orange table chairs, the room reminded me of the citrus aisle at the grocery store. This is where the family ate most meals because the dining room with its wood table and black vinyl chairs was only used on special occasions. Thanksgiving was next week and Dale said that would be a time when we'd all eat at the dining room table.

Buzz and Gerry came in from the garage and started washing the grease from their hands in the kitchen sink. Dale's long face twisted so much that it looked like a wrung washcloth. She seemed irritated at them. She watched them from behind, shaking her head and scratching the top of her brown shag with its frosted tips.

"You two are going to clean up that mess with Comet when

138

you're through. I'm not going to scrub those sinks again."

She curled up her right hand into a fist on her right hip and shook her left index finger at their backs. When she turned back around, her face didn't look like a washcloth anymore. The dark circles around her brown eyes made me think of a chocolate Tootsie Pop.

"Hey, Gem!" little Janis yelled with her scratchy voice.

When I looked at her, she puckered her face and stuck out her tongue. Right then, I wanted to jump across the table and grab hold of her ponytail that stuck up from the middle of her head like a blonde fountain and pull it. She was truly a brat.

"...Take another little piece of my heart now, baby!..." she sang and started swaying her head back and forth. The only thing I liked about her was that she looked like Tabitha from 'Bewitched'.

"Audrey, help me get lunch on the table," Dale said. She pulled off the lace apron she wore and straightened the top of her turquoise pantsuit. Dale had been a kindergarten teacher until she had Buzz. And from what I understood, she divorced her kids' father soon after Janis was born. She had met Gerry at a dog rescue a couple years later.

When Dale was appointed my foster mom, Maureen brought me to her house to meet her. Gerry was introduced to us as the housekeeper. The kids all said she was the housekeeper, too. After being there for awhile, I noticed she didn't do much housekeeping. She also worked at the hospital. It didn't matter to me whether she was the housekeeper or something else because she was always nice to me and I liked her as much as I liked Dale.

Audrey stood up and the ends of her blonde-brown hair lifted up from the top of her large breasts. I don't know why I noticed them. I tried not to look at those over-filled water balloons under her shirt with its print of the giant rings that reminded me of Froot Loops cereal. The trouble was each of her breasts was circled by a loop, one orange and one pink. It was hard not to notice. I usually tried not to look at Audrey at all, with her blue-green eyes and brown-sugar skin. Could she really have been only be two years older than I? She reminded me of Audrey Hepburn. I already had been told that she was named for the movie star. She brushed past me as if I didn't exist. Once again, I felt like a nothing.

Buzz and Gerry slid their chairs out as I took the chair next to Janis. Janis stopped swaying her head and suddenly puckered her lips at me and made a motorboat sound. Drops of her spit sprinkled my arm and now I really wanted to yank that ponytail. She constantly acted younger than five years old but no one seemed to notice as much as I did.

Audrey came back to the table with three plates of food balanced between her hands. As she set a plate in front of Gerry, the other two plates wobbled and she shifted them just in time to keep one of them from dropping on the table. The edges of the plates clanked.

"Audrey, watch my good Corelle!" Dale said.

"I didn't hurt them, Mom. You act like it's the Sango or something."

"You shouldn't smart off to your mother," Gerry said as she chewed a bite of sandwich.

Audrey rolled her eyes and snorted. When she set one of the plates in front of me, she flipped her head away from me so that her hair twirled like a dancer's skirt. The silver from her POW bracelet caught a ray of sunlight and it flared at me. But what I noticed next was really odd: the color of the inside of her hand was yellow-orange. What was wrong with her skin?

"Buzz, Janis, Ovaltine?" Dale said. "Oh, how about you, Gem?"

Buzz and Janis nodded, but I didn't know what it was. I shrugged.

"Chocolate milk, Opal," Buzz said.

Gerry's left arm made a big arc and landed with a pop on the back of Buzz's head. Buzz flinched and rubbed his head and I wanted to laugh.

"Mom, why does Gerry get to hit me like that?" Buzz asked.

"Because I can't reach," Dale answered. "And you need to stop making fun of Gem's name. Just eat. Ovaltine, Gem?"

"Okay."

After helping serve the Ovaltine, Audrey sat down across from me. She kept her head down as she unscrewed the red cap of a plastic bottle of reddish-orange liquid.

"Can I please have some of your carrot juice, Audrey?" Janis asked. "The encyclopedia says carrots are good for my retina."

"Carrot juice?" I said. "How do they squeeze them for their juice?"

"They don't squeeze them," Audrey said.

"They grind them and extract the juice," Janis added.

I couldn't believe how smart Janis was for a little kid.

"Yeah," Dale said. "She's a vegetarian. And the way she's

living off the stuff she's turning into a vegetable."

Dale leaned against the kitchen counter and crossed her arms.

"You're not eating, Mom?" Audrey asked.

"Maybe later," she answered with a shrug.

I picked up my tuna sandwich and went to bite it, but I stopped: little, green fuzzy things stuck out from between the wheat crusts.

"Is my sandwich okay?" I asked.

Janis reached over and pulled up the top slice of bread from my sandwich.

"Don't finger other people's food," Dale hollered. She stepped over to the table and leaned over Audrey. She grabbed the top of my sandwich from Janis.

"Looks okay," she said.

"Nuh-uh. The lettuce looks all wormy," I said.

"Oh. That isn't lettuce. Those are alfalfa sprouts. Audrey says we should eat them on sandwiches instead of lettuce. They're actually pretty tasty."

"They're rich in vitamins and minerals," Janis said.

God she was so smart for such a brat.

Dale put the bread back on my sandwich, and then stepped back to the counter. I took a bite. The alfalfa sprouts tasted like a cross between peanuts and lettuce. They crunched in my mouth and tasted pretty good when I swirled them around in my mouth with the mayonnaise and garlic tuna flavors.

Everyone was eating now, but no one said anything. No one except Janis, who sang:

"...Take another little piece of my heart now baby..."

I pulled out one of the drawers under the captain's bed that sat in the corner of the bedroom next to the windows. I had put my grocery bags and box of stuff inside the drawers. Of course, I didn't unpack them. As long as I was staying here, I might as well use the drawers. I opened the bag with my crayons and sketchpad. It had been awhile since I had drawn and done the voices for my drawings. As I turned back the cover of the sketchpad, I set my crayon box on the shag carpeting, and lay down on my stomach. I flipped past the first half of the sketchpad but stopped for a second. There were the torn edges from where Eugene Aragon had ripped the pages when I first arrived to Hollygrove. But just past the damage was a drawing of the

141

character Samantha from 'Bewitched', in a long, silver dress from when she was crowned Queen of the Witches. That was my favorite show to draw and tell stories about before the 'Partridge Family'.

I remembered saying: 'Darren, I am Queen of the Witches now, and with that much power, I have to be careful.' I ran my fingertip over the drawing and tried to remember – was I five, still with Mom and Dad, or six, after the terrible times, when I did that drawing? There was the peach color I used for her skin, and the goldenrod I used to make her blonde hair. I stared at the drawing a second longer and felt a breath squeeze from deep in my chest as I turned to a blank page.

I pulled out the yellow-gold crayon from the box and began to draw in Mrs. Partridge's hair, but I stopped when I couldn't see the color so well. I looked up at the square, frosted glass light in the middle of the turquoise blue ceiling and saw that one of the bulbs was burned out. I stood up and switched on the Bozo side lamp next to the bed. Its soft, pink light helped the weaker overhead light.

I drew with my right hand and held the sketchpad steady with my left. The carpet pushed into the skin of my left arm and made it feel itchy. I kept on drawing, anyway.

"Okay, Keith," I said.

The brown crayon I now used to draw Keith Partridge's hair scraped softly against the white paper. I grabbed up the peach crayon and traced the outline of Keith's face. I drew in the edges of his mouth with carnation pink. A knock on the bedroom door made me jump.

"Gem?" Dale's voice said.

"Yeah—umm, yes?"

Dale pushed open the door and I could hear the TV from downstairs.

'...I am not a crook...'

"Why don't you come downstairs and watch TV with the rest of the family? 'All in the Family' is going to come on as soon as Tricky Dick finishes his speech."

"Who?"

"The President. Tricky Dick Nixon.'

"Oh. You know, I'm only eleven and a half. Isn't 'All in the Family' just for grown-ups? Can't I just stay in here and draw?"

"You know, you're right about that, Gem."

Dale yawned and stretched her arms and that's when I noticed she was already in her pink robe. She held a couple of dog leashes and I saw the noses of the little brown and little gray dogs poke past the open door.

"Tell you what. Come down in a half hour when 'M*A*S*H' starts. It's important for you to spend time with everyone. Do you know the theme song to 'M*A*S*H'?"

"Yep."

"Leave this door cracked. When you hear it, come on down."

I kept on drawing till I heard the theme song. When it started I sighed, opened the captain's bed drawer again, and put away my crayons and sketchpad.

A few minutes later, I stood at the doorway to the living room and saw Audrey sitting on the hearth in front of the stone fireplace that took up the whole wall. Two swag lamps that looked like orange fireballs hung from gold chains on either side of the fireplace. Audrey read a book with a picture of a man with a big afro on its cover. Janis sat on the floor in front of the hearth. Her right eye was pressed to the eyepiece of a microscope and she covered her left eye with her hand.

"Whew-hew!" Buzz yelled from the couch.

I looked at the TV screen and there were the running nurses in the opening of "M*A*S*H". Buzz hollered when the blonde nurse ran past, with her dog tags bouncing between her breasts. She wasn't the prettiest to me, though. The dark-haired nurse on the right who held onto her hat was beautiful.

"Have a seat," Gerry said. She sat back in the brown recliner and rested her feet on the bottom of the chair.

The blue light of the TV screen reflected off the wormwood paneling on the walls. I stepped to the couch with its big, yellow flowers and sat at the right side, as far from Buzz as I could get. I rested my arm on the rounded arm of the couch.

The show started with a scene in the operating tent.

"That's just what I did, you guys. I was the head surgical nurse, just like 'Hot Lips' there. My nursing staff at County thinks I got all my training at USC, but I learned the tough stuff in Korea."

"Didn't you do any fighting?" Buzz asked. "I mean, kill a couple of the gooks or anything?"

Gerry's legs slammed the footrest of the recliner back into position. She stuck her finger out toward Buzz.

"Don't ever say that again."

Buzz folded his arms and sunk against the back of the couch. Gerry looked over at me, and I didn't know if I was supposed to say

143

something or not. I looked away toward Audrey, who was still reading. And Janis still had her eye to the microscope. Only Buzz said something.

"Must've been tough for you, being there and all."

Gerry sat back in the recliner again.

"I guess you didn't have any boyfriends there," Audrey said over the edges of her book.

"Why would you say something like that?" Gerry asked. "You know better."

Gerry doesn't like men.

"Don't you like men?" I asked.

"I like men. Most men are good human beings. I just don't want to marry a man."

"Does that mean you and Dale are –" I didn't even know what I was going to ask.

"Shh, shh, it's starting, Gem," Gerry said. "We can talk about this another time".

Something is very wrong in this family.

Yes, the voice was right as usual. Dale and Gerry must have been two wives, I concluded. The kids were all Dale's, that much I knew for sure. So where was Dale's husband?

If there was ever a best week to start at a new school, Thanksgiving had to be it. With three days of school behind me, I walked out of my new sixth grade classroom, past the red brick office of James Cook Elementary, through the gate of the chain-link fence, and onto the sidewalk of 236th Street. My new teacher was okay. She was excited that I had already passed the gifted test back in third grade. I was eligible for James Cook's academically talented program, which meant I would get at least a couple hours a week to watch science movies or take special field trips to museums. I didn't care one way or the other. It just meant less time to be bored in class.

I felt happy as I walked the three blocks back to the Buhlerts'. With so much extra time off from school, I thought I might walk to my old street the day after Thanksgiving. The Buhlerts were only about a mile or two from where I lived as a small child until the bad times. Thanksgiving would give me some time to look around at my childhood home and neighborhood. And the best part was I'd be able to check and see if my time capsule was safe.

The wind kicked up and a chill shot through me. It wasn't so smart for me to forget my windbreaker. My arms swelled with goosebumps where they stuck out from my short-sleeved, brown-striped, Hang Ten shirt. I rubbed my arms and they felt like kernels on a corncob. I wondered if this is what they meant by 'catching your death of pneumonia'. From being this cold.

"Lo!" a strange, thick voice cried as I turned the corner of 234th.

I had gotten to the corner of the front lawn of the people who had just moved in. Claws of brown-tipped crab grass grabbed the grainy edge of the sidewalk. The lawn needed to be mowed because it was overrun by the weeds that resembled helicopter blades. I stopped because of the voice and looked past the weeds. Someone stood in the deep shadow of the Brazilian pepper tree.

"Lo!" the weird voice yelled again from the shadow.

I started to walk again, but a little faster. The person followed me and now I got nervous.

"Lo!"

The person stepped into the light and I froze. A girl, or a woman, I couldn't tell which, ran toward me. From the corner of my eye, it seemed like the girl was juggling two volleyballs. But then I realized what they were: her breasts. The biggest ones I ever saw in my life, and they bounced and shook under a navy blue sweatshirt. I now saw her full on and the way her lower body bulged through her faded blue jeans made me think of the Butterball turkey Dale was thawing for Thanksgiving. It was her face that gave me pause.

Her red hair was cut with bangs like Captain Kangaroo, and her face was blotchy like a pomegranate. But it was her eyes. It was as if they didn't belong to her face. They were narrow slits. Was she Japanese? But her nose wasn't flat. She confused me, made me nervous, and fascinated me.

"Lo, what doing?" she said.

Her lips curled around each word, making the syllables thick with her slow speech. And as she rounded her mouth, I could see tiny teeth, like primary teeth, with sharp points.

"Huh?" I said.

"What is name?"

She rocked back and forth, bringing her hands together with a sharp clap. She must have been quite older than me -- she looked like a woman. Why did she speak so oddly? I didn't want to tell her my name. I didn't want her to know it, much less, say it.

145

"What's your name?" I asked.

Her lips opened like she was going to smile, and I noticed cracks and particles of skin. Just like a shedding snake. A pink, pointed tongue stuck out and circled her dry lips.

"Fona."

"Phone ah?"

"Yah."

Like telephone?" I asked.

"Yah. I'm Fona. Lo."

Fona brought her hands to her mouth. They were small, not much bigger than Janis's. She curled her fat fingers into fists, shoving them both halfway into her mouth and laughing. Her laugh sounded like a cross between Herman Munster's laugh and a panting St. Bernard.

"Feona!" a man's voice roared.

I looked at the front stoop of the house. In the shadow of the porch cover, just inside a gray screen door, I could see a man.

"Get in here, Feona!" the man yelled again.

"Oh-kay!" Feona grunted.

She turned and ran. Instead of pumping her arms like most people do when they run, she held them stiffly out and swung them. I watched her till she disappeared into the shadow of the porch. Something was wrong with her, but what? Why was she so odd looking? I didn't know what she really was—a girl or a woman. She was also nice like a little kid, which made her womanly body even stranger.

I couldn't stop thinking about Feona, 'Fona', even during Thanksgiving dinner. I sat with all the Buhlerts and Gerry at the dining room table. Dale carried the turkey in and placed the silver platter in front of Gerry. The whole house smelled like roasted turkey, sage and onion. Dale stepped back quickly and leaned against the dining room doorway.

"Boy oh boy, does that smell good!" Gerry said. "Why don't you take a seat, honey?" Gerry said toward Dale.

Gerry cut into the golden bird. Steam rose from it. The turkey reminded me of Feona in her jeans. I giggled. Gerry raised her eyebrows.

"Something funny, there, Gem?"

I shook my head. Dale took the seat just to the left of Gerry. Gerry glanced at Dale and then stopped carving.

146

"Thanks for the bird, here. It looks terrific."

"Gerry, did you know that turkeys raise their heads to the sky and drown themselves sometimes when it's raining?" Janis said.

"Is that a fact? White meat or dark, Janis?"

"Drumstick, please!"

Gerry carved the right drumstick from the bird and set it on a plate. She passed the plate to Audrey, but she leaned back like there was dog poop on it. She rolled her eyes.

"It's just turkey," Gerry said. "Fix Janis up with trimmings, will you?"

"Potatoes and gravy!" Janis yelled.

"How about you, Audrey? White or dark?"

"Gerry, I can't eat turkey. I'll just have some yams and cranberry sauce. I'm starting the Grape Cure tomorrow and I don't want to be full."

Gerry shook her head.

"The what?" Dale asked.

"The Grape Cure. Adelle Davis says if I just eat grapes for three weeks, it'll keep my body from ever getting cancer. You should do it too, Mom."

Dale leaned back against her chair. She shook her head.

"I most certainly will not and neither will you. You're a growing girl and you need your nutrients. I'm not going to stand by and watch my daughter – my bone-thin, vegetarian daughter -- turn herself into a purple straw. This is where I draw the line."

"Gerry, you're a nurse supervisor. Do you think it would hurt me to just eat grapes?" Audrey asked.

"If you think you can just eat grapes for three weeks, I don't see how it could hurt you much."

Dale slammed a spoonful of green bean casserole on the plate, making a mound of green mess. She pointed the spoon toward Audrey.

"You're doing this to get back at me for not inviting your father."

"You could've asked him," Audrey said.

Another spoonful of green bean casserole slammed onto another plate. This time, a mushroom flew off the plate onto the floor. One of the dogs slurped it up. Dale glanced down at the dog.

"Somebody likes the casserole. Audrey, sweets, it wouldn't be right to have him here. It's been four years," Dale said.

"Good point. I forgot she's here. I'm sure Daddy would just love that."

Gerry grabbed Dale's hand and held it for a second, like they were boyfriend and girlfriend. Dale set the serving spoon down.

"Why don't we all just enjoy our meal, okay?" Gerry said.

Once everyone at the table had been served, stainless steel flatware clinked and clanked against the Sango plates with the yellow daisy borders.

Whip cream spurted from the nozzle on top of the can as I covered my pumpkin pie with a mound of white after dinner. As I swirled the sweet cream and spicy pumpkin of the first bite in my mouth, Gerry cleared her throat.

"Okay, now everybody remember. We're up tomorrow by six to get out by seven. On the dot. No hassles. We have to gas the camper and bikes up at the Gulf station and I don't want to get stuck in a long line at the pumps. That'll get us to California City by eleven."

Gerry took one last bite of pumpkin pie, then dabbed her mouth with a napkin. She pushed away from the table.

"Buzz, when you're finished with your dessert there, come on out to the garage and help me get the bikes loaded on the trailer."

As Gerry headed down the hall toward the front door, I heard her stop in the kitchen where Dale was cleaning up. They whispered a second, and then I heard the smacking sound of a kiss. I was pretty sure right then that Dale's husband wasn't ever going to be invited for dinner.

But I was also disappointed: I forgot that we would be going out of town. I was going to have to wait to explore my childhood home. I sighed.

Audrey stood up and gathered dishes. Janis looked at me, crinkled her nose, and stuck out her tongue. I wanted to smack her face so bad. Then I thought about something: would Dale let me stay home for the weekend? I knew I could take care of myself, and all I had to do was convince her. I got up from the table and walked to the kitchen.

When I got there, Dale stood at the counter and poked at her mashed potatoes. Audrey came in behind me, set a stack of dishes next to the sink without saying anything, and then went back to the dining room. Dale's eyes looked red.

"...Take another piece of my heart now baby..." Janis sang in the dining room.

"Did you enjoy dinner, Gem?" Dale asked.

"Yep."

"Potatoes weren't too lumpy were they?"

"Nope."

"Good. Because we'll be having all of it again tomorrow when we're out in the desert. You excited to watch Gerry and Buzz ride their bikes?"

I shrugged and nodded. I really didn't care.

"I got a question, Dale."

"Okay. I'll try to answer but no guarantees."

For some reason, that reminded me of the kissing sound I heard Dale and Gerry make before. But I wasn't interested in that.

"Dale, do you think I could stay home for the weekend?"

She stopped picking at her mashed potatoes and looked at me. Her eyebrows squished together like I said something confusing.

"By yourself?"

"Yeah. See, I want to go exploring my old neighborhood. That's all."

"First, the answer is no. Second, if we let you do that, Maureen would be here that fast to take you back to Maryvale."

"I just think I'm gonna be bored."

"Even if you decide you don't like to ride, the desert's real pretty at this time of year. Not too hot during the day, and real cold at night. It's very interesting. Sleeping in the Open Road is fun, too."

"You sleep on the street?"

"No. That's our camper."

"Will all the dogs sleep with us, too?"

"Oh, no. They'll be staying back here in the run. Mrs. Haggerty next door will feed and water them."

"How come you don't just bring 'em?"

"I don't want them to get too attached to us. When I get them placed, it just makes it tougher on them."

"Dale?"

Dale took a last morsel of potato from the tip of her fork, and then set the fork down. I glanced at her plate and it didn't look like she had eaten much.

"Yeah. Go 'head, Gem."

"How come Audrey's so mad at you all the time?"

Dale looked down and began to pick her left thumbnail with her right index fingernail. She moved on to picking her left index finger. Obviously, she must have been nervous. I wanted to withdraw the question. My eyes darted around the kitchen, trying to think of something else to ask about.

"Because I don't love her dad anymore."

The way she said that, it sounded like a question to me. Or maybe even a lie. But what did she really mean by that?

"Better get these leftovers into the Tupperware. Don't want tomorrow's dinner to spoil."

I left Dale in the kitchen and heard Janis laughing in the den. When I walked in, the 'Three Stooges' was on the TV. Moe and Larry ran through some sort of old room with Egyptian hieroglyphics covering its walls. As Moe stopped and leaned against a wall, a hole opened up and a claw wrapped in bandages reached out and swiped at him. I always liked this Egyptian mummy episode, even though it was a little scary.

Janis stuck her tongue out, but I didn't care. I tried to remember what my family used to do after Thanksgiving dinner when I was a kid, but all I could remember was Dad asleep in a reclining chair after a football game. TV was better than that. I slid onto the couch and watched the rest of the 'Three Stooges'.

At one-thirty in the afternoon the next day, I sat in a folding chair with blue and red stripes, sketching. Dry, cold wind whistled past my ears, burning their tips as the engine of Buzz's Yamaha sputtered. As Buzz turned the right handle of the motorcycle, the engine revved like a chainsaw. The sound pounded my eardrums. I pressed my hands against my ears to protect them. Suddenly, a cloud of pale, brown desert kicked up into my face as Buzz sped off. I spit dirt and brushed my eyes, opening them just in time to see Buzz swerve around the trunk of a Joshua tree, with its bark that looked like it was covered with gray, sharp feathers. The ends of its branches were twisted claws that reached for Buzz's blue helmet. Oh, if it could snatch him up like those apple trees in 'The Wizard of Oz'. But he made it safe past them.

Leftover sand from his takeoff gritted between my molars. Buzz became a dusty comet weaving through the spindly desert bushes that reminded me of sea urchins from the Jacques Cousteau movies in assembly. Further out, Gerry's bike rose and dipped over small hills of sand and dirt. The farther they rode from the campsite formed by the Buhlert's camper and the Mitchell's (another dirt bike family) tent, the better I felt about the whole thing. I already decided I didn't want to have anything to do with the noisy, dirty motorcycles. And worse, something about them made me nervous. Each rev of the engines made me blink involuntarily. I guess the motorcycles scared me, but I didn't want to tell anybody that.

The girls sat in the camper sipping Cactus Cooler sodas and rattling a cup of dice as they played a game of 'Yahtzee'. Dale reclined just outside the camper door on a plastic lounge chair. A can of Pabst beer sat next to her. I could hear a 'swooshing' sound as she rubbed Coppertone on her arms, all the way to where they peeked out from her short-sleeve, white blouse. She turned her head and I couldn't tell if she was looking at me or not because of the dark blue sunglasses she wore. The back flap of the red bandanna she had tied over her head flapped in the dry, cold wind.

I got up from my chair and scratched the backs of my legs that itched from the dents caused by the plastic chair straps. The drawing of the Partridge Family's bus broken down under a Joshua tree was finished. I laid the sketchpad on the ground and placed a granite rock on top of it. I noticed how my sneakers sunk into the soft dirt of the desert with each step as I crossed over to the twisted Joshua tree. Glancing back once more toward Dale who was now lying back, I pulled out my magnifying glass. I hoped to see a tarantula or scorpion up close. But as I bent down to examine the thick, gray-green base of the tree, I stopped.

Protruding from the dirt was a triangle of metal. It was a rusted brown color with a smooth surface, like the skin of the black olives I used to stick on my fingertips during Thanksgiving dinner when I was little. I didn't know what kind of metal it was. I grabbed a twig and began to dig away at the thing. When it was about half uncovered, I could see it was long and skinny. About the size of a cigar. Or it looked like an extra long chocolate Space Food Stick -- it could feed the whole Sky Lab crew as long as it was. I plucked it from the ground and it felt heavy in my palm. That must have been why it left an impression in the dirt. A stain of orange rust in the pit it left led me to think it must have been made partly of iron.

As I turned it around to examine it, I noticed small dents in its surface. Just like the Chicken Pox scars on my forehead. Did lying in the sand for years make the dents, or did the hammer that made it cause the marks? I couldn't know for sure. A sharp piece at the top looked like a sawed-off rhino horn. Was it a hook? But what kind of a hook was this? It was heavy and long as a ruler. I couldn't figure it out.

I scratched my head and looked around. The motorcycles

hummed in the distance. I thought about bringing my find to Dale, but when I watched her for a second, it seemed like she was asleep. Janis's loud giggles from the open camper windows didn't even disturb her. As I turned my head back to the object, I stopped when I saw the Mitchell's green, dusty tent. My eyes followed the yellow rope that attached to the tent stakes.

That's what it was. A tent stake. Had to be. Miss Dileo, my fourth grade California history teacher, popped into my head. Nomadic Indian tribes had occupied the Mojave Desert for years before Spain ever set foot here she told the class one day. Could I be holding a stake that held down a nomadic Indian's tent? How many hundreds of years old could it be? A shiver electrified my back and goosebumps popped up on my skin. I was holding something ancient and mysterious. Would there be more stakes here? Arrowheads maybe?

I set the stake down. Using the twig from before, I poked around at the base of the tree. I figured that I had to follow some sort of a pattern so I wouldn't go over the same area twice. I made parallel rows of punctures, separating them by five or six inches each time. As I started the third line of holes, the tip of the twig hit something. I dropped to my knees.

With a sort of a karate chop, I landed the side of my right hand into the ground. I swept away an inch of the dirt. Dust flew up my nose and it smelled like wet metal. Nothing was at this level. I karate chopped the dirt again and cleared away the next three inches. This time, my hand grazed across something flat and hard. I was so excited my heart felt like it was slapping the inside of my chest. With the dirt brushed aside, the new object appeared and took on a square, almost pillow shape. I leaned over and blew one last layer of dust off and there it was: a charcoal briquette. I sighed and sat back on my haunches. Someone must've camped here before us and left their barbecue mess.

"What are you doing there?" Dale said from behind me. "Praying to the tree?"

I brushed my hands over the dig site. I was too embarrassed to tell her. I plucked the stake up and tried to slide it into my pants pocket without her seeing it.

"What do you have there?" she asked as she walked up.

I held the stake out to her. Dale pushed her sunglasses over her eyes and squinted at it.

"I think it may be a tent stake from an ancient Indian tribe," I said.

"Hmmm."

Dale nodded and handed it back to me. She dropped her sunglasses back onto her nose.

"You've been digging all this time just for that?"

"No. This was sticking up from the ground. I just pulled it out."

"Then what were you digging for, a free trip to China?"

I chewed on my upper lip. I felt too dumb to answer her.

"I don't know."

"Were you hoping to find another one?"

I stared at the ground and nodded.

"You don't have to feel bad, Gem. It's okay."

"Ever since I watched 'Bewitched' one time when they went to ancient England, I've liked old history stuff."

"So do I. A long time ago, I was going to be a history teacher instead of a kindergarten teacher. That was before I had kids. Did I ever tell you that?"

I shook my head and shrugged.

"Do you like digging up things from the past, too?" I asked.

"No."

She's ashamed of something in her past.

I wondered if my face looked different when the voice said that. She didn't seem to notice anything. I went to shove the stake into my pants pocket but paused.

"Can I bring this stake in for sharing on Monday?"

"Yeah, Gem. That's okay. You oughtta be proud of your special artifact."

I sighed. I wasn't proud of anything and almost everything made me feel like nothing.

"Dale?"

She folded her arms and raised her chin toward me. I almost thought she was going to say something like I didn't have the right to ask questions because I was a foster kid, but she nodded.

"What?" she asked.

"How come you save all those dogs?"

"They've been abandoned and need homes."

"Like foster kids?"

"Yeah. The same thing."

They are substitutes for her own children. She is ashamed of something in her past.

"You seem to take more time with them than Buzz and the girls."

She suddenly pulled up her sunglasses and her eyes were tiny slits of anger. I shouldn't have said that.

"That's enough of the third degree."

She stood up and folded her lounge chair, making a metallic crack with its hinges.

"Come on into the camper and have lunch with the girls."

Dale tucked the folded chair under her left arm, turned, and walked toward the camper. Her navy tennis shoe on her left foot dug into the ground for a second, making her wobble.

A while later, Dale leaned against the camper stove as I finished the last bite of my turkey sandwich. I went to grab the last two of my Wampum barbecued corn chips, but Janis stole one from my paper plate.

"That was mine."

"No it wasn't," Janis said. "It was purchased by my mother so it's mine."

"Janis, don't be such a snot. That's not cool," Audrey said.

Audrey looked up from the book she was reading. She grabbed a handful from the pile of corn chips Dale had placed on her plate--she had started the Grape Cure and wasn't going to eat corn chips--and dropped them onto my plate. I noticed how long her fingers were, and how soft they looked. I wanted to grab them.

"Anybody want a raspberry Zinger?" Dale asked.

"Yippie!" Janis yelled.

"Mom, they have animal fat in them. That's such bad karma to eat those," Audrey said.

I wanted one of the pink-coconut covered, cream-filled cakes. They were one of my favorites. But I didn't want 'bad karma', whatever that was. I didn't want to disappoint Audrey, either. I shook my head.

Cellophane crackled as Janis opened the package and bit into the Zinger. Audrey lifted the book to her face again. The guy with the big afro on its cover reminded me of that singer--Johnny Matthias was it? 'Sathya Sai Baba' the cover read. That wasn't the singer's name. Just as I was about to ask Audrey about the book, Dale stepped out of the camper door. The camper bounced and shook and a second later, the hinges of a lounge chair cracked. Dale must have gone out to lie in the sun again. Motorcycle engines sputtered from a distance then grew

154

louder as they approached the outside of the camper.

"That one hoop-dee-doo was far out," Buzz yelled over the engines.

"Yup," Gerry responded. "You stayed on the bike, though."

Why were they back already? They couldn't have been out riding longer than a half hour. The motorcycles engines stopped and the camper became quiet. I sighed as Janis slid out under the table and ran to the camper door. Audrey pulled her book closer to her face.

"Gimme a ride, Gerry. I wanna ride!" Janis jumped up and down.

"After lunch, little sweetie," Gerry said.

As she stepped up on the camper bumper, the camper dipped and rocked like it was the 1971 earthquake all over again. Gerry's face was a mask of dust, except for around her eyes. A raccoon, just like a dirty raccoon.

"Hey, Gem, wanna learn to handle a bike?" Gerry asked.

She smiled and I could see a trail of mud across her front teeth. Just what I want: to be scared and dirty. I was about to answer when Audrey lowered her book so that I could see her eyes.

"Yeah. Why don't you go learn to ride? I know how to."

That was it for me. No matter how nervous I was I wasn't going to be a baby in front of Audrey.

"Okay."

"You can ride Buzz's bike. It's a 125 and it won't be too much for you to handle."

I had no idea what Gerry meant, but I followed her out of the camper. As we stepped past Dale in her lounge chair, Gerry took off her yellow helmet and shoved it on my head. It felt like a warm, soggy bucket. Dale lowered her sunglasses and squinted.

"What's going on?"

"He wants to learn to ride a bike."

Dale jumped up faster than I had ever seen her move. She yanked her sunglasses off and clutched them in her right hand.

"Just take him for a ride. If he gets hurt, he's got no insurance. And you know that we're violating foster family regulations by just taking him for a ride."

Yea. I had a good excuse to not have to go through with it.

"We can't violate the regulations," Dale went on. "They may come and take him back sooner."

Gerry looked up at the sky, her left hand resting on her hip.

When Dale finished, she looked right at me.

"You wanna learn?"

"Gerry, honey, don't put it to him. He can't decide."

"What do you say, Gem?"

Buzz leaned against his motorcycle and patted it. That wasn't going to convince me. But when Audrey stepped to the door of the camper, I again didn't want to disappoint her.

"It's okay, Dale," I said. "I'll be careful."

Gerry's face broke into a big smile. Audrey nodded.

"This takes the proverbial cake," Dale said. But she slumped into her chair and gave up.

"He'll be fine. I won't let him hurt himself," Gerry said. "Besides, I get a sense that he's a little intimidated and it will be good for him to face his fear."

How did she figure that out? Gerry was amazing.

I followed her over to Buzz's red Yamaha. She threw her right leg over the black, dusty saddle of a seat. She turned the handlebars and straightened the wheels into a line.

"You want to keep the bike on its kickstand until you start her up. To start it, you pull in the clutch here on the left handle -- see how it looks like a bicycle handle brake? Give the left pedal here a kick, and turn the right handlebar, your accelerator, just a little bit."

The motorcycle revved into life, its motor sounding like a chainsaw. It shook and rumbled, jerking a little like a horse.

"Once you got it going, keep hold of the clutch and push forward off the kickstand. Now hop on the back, I want to show you how to throttle and shift."

The wind burned my eyes as Gerry and I thumped in a wide circle around the campsite. I held on tight to Gerry. I watched as she pulled the clutch handle, then popped the small peddle on the left to change gears. Each time, the engine of the motorcycle seemed to change its tune to a higher pitch, from a chainsaw to a buzz saw, from that to a humming jet. The movements seemed pretty easy. We finished the circle and Gerry pulled the motorcycle into camp. She released the accelerator and the clutch.

"Now, you get up front here and you can take me for a ride to make sure you got it."

"...*Who needs wings to fly?...*"

I threw my leg over the motorcycle. My heart pounded. When Gerry climbed on behind me, I felt her thighs against my side.

Something in me felt like a small child again, like a protected little kid again, and it felt good.

"Let's go," Gerry said. "Grab the clutch and kick it on."

I squeezed the clutch handle and the metal was cold in my hand. As I kicked the pedal to start the engine, I felt numb and automatic as a robot. My thighs vibrated and my knees rattled against the red tank. A wisp of gasoline floated past my nose as the engine hammered my ears. The good feeling of Gerry behind me disappeared.

"...Who needs wings to fly?..."

"Okay, slowly let out the clutch and pull back on the throttle."

The motorcycle jerked ahead. The clutch handle sprung from my hand and the engine stalled.

"You're okay," Gerry said. "Ease off the clutch a little slower this time and if it sounds like the bike is gonna stall, just pull back on it."

I started the motorcycle again, and this time, as I eased off the clutch, I remembered to pull back on the throttle and the motorcycle jumped ahead. We bumped over the sand.

"Pull all the way back on the throttle and put your foot on the clutch pedal."

I did that. I felt the weight of Gerry's boot on top of my foot.

"Grab the clutch pedal, now!"

When I grabbed it, I felt Gerry push my foot down, causing the clutch pedal to click, and the engine to rev higher.

"That a boy! We're in second."

Even though I was afraid of the roaring monster underneath me, I liked the feeling of Gerry saying 'that a boy.'

"Now for third!" Gerry yelled.

We rode together, making the same wide circle as before, and shifting through all the gears. We rode up to the campsite. Dale stood with her sunglasses in her hand, her eyebrows raised, making the skin of her forehead look like a stack of pancakes. When we stopped, she put her sunglasses back on and sat.

"Okay, you want to try it alone?" Gerry asked.

I almost said no till I noticed Audrey sitting on the camper bumper. I nodded and Gerry jumped off the back of the bike. I pushed my feet hard against the ground to keep the motorcycle from tipping over. I didn't like the feeling of being on the motorcycle by myself.

"Go, Gem!" Audrey yelled.

157

I started up the motorcycle. The roaring chainsaw of the engine, the heat it was now putting off, and the rumble of the motorcycle conspired to make me nervous.

"*...Who needs wings to fly?...*"

I let out the clutch and pulled back on the throttle and jerked ahead. As the engine began to scream to be shifted, I pulled back on the right handlebar by mistake. The brakes grabbed hold and I flew through the air. In a swirl of beige, red, and blue, I was suddenly on top of a soft bush, staring up at the blue sky. What I thought was the motorcycle's engine turned out to be Buzz's machine gun laugh.

Gerry, Audrey, Janis and Buzz, who was really laughing hard, looked down at me. My face felt hot, but not because anything was wrong with me. Gerry kneeled down and grabbed my wrist and ran her hand over my head and forehead. She removed the helmet.

"Oh, my God, Gem, can you talk?" Dale asked as she ran up.

"Yeah. I'm okay. What happened?"

"You grabbed the wrong handle to shift," Gerry said. "Anything hurt when I do this?"

She pressed the sides and top of my head. I only felt her finger pressure not pain. I shook my head. She ran her hands down my arms and legs, lifting each one.

"Any pain?"

I shook my head. She finished by lightly touching my belly and chest.

"Everything is still in the right place," she said. She helped me to my feet and brushed off my back and pants.

"You should'a' seen how you flew over the handle bars when you grabbed the brake," Buzz laughed. "What a Ruby. Least my bike didn't get nailed."

Audrey rolled her head for a second as she looked at me, shrugged, and then turned back for camp.

"You sure you're okay?" Dale asked.

"Nothing broken or out of joint. He's fine," Gerry answered.

I rubbed a scrape on my elbow later that night as Buzz, Audrey, Janis, Jimmy Mitchell, and I sat around the campfire. Its orange flames crackled and smoked, sending fireflies of cinders into the black desert sky. Dale and Gerry's voices echoed from the camper as they laughed and talked with Jimmy's mom and dad over a game of Parcheesi.

"Pass the marshmallows," Jimmy said.

I watched him as he skewered three marshmallows onto a wire

158

hanger then held it over a lick of flame. The edges of the marshmallows blistered and burned.

"Tell us one of those spooky stories, Buzz," Audrey said.

"Yeah!" Jimmy said.

Buzz leaned back in his chair, dropped his chin with its cluster of blackheads against his chest, and looked around at all of us. His face was very serious.

"Up in Pee Vee, there's this old house that no one's lived in for maybe, you know, fifty years. An old mansion, called the Vanderlips Estate..."

"Pee Vee?" I asked. "You mean Palos Verdes—by Torrance?"

"Yeah. Palos Verdes. The Hill, we call it. Where all the rich people live," Buzz said.

"Ooh, I love these stories," Audrey said.

"They're not just stories, Audrey. They really happened," Buzz said. "All the bad and mysterious stuff that ever happens around Torrance or Lomita always happens on the Hill. They think it was maybe where evil Indian medicine men used to do black magic in the old days. Put hexes on people, eat babies, all kinds of stuff."

"Eat babies?" Janis said.

My skin tightened with chills. I really didn't want to hear anymore.

"Anyways, the legend is that old man Vanderlips and his wife were cannibals. That anytime someone was stupid enough to wander at night on the road by their house, that person would disappear. Sometimes the body would be found, but they could never link up the Vanderlips with the murder.

"And the way they killed their victims...That's part of the story. So this guy and girl were driving up there after prom night at Pee Vee High. They ran out of gas and the guy had to push his sixty-eight Mustang off the road and under an oak tree. When he got back in the car, he told the girl that he was gonna go get some gas, and that she had to leave the headlights on, and the doors locked.

"'There's a blanket in the back seat, so climb back there and cover yourself up. Don't let anybody in the car, and wait for me to come back,' he said."

"He got out of the car and stepped out of the light and into the black night. And you've never seen it darker than on one of the streets on the Hill that don't have streetlights."

I looked around at everybody's faces as Buzz told the story.

Their faces, like yellow and orange masks from the campfire, just stared at Buzz. Were anyone else's teeth chattering like mine, like they were so scared they were cold? I couldn't see if they were.

'...*Who needs wings to fly?*...'

Buzz put his hands over his head as he told the next part of the story, pretending to pull a blanket up over his face. He twisted his face as he told how the girl in the car heard someone or something pulling at the door handles. But what he said next I wasn't going to forget for a long time.

"...So pretty soon, when the tugging at the door handles stopped, the headlights started to flicker. She had been there for over three hours and the battery was draining."

"A battery can't drain that fast," Audrey interrupted.

"Shut up. It was an old car and I think I know more about cars and engines than you do. Anyway, then the headlights went out. When the girl felt brave enough to peek over the edge of the blanket, it was as dark as if she was in a cave.

"The wind kicked up and she heard a weird sound on top of the car. It sounded like this."

Buzz scratched the metal arm of the lawn chair back and forth a couple of times, and the screech of his fingernails on the aluminum sent electric shocks down my back. I didn't want to hear anymore of the story. I just wanted to go into the camper and pull a sleeping bag over my head.

"Another hour went by, and every time the wind kicked up, she heard it." Buzz scratched the arm again. My back chilled again.

"All of a sudden, headlights from another car lit up the inside of the girl's car. She heard a bang on the back window. 'This is the police. Open up immediately.'

"The girl jumped up, scared out of her gourd. Just as she stepped out of the car, the policeman grabbed and pushed her toward his car. 'Go sit in the squad car, miss. And whatever you do, don't look back.'"

"Oh, Buzz, I've heard this one a gazillion times," Audrey said.

"Bitchen', Audrey. Screw up the climax of the story."

"I wanna hear," Jimmy said. "Finish it."

"Yeah, I'm not ascared," Janis said.

Now I felt like a huge baby. Janis, a five-year-old, wasn't even scared? Not even of that scratching sound?

"Okay, I'll finish. So the cop said: 'Whatever you do, don't look

160

back.' But just as the girl slid into the cop car, she turned around. There, hanging from the lowest branch of the oak tree, was her boyfriend. His body was bloody and carved up like a side of beef at the butcher's, with big hunks of his skin and flesh missing. And his hand was hanging down so that the tips of his fingers just touched the top of the Mustang. They swayed with the wind one more time."

Buzz ran his fingernails across the metal arm of his chair again. Janis gasped.

"Cannibals?" Janis said.

"Cannibals," Buzz replied.

"Jeesh" Jimmy exhaled.

My skin shriveled into a thousand goosebumps. I couldn't get the image of the dead man out of my head.

The caramel and ash taste of a toasted marshmallow gummed up my mouth awhile later, helping my goosebumps flatten as I tried to forget about Buzz's story. The camper door popped open. Jimmy's mom and dad stepped down laughing.

"Okay, Jimmy. Let's get to the tent now. Time for bed."

Jimmy kicked sand with the heels of his sneakers. He crammed his hands into his brown cord jacket, and then stood up.

" 'Night everybody."

"Audrey, you and Janis get in here and help me set up the table bed," Dale hollered. "Buzz, come grab sleeping bags for you and Gem."

Audrey, Janis, and Buzz stood up and folded their chairs. I jumped up. I wasn't going to be left by myself in the dark next to the orange embers of the dying fire. I folded my chair and carried it under my arm like everybody else did.

When we got to the open camper door, yellow light spilled onto the pale beige desert sand speckled with some sort of black minerals. The girls leaned their chairs against the ridged aluminum camper side. Hopping up the bumper and through the door, each girl's weight caused the camper to shudder. I looked behind into the blackness of the desert and wanted Buzz to hurry up and get inside. Instead, Buzz set his chair against the side of the camper, then grabbed one of the folding lounge chairs. A rolled up sleeping bag ejected through the camper door and Buzz caught it. He tucked it under his right arm and walked off back toward the campfire.

"Here's your bag, Gem," Gerry said as she tossed a sleeping

bag to me.

"Sleep well," she said. The camper door groaned on its rusting hinges as Gerry pulled it shut. Only the small window in the door gave light through its striped, orange curtains. I looked back toward the campfire and I could see orange sparks twirling as Buzz added more wood to it. I ran for it, clutching the rolled sleeping bag like a Teddy bear. My sneakers sunk and stuck in the soft dirt.

"We really gotta sleep outside?" I asked.

" 'Course. I always do. There ain't enough room in the camper. Guess you're sleeping out, too, Amethyst. Don't forget to grab a lounge chair, though."

"Where are they?"

"The other side of the camper."

I walked back toward the camper, envious of the silhouettes made by the rest of the family as they moved around inside. I kept my eyes on the camper that now looked like a square pumpkin in the dark night. Never looking right or left into the desert with its blackness that seemed to be trying to smother me, I grabbed up a lounge chair and ran back to the campfire.

Setting the chair on the opposite side of the fire from Buzz, I stretched the chair open. I untied the sleeping bag's strings and unrolled it. The long zipper buzzed like an over-sized fly as I pulled it open. As I sat to take off my shoes, Buzz let an explosive fart. Is this what the night was going to be?

"Ahh, nothing like a marshmallow sleeping bag fart, huh?"

I climbed into my sleeping bag. Its red felt lining with a pattern of crossed hunting rifles lay warm against my skin. A soft smell of what I found out later was cedar filled my nose as I slid as deep as I could into the bag. I was not going to let the night get me.

"Hey, Ruby!"

"What, Buzz?" I said through the sleeping bag.

"Stick your head out a second."

"Why, you gonna let one again?"

"No. Just do it."

I stuck my head out and Buzz scratched his fingernails across the arms of the lounge chair. A jolt of adrenaline pumped my skin into gravel. I thought about heating one of the marshmallow hangers in the fire and jamming against his arm. Why did I think that? The thought made me wince.

"Real funny," I said.

I slid back into the bag and did my best to cover my ears. Buzz scratched the chair arms again and again, stopping only to laugh.

I didn't remember when I fell asleep, with Buzz still laughing, but a loud pop and crackle from the fire jolted me awake. My hair clung to the edge of my face that was moist with sweat. The inside of the bag felt like what the Thanksgiving turkey must have felt inside its roasting bag. With my teeth chattering from fear, I lifted my head out of the bag enough so that I could see.

The fire glowed like a heap of orange, gold and black mush. I could barely see Buzz on the other side, but I could hear a thick snore. Avoiding the spooky black desert, I raised my eyes to the sky. The sky was just as black. I couldn't tell where the desert ended and the sky started.

But the stars. The sky looked like a million Christmas trees spread out for me. If they were a million Christmas trees just for me to see, then I belonged to them and they belonged to me. Maybe I wasn't just a useless foster kid tagging along with someone else's family. That made me feel better and a little less afraid.

Suddenly, one star burst into a white blaze and streaked across the sky. A falling star! Another streaked across the other direction. The stars were falling, alone, burning, and dying. The brilliance of the other stars that kept their places in the sky almost seemed to taunt the falling ones. Even the night sky didn't have any need for the falling ones. So maybe I was useless again after all. Just a stupid, useless falling star. Each star that fell made me feel more alone than I ever had.

Ffffllooopppppwhopppppppppppppppppp!!!

Buzz ripped a colossal fart. That took my mind off the falling stars. For now, at least, I wasn't alone.

11.

"Well that was a marathon," Gem said.

"You're telling me—from attachment disorder to lesbians."

"My throat is cracked," Gem said.

"No surprise there," Dr. Friedman said.

"I can't believe it's Friday already. I don't feel cured."

"We have another week of this—give it time. That star bit was pretty poetic for a kid. But it also was pretty accurate. You were alone and a tag-along as a foster kid. That's why you developed the detachment disorder."

"We covered all that twenty-six years ago. I told you there was no point in going through this."

Gem stood up and handed Dr. Friedman the manuscript. She slapped his hand away and then made a fist.

"Right in the kisser if you try that again. I don't remember you ever mentioning the lesbians before. It was a tough time for gay people back then."

"Why should I? They were really good to me. I didn't even think about that."

"I guess you could say being a foster kid had its small advantages."

"What the hell?"

Dr. Friedman stood up and stretched. Her shoulder clicked as she raised her arms over her head.

"Wow, you sound like the Tinman," Gem said. "Being a foster kid had no advantages at all."

"Sure it did. Think about it. You were exposed to all types of different people. They each had some affect on you, bad or good. Most of us are raised pretty isolated and narrow."

"You know who you are and what you come from," Gem countered.

"That security has a price. Trust me, I have treated plenty of people raised in 'ideal' homes and suburbs like Torrance. Rigid, close-minded, uptight, a lot of OCD and depression there, too. Too much expectation and disillusionment when life hits back too hard outside the white picket fences."

"Speaking of poetic."

"But nothing much about Dad, yet, and he's really the focus."

"Then why don't we skip ahead and get this done faster?"

Dr. Friedman grabbed the manuscript, rolled it up and pretended she was about to strike him with it.

"No chance unless you call it quits. Otherwise, see you tomorrow at ten."

Gem watched later that evening as Kelly's beautiful fingers connected the sections of her platinum flute together. He lay in their cherry, four-poster bed with his hands clasped behind his head. Cool air from the open French doors leading to the bedroom balcony blew in across his chest. From all the discussions in the last week's of therapy, his body felt like a tight coil. Kelly pulled the overstuffed, white satin chair toward the bed. She sat down on the edge of the chair, fluffing her eggshell night gown out as she sat. Gem smiled at her.

"You are married to the west coast expert on Mozart's flute compositions, after all. Hope I can still play."

"Cuppy, I don't know. It may keep me awake."

"Only if I call Herb and ask him to bring over his harp. Then you won't sleep. But Mozart K 299 will help you, I promise."

Gem wasn't convinced. His brain was firing off troubling memories and dark feelings of sadness and anxiety.

"Just roll over, Cupper. Focus on the music, okay?" Kelly said. "Here comes the Andantino. Pardon any squeaks—it has been awhile."

With that, Kelly began to play. The soft, rich tones of the piece almost immediately calmed Gem. He watched the fluid movement of Kelly's hands, and the dance her fingertips performed on the flute accompanied by her soft breaths. Images of his dad now blended into houses lined up on a street. His mind followed the music and now he saw Dale again and Mrs. Wagner. He floated over the sump and fell asleep.

The next morning, Gem was still waking up as he entered the parking garage at Dr. Friedman's office. In the same way she taught him how to live and love, Kelly's love-filled flute recital brought him to his deepest night's sleep in weeks. Tired, but grateful for his lovely Kelly, he stepped out of the car and walked toward the parking garage elevator.

12.

It felt like someone were pushing me as the wind caught my windbreaker jacket, almost magic. I held my arms over my head like a goal post, stretching the blue jacket between them to make a sail. When the wind hit the jacket, my roller skates started to glide over the sidewalk, their metal wheels scratching against the cement.

This Sunday was the first time I could play outside since the rain had trapped me in the house with Buzz, Audrey, and Janis. It was also the day I decided to break in my new skates. Their black leather sides were stiff and shiny and their wheels still looked like smooth aluminum. Maureen always brought me a Christmas present, and I couldn't believe she thought of new skates this time.

Skating always made me feel light, like I was flying, and I could move fast, much faster than I could run the bases on the field. As I flew along the sidewalk, the bottoms of my feet tickled from the vibration of the skate wheels against the cement. I felt the bump of one of the sidewalk seams. Step on a crack, break your mother's back. But rolling over a crack was okay, wasn't it? Besides, my mom was dead so it didn't matter.

When I got to the end of 234th Street, the wind stopped and so did my skates. I lifted my right leg and pumped it against the sidewalk to keep momentum.

Just at the corner of 234th and Crenshaw, cars blared past me in both directions, and I had to stop to make up my mind. Audrey had told me the story of an old house in a field at the end of 237th Street where devil-worshipping hippies lived. '...It was all glowing, orange, and yellow, and red, like a fire that one night...' she had said. 'We stopped to see what was going on and heard weird screams and

167

mumbling -- like prayers being said backward... Stacy, my friend with her learner's permit, drove off really fast...We never figured out what was going on...'

I was curious to see the house, especially if any devil-worshipping hippies had been staying there. But what made it hard for me to decide was what was over on 240th Street. I had wanted to go there since Thanksgiving, but because the Buhlerts were always dragging me off to the desert for dirt biking or the mountains for snow sledding, this was the first chance I had to try. I could skate that far and back, too, and what was there was something I really wanted to see again: the house where I was born and lived with Mom and Dad before all the awful times. And just outside, next to the backyard, I could check the sump to see if my coffee can time capsule was still buried safe. I chewed on the edge of my index fingernail as I tried to decide which way to go.

I was just a little kid when I put together my time capsule, so whatever I'd find inside it would probably be little kid stuff. Besides, a spooky house where crazy hippies once lived could be real fun to explore. I decided to go look at the house and dig for the time capsule some other time. I raised and pumped my right leg. My sneakers, with their laces tied together and strung over my shoulder, bounced against my chest. The cold air made my eyes water.

I got to the field at the end of 237th Street. The sidewalk ended right where the field started. I would have sat and rested while I changed into my sneakers, but the field was still muddy from the rain. So I bent over to change out of my skates, using a broken picket fence overgrown with thick, green ivy to lean against for support.

After I finished, I stepped around the fence. I could just see a roof sticking up over the bushes and weeds. My shoes sunk into the soggy ground as I walked toward the roof, and as I got closer, the house started to appear through the weeds like a ghost rising from a grave. I could now see that the windows had all been broken out. They looked at me like a pair of black, square eyes.

'Who needs wings to fly?...'

I knew why this time I was hearing the song: the old house looked wrong. It didn't belong. It reminded me of the pictures of the WWII airplanes crashed under the ocean I saw once in National Geographic. When something was where it didn't belong, it was creepy.

The sides of the house were all blistered and some paint and plaster had peeled off, lying around the edges of it like a hard-boiled eggshell. I could see that the house had no door, either. All around the outside of the house the feathery weeds that smelled like licorice grew, just like the ones that grew around the sump. And even though the wind that helped me sail on my skates before still blew around me, it seemed to stop in front of the house.

I looked to the far side of the field and saw the edge of an asphalt parking lot. I figured there must be a store or something just around the other side. Even so, I felt nervous to be in front of the house. What did I have to be afraid of? The hippies were all gone.

"What the hell you doin'?" a man's voice yelled.

I jumped back and almost fell onto my butt. A skinny man, with bushy long, red hair and a scraggly beard stood in the doorway of the house. A trail of wiry, red hair grew down the middle of his chest and stomach, like a competition stripe on a Hotwheels car.

"Get lost, punk!"

The man stepped out from the doorway and now I noticed he was barefoot.

"Are there hippies here?"

"Huh?" the man said. He wiped off the corner of his red mustache with the back of his dirty hand. His fingernails were caked with black dirt.

"Don't crazy hippies live here?"

"Punk, I don't got no idea what you talkin' 'bout. You got a nickel for a Viet Nam vet?"

He wrinkled his nose when he said that, just before curling up his lip to show his slimy, black-brown teeth. There was only one thing I could think of to do: run! My stupid sneakers dug and pulled as they stuck in the wet dirt, but I kept running anyway.

"Send your sister next time, punk!" the man yelled.

By the time I skated back from 237th Street, after changing out of my sneakers on Pennsylvania Avenue and keeping a lookout for the spooky man over my shoulder the whole time, my face and neck dripped with sweat. I saw Buzz and Janis standing in the street with a few other neighbor kids. I was actually glad to see Buzz. Now that I was safe, I slowed down my stride.

I rolled down the sidewalk and into the street, my metal wheels rattling louder as they hit the asphalt. Just as I got to within a couple feet of Buzz, my throat hit something solid and everything turned upside down.

169

"Buzz, you shouldn't a done that!" I heard another kid say over laughter.

Buzz now stood over me and I could still feel my skate wheels turning. I was flat on my back in the street.

"You're okay, ain't you, Opal?" Buzz said.

I could feel the other kids staring at me. My face warmed up from being embarrassed. I nodded and started to get up. Buzz slammed me back down with his hand.

"Hold it. Someone wants to meet you!"

Buzz waved. I struggled against Buzz's grip, but I couldn't get myself free. I panicked, and the sunlight, the laughing kids, and the blue sky all seemed to turn dark. The harder I pushed against Buzz's arm, the harder Buzz held me down. Things turned darker and darker, almost as if my eyes were shut. I was so mad.

"Yeah, over here!" Buzz yelled.

I managed to twist my head around in time to see Feona running up. Her breasts bounced under her light blue sweatshirt.

"Feona, come give your boyfriend a kiss!"

Feona's face folded into a giant smile, making the slits of her eyelids almost fold into the corners of her grinning mouth.

"Oh-kay!" she said.

She waddled like a penguin toward Buzz and me, and as she squatted down near my head, she puckered her lips. Now all I saw was black and I hated Buzz. I felt like I could kill him. I twisted and squirmed and knocked Buzz's arm loose. I jumped up, knocking Feona to the asphalt. Everyone laughed.

"Jees, Sapphire," Buzz said. "It was only a little kiss."

My face was on fire, and I felt something pressing in my chest. I pumped both feet to get away from Buzz and the other jerks. As my metal wheels scratched and shrieked against the asphalt, I heard Feona crying. I didn't care because it made me sick to think of her kissing me.

I skated as fast as my legs would take me. I figured someone watching me right then might have been able to see puffs of smoke from where my cord pants rubbed together between my legs. That's how fast I was going. All I wanted to do was get away from the laughs and from Buzz's nasty face. It all reminded me of the times I spent in Hollygrove when I was a guppy. I remembered Eugene Aragon, and the other teenagers with scraggly mustaches and chins lined with blackheads. The ones with the blackheads always seemed the meanest. All of it swirled in my head and made me feel like nothing again. A stupid, worthless, foster kid. So I skated faster and faster, trying to get away from the bad feelings. I didn't know where I was going.

You need help. Skate to 240th Street.

Yeah, the voice was right again. That street was like a magnet, and as I rolled around onto Crenshaw, the lonely feelings faded.

When I rounded the corner of Pennsylvania Avenue, I recognized the bungalow house with the gray, clapboard sides. Its front lawn of crab grass and dandelions grew all the way to the stairs that went up to the long porch. I stopped to look at the house.

Something about the porch pulled like a string inside me. Fireworks, I remembered: swirling, sparking pinwheels and screeching Piccolo Petes in front of that porch; homemade peach ice cream being scooped from a big wooden bucket. I felt happy for a second and I could almost see shadows of neighbors standing around together for Fourth of July.

Who lived there again, I tried to remember. The name of the family just wouldn't come to me.

I got frustrated trying to remember so after about a minute, I skated away. I got to the curb on the corner of Vine Street and 240th. I recognized the green, metal street sign that marked the corner. I looked around and also recognized the house on the right.

It was gray with black trim, and I remembered something about this house, too. A big family, a big, Mormon family--that was it. The Curtis's. They had a boy my age -- Seth. I could see Seth's brown hair and brown eyes as we laughed about a "Three Stooges" episode on Channel 52.

I reached out and grabbed the metal street sign pole. It was so cold, it made my skin tingle. When I looked across the small side street, my breath seemed to leave me: the gold house with the brown trim. It was my home once. The new owners hadn't repainted it. Then there was the pepper tree that grew the bb-sized red berries. It was still there, not much taller than it was then. It grew out of the middle of the narrow strip of lawn--the 'boulevard'--that separated the sidewalk from the street.

I skated across the street. When I got to the corner, I looked closer at the house. The wooden plant shelf that wrapped around one side of the house was still there. My stomach began to tighten.

'*...Who needs wings to fly?...*'

The song? I wasn't feeling afraid. What was going on? I skated around to the front of the house and recognized the two front

171

windows with their mullions and small panes. A rectangle of red bricks separated the two windows. That was our fireplace. I recalled pumpkins cut from orange construction paper, and the twisting, tall hat of the paper witch hanging in the windows for Halloween. I saw in my mind the windows painted with snow-covered trees that surrounded a cottage. Mom and I painted a Christmas scene every year I could remember. I could almost smell the wet-flour odor of the tiny jars of poster paint.

'...*Who needs wings to fly?...*'

I rounded the other corner of the front lawn, and at the end of the lawn, I saw the chain-link fence and the weeds growing green over and through it. Skating closer to the jungle of growth, I looked at the sump. I could just see through the thick bushes. Would I see the dragonflies that used to buzz its murky, yellow-green surface? I didn't, so I leaned closer. What about the baby toads that would skitter through the fence and invade the backyard? I didn't see them, either, but it had to be spring for them to come out, anyway. I stepped to a thinner growth of weeds and saw that the sump was now a brown, dry pit that smelled like dead fish and molded vegetables. It wasn't the watery pond it was that flooded during winter rainstorms when I was little, turning 240th Street into a silver lake and our house into an island. I could almost feel the cold water against my yellow rain boots, and see the lightning flashes over the O'Neill's house across the street.

My eyes followed the edge of the brown pit as it sloped up toward the backyard of my old house, and I had the urge to climb the fence. Somewhere, under the weeds and bushes, was the 'x' made from two pink, plastic rulers tied together with a shoestring. Just like in the pirate movies I loved when I was little, the plastic 'x' marked the spot where I buried my time capsule. The coffee can of red tin contained treasures from six years before. I couldn't remember what I put in the can besides a gold crayon and a blue, puree marble. Not being able to remember made me want to dig it up even more.

I was going to have to take off my skates, change into my sneakers, and climb the fence. As I thought about it, the sun dropped behind the Palos Verdes Peninsula and the shadow cast by the Hill now crept over me, making it feel like it was already midnight. I didn't think it would be too smart to try to climb the fence when it was getting dark.

Too late. I had to go. I promised myself I would come back the next Saturday or Sunday. When I skated back around to the front of the house, I stopped and looked at black stains on the sidewalk. Those were burn marks left by the smoke snakes lit on Fourth of July. I remembered lighting the aspirin-sized, black pellets and watching as the snakes of gray ash twisted from them. It felt weird to see those burn marks. Almost as if it were just yesterday when I lit them. I looked up from the burn marks and saw the cement path from the sidewalk up to the porch of the house. I could almost hear the clomp of Dad's work boots against the two cement porch steps the day the police took him away. As I turned to skate, I felt something I hadn't felt in a long time: my face was warm, and my face was wet. Tears. I skated away.

When I got back to the Buhlerts', it was almost dark. The garage was filled with blue and white light from the fluorescent bulbs overhead, and I could see Gerry and Buzz working on Buzz's motorcycle again. Buzz looked over his shoulder and made a face as I skated up to the front door. Gerry smiled and waved a greasy hand.

I took off my skates and walked into the house. Dale stood in the doorway of the kitchen, her hands rolled into fists on her hips. Her face looked pinched, like she just drank a glass of lemon juice.

"Where have you been?" she asked.

I didn't want to tell her.

"Just skatin'."

"Skating where? It's almost dinner."

I shrugged.

"Around."

"I was getting worried. I was just about ready to call Maureen to report you missing."

"I just wanted to skate. Guess I lost track of time or something."

"I placed two of the dogs today and I wanted to bring you along so you could see how rescue and adoption work."

I realized by the way she said that, she was balling me out. I shrugged and turned to go up stairs. She stopped me.

"Wait a second. I'm not angry anymore. Have a seat and tell me where you skated."

I sat down at the kitchen table. Pork chops sizzled in a fry pan and as Dale poked them with a fork, I could smell cooked onion and apple.

"I skated to my old house."

"All the way over on 240th?" she said over her shoulder.

"Yeah, it's a gold and brown house. I remembered a lot of

173

stuff and it was weird to be there again."

"I would have liked to have taken you there myself. Memories can be real tough if you're not ready for them. Especially if you see reminders of things you don't want to remember."

I thought about Dad getting taken down the front steps by the police. Dale flipped one of the pork chops over so hard it slammed into the pan and spattered oil onto her arm.

"Ouch. Damn that hurt."

Dale lifted her wrist to her mouth and sucked on it a second.

"Jeesh. Almost the same spot I burned a couple weeks ago making Sizzle Burgers."

"I don't like to think about a long time ago when I was a little kid," I said.

Dale twisted the cold-water faucet and held her arm under the stream. She rubbed at it.

"I've got a lot that I don't want to remember, too, believe me. Some people aren't ever going to let me forget."

I wondered what she meant. Dale had kids, a two-story house, and Gerry. What could make her so sad?

Dale loaded the pork chops on a plate a few minutes later. She pulled a plastic bag from boiling water, opened it, and poured peas and little onions covered in white sauce into a serving bowl.

I finished the drawing of my mom and dad one afternoon a few days later. After I skated to my old house and saw the sump and everything, I couldn't stop thinking about them. I decided to draw them as best as I could remember them.

"You're a good boy and we love you," I said, looking at my mom.

"Let's watch some TV. Our favorite show is on," I said, doing the lower voice of my dad.

I sighed and pulled the page out of my sketchpad.

"I'm just a stupid spaz" I said as I wadded it up. Hearing a squeaking sound like a mouse outside my window, I looked down.

I saw the top of the camper in its space in the backyard. It bounced and wiggled. Who was inside it? Gerry was still at the hospital, Audrey and Janis were downstairs watching 'Love American Style' re-runs, and Buzz was still at wrestling practice. Should I call the cops? The camper shook again. I ran downstairs.

Sneaking around the house to the side yard where the camper

sat, I saw that the door was swung wide open. "La-la-la-la" a deep woman's voice sang. A frying pan clanged and thudded.

I jumped to the open door.

"Uh-oh!" the voice said. It was Feona. She jumped up.

"What're you doing?" I asked.

"I play house. Uh-oh."

"This is not your property!" I yelled. Something about her squinting eyes and little face made me nervous.

"I am going."

Feona waddled to the camper door and jumped down.

"I'm gonna tell!" I said.

"No. I not want to get in no trouble."

As Feona ran to the curb, I couldn't take my eyes off her sweatshirt. Her breasts were bouncing and heaving. That's when I knew what I wanted to do.

She has the brain of a five-year-old, and she won't live for very long.

I didn't know what that was supposed to mean. All I knew is what I wanted to do.

"I won't tell if you come and do something," I said.

"Oh-kay."

She turned back around and stood facing me, her thick arms loose and useless against her chubby sides. I looked to see if anyone was walking down the street. It was clear.

"Go to the other side of the camper. By the fence."

Feona stepped around the camper, making her arms swing like she was pitching softballs. I followed behind her. The brick backyard wall made a dark shadow against the camper.

"What doing?" Feona asked.

"All right, Feona. I won't tell anybody about what you did if you lift up your sweatshirt."

"Can't. I can't show no boobies. It is bad."

"It's just you and me. You won't get in trouble."

"Can't"

Feona shook her head and tried to step around me. I put my arm up and blocked her.

"Okay. Then I'm gonna go tell on you."

Feona shook her head again. Her face turned red, making the bangs of her hair look like orange wire.

"You make me cry. You make Fona cry."

"Shh! Shh!" I slapped the air.

175

Feona raised her hand and wiped her eyes.

"Fona go home now to tell on you!"

I grabbed her shoulder and held tight as she tried to free herself. My fingers dug into her thick flesh.

"Ow! You hurt me!"

"You wanna play a game?"

Feona's face lit up like pumpkin.

"I want to play game! I get to play! Yea! Yea!"

"But if you lose, you know what you have to do?"

"What?"

I grabbed the bottom of my striped shirt and started to lift it up.

"I wash clothes with Biz?"

"No. You gotta do this."

I lifted my shirt a little higher.

"Uh-oh. Show boobies?"

"Yep. Or we don't play, and then I tell on you."

"Oh-kay. I will 'cause want to play!"

"Here. Sit down across from me."

The cement of the driveway was cold against my butt. Feona plopped down across from me and folded her legs Indian style.

"You know how to play 'rock-paper-scissors?'"

"Yeah! I know how!" Feona said. She started to clap her hands in excitement, but I grabbed them.

"Shh. We won't be able to play if you clap."

"Oh-kay."

"Here we go!" I said, making a fist of my right hand and holding it out toward Feona. Feona grinned and held her fist out toward me.

"Rock!" I said.

"Paber!" Feona said, flattening out her hand.

"Scissors!" I yelled.

But Feona made scissors as soon as I did. It was a draw.

"I want to play again!"

"Okay."

I held my fist out again. Feona matched it.

"Rock-paper-scissors!" I said really fast. I kept my hand in its fist, but Feona, staring at her hand, extended her fingers to make scissors.

"You lose!"

"Oh, no!" Feona said. She piled both of her hands on her forehead and rocked forward.

"You know what you have to do!"

"Oh-kay!"

Feona grabbed the bottom of her sweatshirt and rolled the material up like she was rolling carpet. When I caught the first glimpse of her white and pink belly, I felt a tingle in my penis.

"Oh-kay!" Feona said.

"Nope, you gotta go all the way up!"

"Can't or I get in trouble!"

"I won't play anymore."

Feona snorted. She pulled the sweatshirt higher and I now saw the white cotton of her bra that held two breasts. They weren't as big as kick balls as I once thought, they were bigger! My penis started to swell, and it scared me. That only happened when I had to go pee in the morning when I got up or else if I leaned against something for a while. Why did it happen now?

"What's going on?" I heard over my shoulder.

"Uh-oh!" Feona said.

I jumped to my feet and turned around. Audrey stood with her hands on her hips.

"Feona, you go home!" Audrey said.

"Oh-kay."

Feona waddled past me and ran across the street to her front yard. Audrey's eyebrows twisted with confusion.

"Aren't you a little old to play doctor?" she said.

That made me think of my dad for a moment. I didn't know how to answer. I was scared first for getting caught. But I was also embarrassed that it was Audrey who caught me.

"She just lifts her sweatshirt up sometimes," I said.

"Oh why would she do that?"

"Because she's got a brain of a five-year-old and will die young."

"Ooh, why'd you say that?"

"I don't know."

Audrey grabbed her hip with her left hand and started twisting the end of her hair with her right. She looked up toward the sky for a second.

"I should tell on you. You might grow up to be a pervert."

"Please, don't."

"What will you do for me?"

Any special feelings I had felt for Audrey before now disappeared when she said that.

"What do you want?"

She looked up at the sky again. This wasn't going to turn out too well.

"I was on my way to Takahashi's Store. I didn't feel like walking and so I was gonna offer you a quarter to go for me."

"Okay."

"But if you really don't want to get in trouble, you gotta go for free."

"I can do that."

"Anytime I ask."

I dropped my head. Now I really didn't like Audrey. She held out seventy-five cents.

"Here. I want a Scooter Pie -- chocolate, not vanilla -- and a Delaware Punch."

"I thought you only ate health foods like carrot juice."

"Stupid. I'm a vegetarian. That's all."

Audrey turned and walked back toward the front door.

"Wait a sec," I said.

"What, pervert?"

"Where's the store?"

"Up on 235th. Across from the Self Realization Fellowship Center. You'll see."

I turned to walk.

"The snack rack is right by the cash registers!" I heard her yell over my shoulder. "Chocolate, not vanilla!"

I hadn't yet walked this direction down 240th Street. My school was down off Crenshaw and 238th. My childhood home was in the same direction. There was no need for me to walk up to Arlington. Not until now. And as I turned the corner to walk the block, the voice said:

Memorize this walk. She's blackmailing you and you will be walking to the store for her all the time.

The voice was right as usual. But the blackmail was nothing compared to what she would eventually do to her family. I picked up a twig and ran the tip of it along the chain-link fence I walked past. My penis swelling up. Audrey calling me a pervert. What was wrong with me? '...*Who needs wings to fly?*...' The twig and each link it caught made a beat, sort of a song. The clicking song helped me forget about my worries.

Up on the right, I could see the red and white sign for Takahashi's Store. Just before I dropped my eyes back to the ground, I noticed a tall, golden-yellow tower. The roof of the tower was covered with the red, round brick tiles I had seen on pictures of the missions in my California History book.

As I got closer to the edge of Takahashi's parking lot, I could see the arches at the top of the tower. Meeting the tower about a third of the way up was a lower roof of the red, round tiles. Just below the roof, I could see a round, stained-glass window. Below the window, another roof of red tiles stuck out over a long porch. A sign in black letters spelled out: 'Self Realization Fellowship Center' just above the portico.

When I saw the portico, which was actually four arches and columns that met cement steps, my stomach twisted. Wasn't this a Catholic church once? I ran across the street to get a closer look.

The big, gold building was like the sun bursting through rain clouds. As I stood in front of the portico, I started to remember something: Mom's coffin. I could remember people dressed in black like Mrs. Wagner and Mrs. Nielsen, and the long, black car that carried the coffin. I stepped closer to the portico, and seeing the steps again made a lump grow in my throat. I realized this used to be our church: the place where I was baptized; where the choir sang Christmas songs; and the place of Mom's funeral. I didn't know why, but I had the urge to lie down on the steps and curl up for a nap.

Heavy wooden doors with black iron hinges sat inside the shaded portico. I could remember what those hinges sounded like when the doors were opened. I could almost smell the smoke that came from the silver ball the priest swung toward the coffin: Ivory soap and cigars. Just as I thought about hopping up the steps to go inside, I heard the latch on the door. I turned and ran across the street to Takahashi's store, away from the coffin, away from the ghosts in my memory, away from our church that was now the SRF Centre.

When everyone was finished eating that night, I went up to my room and pulled out my sketchpad. Instead of an episode of the 'Partridge Family', I sketched the front of the church. As I filled in the walls with the yellow-orange crayon, and carefully drew the round roof tiles with Indian red, I felt like my former church had a secret to tell me. It was like the church was alive, and it wanted to tell me something. Why was it the Self Realization Fellowship Centre now? What was the SRF anyway? A government bureau or something else sinister? I didn't know, but as I finished coloring in the stained-glass window with red, blue, yellow, and green, I wanted to do some more sketching of the church, and the tower. I'd be going back to SRF Center soon.

I flipped the page, and thought of Feona. What I really thought about was Feona's breasts, big and bulging in her giant bra. I pulled out the peach crayon and began to draw the half-circles of the tops of her breasts. As I drew in the outline of her bra, I wondered if I could get her to take it off. What then? Why was I thinking like this? And why, just as I drew the straps of her bra, did I feel my penis swell again? I tore out the drawing of Feona's breasts, ripped it up, and slammed my sketchpad shut. I was sick, dirty. Maybe I was a pervert and there was no one to talk to about any of it.

The next Saturday, I asked Dale if I could take a walk for the afternoon. When she said yes, I slipped on my windbreaker and sneaked my sketchpad and crayons inside its folds.

"Get back here by four," she hollered.

I was so set on getting to the SRF Centre to draw it that I hardly noticed the noise as my sneakers slapped the ground with each step. Fluffy white clouds danced past the sun. The air stung my nose with its cold.

The red and white sign of Takahashi's seemed to point to the SRF Centre. As I stood looking at the front of the SRF Centre from across the street, the clouds made inkblots of shadow on its yellow walls. The sun made the whole place sparkle. My eyes followed the roof until they landed on the steeple. It stood straight and mighty as it rose to the sky. What was it about the tower that was so interesting?

This old place makes you feel safe, the voice said.

I kept an eye out long enough to make sure no one was walking around the outside of the SRF Centre. When I was sure no one was around, I crossed the street. Once I made it to the portico, the cement stair felt cool as I sat. I pressed my hand against the side of the steeple and felt the stucco gouge into my palm. Sitting on these steps made me feel like I was sitting on someone's lap. Calm. Okay. I didn't know why, but I felt so comfortable. It gave me the same feeling as the sump did, or seeing my childhood house. It was like each of them was a tape recorder of my life and if I could just figure it out, they would play

180

back my life to me. They could maybe tell me who I was, who I was becoming, and maybe feel less alone.

I opened up my sketchpad and began the fourth drawing of something that wasn't from a TV show. More important than the one of Mom and Dad, the bad one of Feona's boobies, and the one of the whole church, this drawing I was about to do of the steeple meant so much. I could remember so many Sundays when the church bells would ring and I would walk between Mom and Dad holding their hands. Other families would pass and greet us on the way into the church. The bell also rang at the end of Mass and that meant powdered sugar donuts and fruit punch in the parish hall waited next door. That was it -- the tower reminded me of those times.

I began the sketch by laying out two parallel lines that would come to be the sides of the tower. As I raised my eyes to add more detail, I suddenly remembered the steeple on a gray, rainy day. Its roof seemed to puncture the gray clouds. Was it my birthday? My fourth birthday, was that it? I wasn't sure, but it seemed like it might have been. As I drew in the arches of the bell niche at the top of the steeple, I thought they looked sort of like, what? Eyebrows. That was it. The arches looked like eyebrows over smiling eyes.

My hand glided to the top of the drawing to sketch in the roof with its red brick tiles. I stopped for a second to look at the peak of the tower to figure out what was different. It used to have a cross on it—that's it. I guessed that the government agents who worked for SRF didn't have any use for a cross.

I picked through the well-worn tips of my crayons to decide which yellow I should use for the stucco. The three choices seemed either too lemony or too orange. I decided on plain yellow and also determined that I would color a light layer of brown over it. After coloring in with the yellow, I began to go over it with the brown crayon. Crayons always seemed to scratch the paper as I used them, but coloring on top of another layer of crayon felt like gliding over ice.

The creak of a wooden window sash startled me. I looked up across the street and saw what looked like a one-story house. It was a big house with the same red brick roof the church had, with ivy and thick bushes growing all over the side that faced me. I could see one window and a shadow on the other side of a screen. A song I knew from the radio played through the open window.

'...He was born in the summer of his twenty-seventh year...'

I recognized John Denver's voice. Who played the record?

Who lived there? Why did the house match the church?

'*...Rocky Mountain high, Colorado...*'

I lost my curiosity as the music soothed me. The sun warmed my back, and a light, crisp wind blew against my face. All of it made me feel comfortable, like I belonged on these steps, and like I had been sitting on them a million years. I took a deep breath of the wind that now smelled like the sea.

I went back to work on the tower. When I finished coloring the brown over the yellow, the drawing was done. But the tower stood alone on the white page. I couldn't decide what else I should add.

Then I thought of Mom and Dad. Or, at least I thought of a picture I had of them. Dad wore a black suit, and Mom wore a pink dress with a small, pink hat with netting that spilled over her eyes. Were they in their church clothes? I decided to draw them standing at the base of the steeple.

I pulled out the carnation-pink crayon and began to draw Mom's dress in the photo. Once I added her head, it was time to draw her hair. But it was difficult to choose the right color for her hair. I paused and considered a few different shades of brown and brown-red.

"What are you doing there?" a voice boomed from behind.

I jumped up, grabbing my sketchpad, and scattering my small box of crayons in all directions. A man in white pants and a shirt with a tight collar walked toward me. I could see a red dot in the middle of his forehead.

"Huh?" was all I could get out. I was so startled.

"You don't belong here," the man said. "What are you hiding behind your back?" I had never heard an accent like that—sort of low and almost Irish. There was a sing-song quality to it. He quickened his pace.

"I gotta go."

I turned to run and the man pulled my sketchpad from me.

"You steal this from the temple or something?"

"That's just my --"

The man raised his arm and I thought he was going to hit me. I darted across the street and the man was yelling something at my back. I ran to the bottom of Takahashi's store sign, hid behind one of the metal posts, and watched him. What was he going to do with my sketchpad? The man crossed back toward the house, turned and glanced back in my direction, his hollow face scowling over his high cheekbones. He shook his head covered in thinning gray hair and

182

walked the rest of the way into the house. My sketchpad disappeared.

13.

By the time I had run to the corner of 234th Street, I was out of breath and very upset. Losing my small pack of crayons didn't matter. I still had a whole sixty-four box left that Jennifer had given me. It was my sketchpad. All of my drawings, all of my stories, all of my world--gone. I stomped my feet hard against the sidewalk. I stopped.

Three houses down from the Buhlerts, on the grass boulevard, Feona lay on her side. She didn't belong there. The whole neighborhood was bothered about Feona sitting on porches without being invited or picking dandelions from anyone's lawn whenever she decided to sit. No one in her family ever seemed to be around to take care of her. So when I saw her laying there, another place she didn't belong, it made me mad.

I ran up and now saw that she was asleep, her thick, pink-blotched right arm stretched out and supporting her big head like a pillow. The dichondra grass lay flattened in a crater all around her body. She looked like a sleeping baby and for some reason that made me angrier. She was just too big to look like that. And I knew I would get in trouble if I ever even walked on Dale's dichondra, so laying on this neighbor's had to be really bad. Someone had to do something about it, and I was so mad now I was going to do just that.

"Get up! It's against the rules for you to sleep on the boulevard."

Feona rolled over onto her back and started to cry. She kicked her legs like she was riding a bike and I thought she looked like a baby again.

"Go home! You're not supposed to be here."

184

I lifted my leg as if I was going to kick her but she saw me and jumped up.

"You scareded me! I go home."

Feona turned to run. Her jeans were smudged with grass stains.

"Don't ever sleep here again!" I yelled. Feona ran across the street, flailing her thick arms and crying. I remembered my sketchpad and started to feel mad again.

I ran the half block to the Buhlert's. All I could think about was my sketchpad and that mean man with the weird accent who took it. Another thought interrupted my anger: should I just tell Dale about it and see if she could get it back? But I would get in trouble for sitting on the old church steps without permission. I stood on the front porch of the Buhlerts as all these different ideas rolled around in my head. Reaching up to run my hand along the front door window with its yellow-orange glass bumps, I didn't know what I was going to do. I heard the garage door creak open behind me.

A wrench banged against a pipe. Buzz and Gerry were together working and talking like they always were. Buzz started to laugh. The way he wheezed and snorted with that laugh of his reminded me of a barking seal. I hated Buzz mostly all the time since he was just like the teenage boys at Maryvale. He was a real Buckaroo of a jerk. Even though Gerry was nice to me, I felt like a nobody whenever Buzz and Gerry did their stuff with motorcycles. They didn't like baseball or basketball like I did—just motorcycles and football.

Janis bugged me when she was a brat, which was mostly all the time. Now that I was Audrey's store slave, I didn't like her much, either.

Dale took the most time with me, but she was always either tired or out rescuing a stray dog. I had the urge to run upstairs, grab my paper bags of stuff, and go. Why did I even end up at this weird place? With this weird family: a foster mom who held hands and kissed her housekeeper who really wasn't a housekeeper and the SRF Centre with the thief?

People who live in two story houses aren't always happy like the Partridges.

The last time I heard the voice, it was telling me I felt safe. Now it just made me sigh. I grabbed the doorknob. I decided I needed to talk to Dale about my sketchpad.

Just as I grabbed the knob, the door flew open and jerked my arm. It hurt so bad I grabbed my shoulder.

"Where's Gerry?" Dale yelled.

185

She stood in the doorway, holding the top of her light pink robe with its shiny, diamond-shaped quilted puffs. On her head was an orange towel wrapped around her hair and twisted like a doughnut. Her eyes were big as drawn-on clown eyes. She held some sort of folded papers in her hand. She waived them at me.

I shrugged and she ran past me. A breeze of that fruity-smelling shampoo -- Herbal Essence -- floated past my nose. I always remembered that shampoo because of the bottle with the cartoon of the girl with the long hair that just covered her breasts.

"Calm down, let me read it," Gerry said from the garage. The metallic clank of a wrench hitting the floor followed next.

When I stepped around the corner, I saw Dale standing, holding her hands to her face. Gerry read the papers again and again and shook her head. Buzz sat on the floor next to his motorcycle, twisting his right hand over and over. The garage echoed with the rattle of a ratchet.

Gerry walked into the house, rubbing her hands onto a dirty rag. Dale held the top of her robe and sat on a milk crate near the workbench. Her eyes seemed to drift off. Gerry came back out a couple minutes later.

"He's out of the office till Monday. I don't get it—did someone set up a private eye?"

"I can't face him in a hearing, I just can't," Dale said.

Gerry touched Dale's face softly, and then turned and crouched down next to Buzz again. Dale looked like cotton candy standing in the middle of the gray and dirty garage. She turned and walked out past me. Her bare feet slapped against the driveway. Buzz looked over his shoulder.

"What do you want, Amethyst?"

Gerry popped him on the back of the head. I walked to the front porch and sat. I couldn't talk to Dale about my sketchpad, not now, not with whatever trouble was brewing for them. All I really wanted to do was draw. How could I get my sketchpad? What was I going to do?

The next night, Saturday, I determined what I would do. Buzz and Audrey had each gone out with friends for the night, and Janis was in bed. Gerry and Dale were upstairs in Dale's bedroom watching M*A*S*H. It was only nine o'clock and I wasn't sleepy. I put on my blue jeans and a dark blue shirt, slipped my skates over my shoulder,

186

and stepped slowly down the stairs and out the front door.

Once I got a few houses down, I put on my skates. Usually I was scared at night being outside, sure that the Zodiac killer or Bigfoot was just around a dark corner. But as my skate wheels rumbled and scratched against the sidewalk, making my feet tickle in that way I was so used to during the day, somehow I felt okay being out at night.

In no more than twenty minutes, I was taking my skates off on the stairs of the SRF Centre. I was looking across the street at the house the man with the dot on his forehead went into after he took my sketchpad. How was I going to get inside? And even then, how would I find my sketchpad once I got in? No matter what, I needed my sketchpad, so nothing was going to stop me. Then I remembered that John Denver music I heard from one of the side windows when I was here before. I could just see that window through the ivy that now looked like black diamonds. There was no light on in that part of the house. I decided that would be my access in.

I crossed the street and stood at the window. Through the screen, I could see that the wooden sash was raised about three inches. The smell of something like the burned cinnamon that sometimes happened if you baked Pop 'n' Fresh cinnamon rolls too long hit my nose. But then it went from burnt cinnamon to something almost like Old Spice. I grabbed the edge of the screen and its cold metal stung my fingertips. I tugged and it made a popping sound as it detached from the window frame. I dropped to the ground and lay flat on my stomach like I had seen on 'Get Smart.' My heart pounded so hard it seemed to make my chest rise up and down as if I was doing push-ups. I waited a few seconds to see if light from the window would hit the ground around me and spoil my plan. But it didn't.

I got back up on my feet and looked around once more. The street was empty in both directions, and the man's house was quiet. I took a deep breath and grabbed hold of the wooden window sash. Standing on tiptoes, I used all my strength to push it. At first, it seemed as if it was frozen, and then all of a sudden, it loosened and scratched as it rose up. Then it stopped again. Jammed. No matter how hard I pushed, it wouldn't budge. I let go of it and stepped back. Could I get through the foot-and-a-half opening? No matter what, I needed my sketchpad. I took my skates from over my shoulder and set them on the ground. I rubbed my palms together and then grabbed the windowsill and pulled myself up.

My head and shoulders made it through the opening okay.

187

Using my palms, I pushed against the inside wall and slid my chest and stomach through. But just as I was almost inside, my thighs and butt got stuck. I twisted and turned and that's when the light came on.

I panicked and tried to pull my body back out, but the sash suddenly loosened and fell, pinning me against the windowsill. A man in an orange robe, much younger than the one who took my sketchpad, stood with his hands on his hips.

"What are you doing here?"

"I'm not a burglar. I swear!"

He must have heard how young I was because he stepped closer, dropping one of his hands from his hip and running it over his shaved head. Just above his large brown eyes I noticed a red dot similar to the other man's.

"I'm calling the police."

"Please don't. Just open the window so I can get loose and I'll go away."

He reached for the phone receiver.

"I didn't come to steal anything. Please."

The man paused, still holding the telephone. Something in his brown eyes made me feel as though he was about to start laughing.

"Breaking into a residence is against the law."

"If the cops come, they'll make me go back to Maryvale. Please."

He set the phone back on the receiver. He leaned against his desk and the orange material of his robe made a soft rubbing sound.

"All right for now. But you have a lot to explain first. What's your name?"

"Gem O'Connell."

"Oh," the man said. "I see."

The way he said that made me think he might recognize me somehow.

"I'm Brother Paramananda."

"This window really hurts. Would you please open it wider, Brother Puh--"

"Call me Brother Par. Yes. But don't run away, because I have something for you."

Brother Par grabbed the sash and pushed it up. I slid back out the window and stood up. I rubbed my back as I leaned into the open window.

"What?"

"Come around to the front door and I'll show you."

When I got to the front door, I saw Brother Par flipping through my sketchpad and shaking his head. That made me angry.

"If you don't like my drawings, don't look at them. Please give me back my sketchpad. It belongs to me."

"It's a good thing you put your name on the cover. You wouldn't want to lose all your work. I like your drawings. I like them very much."

"Please just give it to me."

"We have children's art classes here at the ashram. I've seen a lot of children's artwork. Yours is very different."

Brother Par closed my sketchpad and handed it to me. I turned to run and Brother Par grabbed my shoulder.

"Hang on. We still have to talk to your parents about your bad behavior. No matter what the reason, you don't break into someone's house. This is not what we do at all."

"You can't call my parents. Mom's dead and Dad went away a long time ago."

Brother Par paused. He nodded and I noticed he shut his eyes a moment before he spoke.

"That is God's way for you but very sad. It won't always be—it's just right now. Who takes care of you, then?"

"I live in a foster home."

"Do they know you're out this late?"

I looked down and touched the porch with the toe of my sneaker.

"No one knows because my foster moms are upstairs watching M*A*S*H right now."

"You have more than one foster mother?"

"I think so. Dale stays home and takes care of the house. Gerry—she's a nurse supervisor at County-USC Hospital. She's supposed to be just a housekeeper at Dale's but she doesn't do any housework."

Brother Par's eyebrows crinkled up and he shrugged.

"God is everywhere and he has no favorites, don't you think? At any rate, I don't see any reason to have to make a fuss about all this."

I was ready to take off but when he said that, it made me like him. I noticed a bowl of fruit on a table just inside the front door and my stomach growled.

189

"Can I have a banana, please?"

"Certainly. Have you eaten dinner?"

I nodded. He handed me the banana and I started to peel it. He raised his eyebrows and I paused.

"Sorry—thank you."

"Do you want to come in and sit for a minute?"

"Sure."

I followed Brother Par into the front room. Bright floor mosaic tiles made shapes of pretty flowers. I paused to look at them. I had never seen such a floor.

"Nice floor," I said through a mouthful of banana.

"Those are lotus flowers. They're very sacred."

Brother Par picked up two big, green velvet cushions with buttons in the middle. He placed them on the floor in the middle of the room and sat crossed-legged on one. He nodded for me to take the other cushion. I sat but looked around the room to see four brass lights shaped liked onions and the light from them burned soft yellow. Water was trickling down a fountain from another room. As I ate the banana, I noticed two big paintings: one of a man with an elephant head all painted with blue tones. Opposite him was a man with four arms. So weird, but still so pretty. Then I noticed a smaller painting of Jesus looking up and praying, and just below it was an alabaster statue of Buddha. A little trail of smoke was coming from what looked like a miniature, burning Red Devil Cone next to a framed photo of a man with long, black hair from what looked like the 1930's. Those things sat on the only furniture in the room: a heavily carved, dark wooden table.

"What does that saying mean?" I asked, pointing to gold lettering going across the wall near the ceiling where the table sat.

"But it takes so long, my Lord," Brother Par said.

"Duh—I can read it. What does it mean?"

Brother Par tipped his chin at me and raised an eyebrow. I guess he didn't appreciate my smart aleck tone.

"Have you ever heard of The Beatles?"

I nodded.

"George Harrison used to be a part of that group. He wrote a song called 'My Sweet Lord.' That's a line from it."

I swallowed a too-sweet bite of banana.

"Why'd you paint rock-n-roll words on your wall?"

Brother Par broke out into a grin.

"George Harrison donated a lot of money to our fellowship

and it allowed us to buy the old church across the street and the convent as well. That's where we're sitting right now, though instead of a convent, we call it the 'ashram'. Brothers and sisters live here."

I pointed back at the words. "Well what's taking so long?"

Brother Par laughed. He reached out for the banana peel as I finished the last bite.

"It takes so long to recognize that God isn't someplace else, but right inside each of us, everyone and everything on the earth."

I didn't like what he said. I sighed.

"God and Jesus are in heaven. The only way to get to them is to pray and be good."

"Gem, yes, God and Jesus are there, but also all around us. We're all one in God and our task is right actions so that we bring out the God in ourselves and others. It is difficult to do that as we toil in the pain of our individual lives. Our way isn't prayer but meditation."

I folded my arms. So this was like TM.

"So you do TM here?"

"You know about Transcendental Meditation? "

I nodded and raised my eyebrows with certainty.

"Some of the brothers and sisters practice that. And some of the brothers and sisters meditate on images of Christ, too. Or Buddha, or Lao, or Mohammed—all the great sages."

I shook my head.

"Sounds like you're all going to hell to me. And you took over a church—that can't be good."

"The church was heavily damaged in the earthquake a couple years ago. The parish didn't have the funds to repair it so the parishioners dispersed. Thanks to the donations from Brother George, we repaired it and made it into our center."

Brother Par stood up. I never saw a man rise up from the floor like he did. It was as if he was floating as he stood, his arms and legs held in such a way that he glided up from the cushion like an eel.

"Gem, you can come back here any time. You'll see that we're not going to hell, we're making God's presence known and acting on it."

As I turned to go, a scene from Star Trek popped into my head. It was because Brother Par's face looked like an actor.

"Were you ever in the show Star Trek?"

Brother Par's face changed from his peaceful smile to slightly confused. He brought his hand up to his mouth and tapped his lips with his index finger as if he wasn't sure what to say.

"I was an actor once, yes."

"You fought with Captain Kirk a little, right?"

Brother Par stepped over and patted my back.

"You're an observant boy. I think you would definitely benefit from coming back to the center and ashram. Please do."

I started to walk toward the door. As I felt my sketchpad rub underneath my left arm, I paused and looked back toward Brother Par.

"Did you really like my drawings?"

"Very much."

"'Cause I don't let no one else even look at them. Next to baseball, drawing is my favorite thing to do. Want me to tell you about some?"

"Okay."

I flipped the cover of my sketchpad and began to tell Brother Par about the episodes from the TV shows I had made up. I also showed him the drawings and story I made up about the twin ladies who married the twin men. No matter what I showed him, Brother Par nodded, asked questions, and listened. I closed the sketchpad.

"I like you," I said. "No one except my mom, and Maureen, ever asked me so much about my drawings."

"Maureen?"

"That's my social case worker."

"I see. Maybe if you shared them, more people would ask questions."

"Nope. No one cares about me, and for sure no one cares about my drawings. So I don't even bother to show 'em anymore."

"Gem, you're Irish, right?"

I shrugged.

"How old are you?"

"Eleven-and –a-half, going on twelve in June."

"Were you ever baptized?"

"Yep. I even went to the church across the street a long time ago when I was just a little kid."

"So you're Catholic, then."

"Not anymore. It was just when my mom and dad were still around."

"How old were you when your mother died?"

I stood up and pulled my sketchpad from the table.

"I don't wanna talk about that. I gotta go now, anyway."

192

"Wait a second. There's one more thing to discuss. You broke into my room and we haven't talked about the consequences for that."

My shoulders slumped down: here it comes.

"I didn't know it was your room. I had to get my sketchpad."

I hoped that would do it. I turned to go again and Brother Par took my shoulder.

"Do you understand that it doesn't matter why you did it? That you chose to do something wrong is the problem. Right actions reveal God—wrong actions hide God from us because we are acting only for ourselves and in doing so, what you did was turned away from God within you."

I trusted what Brother Par said. I nodded, slipped my sketchpad under my arm, and then turned to go. When I got to the doorway, I stopped and looked back at Brother Par. I liked him a lot. I felt something new: for once, I wasn't just a nothing foster kid tagging along with somebody's family. I mattered a little maybe after all.

"I really can come back here whenever I want?"

For the next few weeks, I snuck away whenever I could and spent all of my free time with Brother Par. I didn't want to tell Dale, Gerry, or anybody else about our friendship—it was something I wanted for my very own. Brother Par and I talked about everything I wanted to: bad feelings, Disneyland, The Three Stooges, everything that mattered. I learned about growing roses, and about God being in everything and being everywhere. I didn't talk about how often I felt like just a nothing foster kid, or the bad things I did sometimes because I wanted another kid to feel like me, or even less than me. But lately, whenever bad thoughts or sad feelings came up, I would breathe the way Brother Par taught. He said it was the first step in meditation and counting my breaths sometimes made my sad feelings go away.

We decided one Friday night to share the thing we each loved the most. The meditation cushions we sat on began to feel real comfortable and I could sit cross-legged longer than Brother Par.

"...Sunshine almost always makes me high..."

John Denver's soft voice and guitar made me almost sleepy as the song ended. Brother Par got up from the mediation cushion and clicked off the eight-track tape player. He had the player and a small TV the secretary of the ashram owned on a bright brass cart he had wheeled in from the office in the back. I slipped my fingers into the box of Crackerjacks on my lap and grabbed up a peanut. It crunched with molasses and brown sugar.

"That's my favorite song of his. Did you like it?" Brother Par asked.

"Yeah."

"Instead of the dull songs that appear in the school musical textbooks, I always teach music to the visiting kids with my eight track player and John Denver. Let's listen a little more, then."

Brother Par reached for the brown, wood-grain eight-track player clicked and popped it back on. John Denver's voice began:

"...He was born in the summer of his twenty-seventh year..."

"Wait a second," I said.

Brother Par stopped the player.

"What's wrong?" he asked.

"What time is it?"

Brother Par stood up and left the room for a moment. He walked back in.

"The clock in the kitchen says it's almost eight-thirty."

"It's time for the 'Partridge Family.' You gotta turn the TV on quick."

"Okay, but it won't be over till nine. That's too late for you to be out."

"Everybody is upstairs again. They don't even know I'm gone. I'm glad I saved half my box of Crackerjacks."

Brother Par turned on the Zenith TV. The brown box popped and crackled as the television warmed up. As the picture came on with an electrical fizz, I noticed the black and white picture.

"Where's all the color?"

Brother Par shook his head.

"We're lucky the ashram has a TV set at all. It's the best we can do I'm afraid."

I sighed.

"...Mama, that's a spicy meat a ball..." the big Italian man said on the commercial as he sat at a wooden table. I reached up to the plastic knob and turned the channel.

"It's on channel seven," I said.

When I stopped the dial, the TV screen showed a news reporter sitting at his desk.

"...and the Symbionese Liberation Army makes another threat against kidnapped heiress Patricia Hearst's life. Film at eleven on Eyewitness News..."

Now the screen became a montage of different people holding

their stomachs and making sick faces.

"...*Plop, plop, fizz, fizz, oh what a relief it is...*"

I turned the volume knob down.

"I hate commercials."

As I sat back on the meditation cushion, I noticed a pile of what looked like shiny pistachio shells next to the old-time photo I now knew was Paramahansa Yogananda, the founder of the Self Realization Fellowship. Gray flashes of light from the screen made the pile of shells sparkle. I couldn't resist so I walked over and picked up them up. It was a string of rough beads with what looked like a tuft of orange hair sticking out from one larger bead. As I held the beads, a strange feeling of warmth went through me, and then sadness. The beads reminded me of something.

"Hey, are these rosary beads?"

Brother Par leaned toward me from his cushion.

I handed the beads to Brother Par. The beads stuck to Brother Par's fingers where I had touched them with my sticky Crackerjack fingers. He wiped them on his orange shirt cuff and dropped them into his pocket.

"These beads help us keep track of our meditation. There are one hundred eight of them, representing the scriptures of the Upanishads. If you want sometime, I can show you--"

"Shh!" I said. I turned up the volume on the TV.

"...*Hello world there's a song that we're singing, come on get happy...*" the 'Partridge Family' theme song began.

Brother Par and I watched the episode. By the time it was over, I was yawning and stretching. Brother Par turned off the TV.

"Wasn't that a fun show?" I asked.

"I liked it all right. I met Shirley Jones at a Hollywood party once. She was very nice. But why do you like it so much?"

A jolt of excitement shot through me when he said he met her. But then I felt too embarrassed to mention that I once tried to run away to her house in Beverly Hills so she could adopt me. I shrugged.

"'Cause I like that it's a whole family together. It's not as good as 'The Waltons', with a mom and dad, even a grandma and grandpa. But at least it's a family with a mom, and Danny is funny. I guess that's why."

I didn't want to tell Brother Par the other, new reason I liked the show: the last few times I watched it, whenever Laurie Partridge was on, I got a tingling feeling in my penis. I wasn't going to tell anybody that, even him.

"I watch the 'Waltons' also. They spend a lot of time trying to do the right thing. Right actions point to God and improve our karma," Brother Par said.

"How come you care so much about that?"

Brother Par scratched the top of his head. He leaned back and stretched out his legs.

"Karma is the memory your soul carries with it for all its deeds from this life and your previous ones."

"I don't understand. You mean my life when I was a little kid?"

Brother Par smiled. He placed his right hand into the palm of his left hand and nodded.

"Just think of it this way. Every time you do something bad just because you feel like it, you sort of stain your soul. You have to stop staining your soul and also work on cleaning up the old stains. Then you can be one with God and see the right way always."

I suddenly recalled getting Feona to show me her boobs, and hiding Wheezing Marty's inhaler. Those were stains for sure. But what about feeling like a useless foster kid most of the time. Was that bad, too?

"So is karmel—"

"Karma."

"Okay. Does it only count for things you do? Like if you sometimes have bad thoughts, do they make stains you gotta wash out?"

"The human mind is like a lotus flower, Gem. A thousand petals. Sometimes there are wilted petals—those are your bad thoughts. We meditate and it helps the mind refocus on all the best parts of the flower—where God lives inside you. So only our actions stain our souls and make karma. Right actions clear away the stains."

"Hurting other people makes stains."

"Yes."

"Lying."

"Yes"

"Shutting a cat inside a trashcan?"

"Yes. All wrong actions make stains."

"I don't understand, Brother Par. I think it's just easier to go to confession or pray to Jesus to forgive you."

He shrugged and nodded 'okay'. I didn't want to tell him that Jesus stopped answering my prayers a long time ago and that Mom

196

never helped, either.

"I gotta go now. Brother Par, will you always be here?"

"For as long as my karma allows, Gem."

"Good. 'Cause you're the only grown-up I like to talk to, even if you meditate and talk about strange things. Thank you for the Crackerjacks."

As I walked back to the Buhlerts, I hoped Brother Par wouldn't discover that I took his Crackerjack prize. I assumed that would count as another stain.

When I got back to the Buhlerts, Buzz, Audrey, and Janis were all watching TV. Buzz looked up.

"Well if it ain't Opal!"

"What are you all—"

"Shhhh!" Audrey said waving her hand toward me. I sat down next to Janis. An anchorman addressed the camera.

"...Holly Ann Lark was last seen three days ago walking up Cabrillo Avenue in Torrance," the news anchor said. "We now go to Wayne Satz who is live at the Lark home. Wayne."

"Thank you, John. I'm here in the Lark home with Mr. and Mrs. Robert Lark..."

I saw that Mr. Lark, with his short gray hair and round glasses, looked as old as Gerry. Mrs. Lark leaned against him, her red hair with its big bottom curls pushing against his shoulder. I noticed her eyes had purple and brown circles around them. My eyes moved past Mr. and Mrs. Lark. I noticed the lime green, velvet couch they sat on. I thought they must be rich to own a couch like that.

"Mr. Lark," Wayne Satz said. "What would you like to say to the person who has your daughter?"

The man cleared his throat, and I noticed a scar he had over his upper lip.

"We just want to tell you that we love Holly Ann very much. She's a good girl, and we want her back."

Mrs. Lark snorted and wiped her nose. She held up a picture of Holly Ann. I recognized the blue and white cloudy background of a school picture. Her hair was long, blonde and freshly brushed, and her eyeteeth stuck out just a little from her big, bright smile. She was my age, I realized, and it was then that I saw her eyes. Even though the photo wiggled in Mrs. Lark's hand, her cocoa brown eyes with eyelashes that made me think of Bambi hypnotized me. She was prettier than Audrey, and it was as if she was standing in the living room instead of being a photo on the TV screen. Something like a tickle started in my chest, and then shot down like a jolt to my penis, just like when I looked at Buzz's poster of Raquel Welch. Something was very wrong with me, I knew. Right then, Mrs. Lark lowered the picture.

The camera moved in close on Mrs. Lark's face, but I could only think of Holly Ann at that second. I couldn't hear what Mrs. Lark said next.

"Holly Ann," Mrs. Lark said. "My girl..."

That night was the first time in my life I couldn't fall asleep. I thought of Holly Ann's face again, and those brown, smiling eyes. When I did fall asleep, I woke up at some point in the night -- that never happened before -- and all I could think about was her face. Who had taken her and where was she? Somehow I wanted to go find her, rescue her, and bring her home. And then what? The same thoughts, then I'd sleep, and then I'd wake up and think about her. A lot seemed to be changing in me including the weird hair the boy-to-man movie talked about. It started growing above my penis and under my arms. I had begun 'puberty' and the very thought of it made me nervous. So not sleeping seemed to be another thing I would have to deal with.

It was about an hour before we all had to get up on Friday morning. I felt horrible from not sleeping and Holly Ann's face popped into my mind. Even though Brother Par had said all that stuff about God being inside me and everywhere, I still thought it was possible that Jesus and God were in heaven and could hear my prayers. I decided to try and pray one more time for God to keep Holly safe and to help me find her. Meditation wouldn't work for that.

I crossed myself like I remembered from church when I was a kid, touching my forehead, my belly, my left shoulder, and finally my right one.

"Umm," I said, folding and unfolding my hands as I looked toward the bumps on the ceiling that made me think of cottage cheese.

"God, uh, oh."

I crossed myself again and squeezed my eyes shut.

"In the name of the Father, and of the Son, and of the Holy, uhh, the holy ghoul...oh, Spirit."

I understood that when you prayed to God, it had to rhyme like the 'Our Father' prayer or like a spell on 'Bewitched'. I figured God wouldn't hear it otherwise.

"Dear God, Holly Ann is somewhere far," I said. "Please bring her to me, no matter how far. I want to meet her eyes that are brown, so hear my prayer and bring her around. With all the stars and clouds above, bring to me the one…uh…I love."

I dropped my hands. I got it to rhyme, but where did I come up with 'love'? Is that what I felt for Holly? Was this like love I heard about in songs, on TV, and at the movies? If not that, then why couldn't I stop thinking about her? I shrugged and felt happy about the prayer. I pulled open the captain's bed drawer to get my clothes out to get ready for school. I stopped for a second.

"Oh, Amen. In the name of the Father, of the Son, and the Holy Spirit. And, uh, God? Something else just for me: I'm not ready to be grown up. Please don't make all that hair grow too fast."

When I went down stairs awhile later, the house was busy with its usual chaos and commotion. Janis was sitting in front of the TV. Hobo Kelly, a local kids show host -- I could never tell if the actor was a man or a woman -- was dressed in a ragged coat, patched jeans, and a stained, twisted sailor's hat like Gilligan's. Hobo Kelly dropped a bucket of trash into the top of what looked like a washing machine.

"*Now like magic, I'll twist the crank three times,*" Hobo Kelly said with an Irish accent. "*…and this garbage will magically turn into special toys and treasures…*"

I had watched this show since I was a baby, but now, with puberty having begun, I felt something I had never felt before: as if I was turning into someone else and maybe forget who I was. Just like her garbage was turning into toys. If this was growing up, I wanted no part of it. What I didn't know then was in the same way that puberty started because the time was right, I was about to learn more about life, death, and myself than I ever had before because the time was right.

14.

I had just run home from school and saw a police car and a child protective services van in front of the house. I knew what that van meant. Most kids were hauled into Hollygrove or Maryvale in those vans. No one was going to take me back that was final. I sneaked around to the rear of the house to eavesdrop. The windows of the family room were always open to allow the afternoon ocean breeze to flow through the house. I got around to the windows and saw they were cracked. I raised my head so that my eyes peeked up over the ledge. I could see Gerry and Dale pacing around two people—a man and a stocky, thin-lipped woman. The woman's navy pants were almost as tight as her lips. Buzz and Janis stood together and I was surprised to see Buzz holding Janis's hand. Audrey stood off from everybody, her arms folded as if she were in charge of everything. Gerry and Dale's gray and blue, plaid luggage was stacked near Audrey.

"You can't do this," Gerry said. "We haven't even had the hearing yet."

"The children need to be placed with their father until such time as the fitness of this home can be determined," the man said.

The stocky woman reached over and picked up Janis. She threw a tantrum.

Dale pointed at Audrey. Her thin hand shook at her daughter.

"This is your fault. You told your dad, didn't you?"

"This isn't natural, Mom," she replied. "You and Gerry are living a lie. It isn't right. It will never been right."

She turned her back and grabbed the handle of one of the suitcases. Buzz looked back and forth between Dale and Gerry. I thought I could see tears forming in his eyes. He moved his lips like a fish, but no sound came out.

"You knew she wasn't a housekeeper, too, Buzz," Audrey said. "You're just as much to blame."

"Where is the ward of the court?" the man in the black blazer asked. He flipped two pages on a clip board.

"He's been outside playing," Dale said. Her voice choked with sadness. "He's due home any time now. Why isn't Maureen here to pick him up?"

Who needs wings to fly?...Who needs wings to fly?...

The song started in my head. I didn't want to leave Dale and Gerry, and especially, Brother Par. But I wasn't going to wait for Maureen or this other lady to haul me back.

Who needs wings to fly?

I hopped over the back fence and ran toward the SRF Center. My eyes stung from my tears and the wind.

"...We talked of poems, and prayers, and promises, and things that we believe in..." John Denver's voice floated from the front windows of the ashram. Brother Par must have been nearby. I knocked on the door. The door opened and the gaunt man who took my sketchpad before looked down at me.

"What can I do for you?" he asked.

"Brother Par! I need to talk to Brother Par."

John Denver's music stopped. Brother Par appeared behind the man.

"Gem?" he said.

"I need to talk, Brother Par."

Brother Par laid his hand on the other man's shoulder.

"It's all right, Brother Dihr. I'll handle it from here."

Brother Dihr nodded and walked away. He paused and looked over his shoulder suspiciously at me, then left.

"I'm in trouble. You gotta help me."

"Come on in. Let's go to the water room."

Brother Par led me from the hallway into the water room. I began to calm as I looked at the full wall of the room covered by a small water fall that trickled softly down rectangular, gray rocks. The water made the rocks sparkle. The rivulets ended in a half-moon circle of the same rocks that was about one foot deep. I ran to the wall and placed my hand under one of the streams. It was only the second time I had been in the room in all my visits and the first time was very brief.

"A waterfall in a house is amazing."

"Water is a sacred element in our way. It is the lifeline of being. We meditate with the sound of water to remind us of balance in life."

I pulled my hand away and could smell a bit of chlorine. Just like swimming pool water I concluded. The base of the waterfall was deep enough for someone to stand in as well..

"Do you ever go into the water? It's nice and cool."

Brother Par smiled that smile I never could quite figure out. I guess it was part of his mystery. It always made me feel better and safe so I didn't mind no matter what it meant. He shook his head. He led me to a mat made of some sort of grass or straw. We both sat. He crossed his legs as usual, stretched his neck by leaning his head toward his right and left shoulders, then nodded.

"Now what's your trouble, Gem?"

The way he asked the question was so soothing and kind. He really meant it. That's the only explanation I have for what happened next. My face went white-hot and I burst into tears.

"I don't wanna go back. Please don't make me..."

My words were squeaks between sobs. Through my flood of tears, I could see Brother Par's face go from peaceful to a worried tension. He placed his hand on my shoulder and I cried even more. I don't know how long it went on, but pretty soon, I rubbed the wetness from my face. My cheeks cooled down.

Brother Par left for a moment then came back with a glass of water. The glass looked like bubbled rubies. I drank a big gulp, then another. I handed it back to Brother Par.

"Where do you have to go, Gem?"

I told him all about what had just happened at the Buhlerts. He listened and nodded as he always did. When I finished telling him, I noticed he had placed his right hand into his open left palm. I knew that meant he was thinking.

"So I just can't go back to Maryvale or anywhere else. I have been bounced around for over four years now and I can't stand it anymore. Maybe I can stay here and become a brother like you."

Brother Par nodded and stood up in that graceful, serpentine way. I now knew that yoga was the reason he moved so smoothly. I had been so upset and focused on telling him what happened that I hadn't noticed the other walls of the room. One had what looked like a giant wheel painted on it. The wheel had something like a swirling sun in the middle of it and eight spokes all painted in a rainbow of colors. A giant painting of Paramahansa Yogananda hung on the other wall.

202

There were photos of other men and women in robes and saris. The late afternoon sun coming from the windows cast a yellow-orange glow over everything.

"I need to speak to Brother Dihr and Sister Amata I don't want you to be fearful, Gem. I am here to help."

Brother Par started to leave and then turned.

"Gem, while I'm gone, I want you to do me a favor."

"Okay."

"Close your eyes and just listen to the water cascading down. It will help calm you."

"Maybe you can finally teach me to meditate?"

Brother Par smiled. He nodded and left the room. I closed my eyes and for a little while listened to the water. Since it made me feel a little sleepy, I got up after a few minutes and went over to the wall with the photos. There were a few photos in ornate brass frames with etched name plates at the bottom. One was a profile of what looked like a black man with a large afro. The words below said 'Sai Baba'. I recognized him from the book Audrey had been reading. Another was a woman with white hair who looked like she could have been from Kansas or Minnesota. The name plate read 'Meera Mata'. The last photo was of George Harrison standing next to a skinny older man with long hair and a graying bear. It read 'Maharishi Mahesh Yogi.' I would learn more about all these people when I was in college, but at that moment, I shrugged and sat back down.

I closed my eyes and listened to the water trickle down. Since that was the only noise in the room other than the sound of my own breathing, it grew louder. Somehow it made me feel nervous so I opened my eyes. It bored me, so I started to pick at the skin around my thumb nails. Finally, Brother Par returned.

"Gem, the other brothers and sisters have agreed that I can let you stay for the night. We have a small room off the main hall where novitiates into the SRF order usually stay, but since we have no one new joining, you can stay there."

I almost started crying again. My chest lightened and my shoulders relaxed.

"What happens after I spend the night?"

"We can talk about that tomorrow, Gem."

"But I'm a runaway foster kid. Won't you get in trouble for helping me?"

"Tomorrow, Gem. You're safe here for now. We'll figure

things out. Trust me."

"But I don't have any of my stuff. Not even a toothbrush."

"We'll take care of that for now. Don't be anxious about these things. They can all be handled later."

Brother Par led me to the room. Unlike the main room and the water room with all the photos and paintings, this room was undecorated. There was an orange and yellow corner group of two couches and a small, wooden lamp. There was one of those metal cups with a burned incense cone so the room spelled of spice, but the room was bare other than the brown shag carpeting. Brother Par left for a couple minutes and returned with a pillow, sheet, a blanket, and also something like orange pajamas. They looked similar to what he was wearing.

"We'll get a bed set up for you. You can change into these churidars and pajama top."

Brother Par held up the orange pajamas. But there was one thing missing in the room. I really wanted to catch up with the news about Holly. I needed to know if she was safe at home by now.

"You think I could use that TV on the cart?"

"Yes, but I don't want you in here just watching TV. You asked to learn to meditate so we'll do that first tonight, Okay? After dinner."

I felt safe with Brother Par and at the ashram. I believed that he would work out a plan for me to stay until I grew up. I breathed a sigh of relief imagining that I might be at the ashram forever. I would find out soon that I was mistaken.

Dinner was in the dining room in the rear of the ashram. As with other rooms in the house, we sat on floor cushions at a low table. Brother Par sat at the head opposite Brother Dihr who like before, kept an eye on me throughout the meal. Three women in long saris of bright colors--turquoise, deep violet, and burgundy—sat at the right side of the table. Two other men younger than Brother Par sat opposite the ladies. Their shaved heads reflected the low-hanging lamp above the middle of the table. No one spoke as we ate the bowls of something that reminded me of chili but was spicy like pumpkin pie. There was no ground beef in it but I really didn't miss it. Plus, a flat bread with onion flavor made up for the lack of meat. Green and red vegetables in a curry and butter sauce were also passed around. My mouth felt almost electric with spices and rich flavors that were nothing like tuna salad or Kraft macaroni and cheese. Fresh fruit and dates were passed around along with steaming cups of dark tea. I grabbed a banana.

"Gem, let's go to the water room again so that you can learn the practice."

Brother Par stood up and nodded at everybody. I wasn't sure what to say so I just stood up and bowed. When I turned around, I thought I heard a couple of the ladies giggle.

When we stepped into the water room, it was dark. Brother Par lit two brass lamps in the corners of the room. He also lit a cone of incense. The room now glowed with amber light and became pungent with the incense. Despite the trickling sounds of the water fall, I could still hear the occasional traffic and horns on Eshelman Avenue.

Brother Par laid two cushions on the reed mats, this time side-by-side. He stepped over to the photo of Yogananda, put his hands together and bowed. Next he eased onto one of cushions and crossed his legs in the pretzel form I had seen so many times before. He tapped the cushion next to him. It was all a bit strange to me, but I went ahead and sat next to him.

"Before we start, I want you to close your eyes."

I closed my eyes and nodded.

"Now, place the tip of your tongue above your front teeth, then move it to the roof of your mouth and hold it. Got it?"

I nodded again. I immediately started rubbing the tip of my tongue along the ridges of the roof of my mouth. I guess he could see that.

"No, Gem. Keep your tongue still."

I moved my tongue up and nodded.

"Now I want you to take a deep breath with your nose as I count to four."

I took the breath as he counted to four.

"Good. Now hold the breath till I stop counting."

I held my breath as he counted to five.

"Good. Now, exhale till I finish counting."

He counted to eight.

"Excellent. Now we're going to take another breath and do the same thing again."

I took three more breaths following Brother Par's counting. My heart beat slower and my head felt a little heavy, like waking up. Brother Par tapped my shoulder and nodded.

"Now that you're more relaxed, listen carefully. I want you to

205

repeat the words I'm about to say. Say them exactly as I say them."

"Okay."

"Use a quiet voice, almost a whisper."

"Okay."

"Here we go."

"Here we go," I repeated.

Brother Par shook his head and smiled.

"Not those words."

I shrugged and nodded.

"Om."

"Home"

"No, say 'home' without the 'h'."

"Okay. Om."

"Good. Now just stretch it out a little until it makes your throat vibrate. "Oohhmmmm…Ohhhmmmmm"

"Ohhhmmmmm."

It did make my throat vibrate, almost tickle.

"What's that mean?"

"We believe it's the sound the universe makes."

"Isn't the universe a vacuum so it doesn't make any sound at all? Only if a star explodes or something like that."

Brother Par nodded and raised his palm.

"Let's have questions after, okay?"

I nodded.

"Ohmmm," he said.

"Ohmmm," I repeated. He nodded.

"Okay, now repeat this phrase: ohhmm, shanti."

"Om, om, om… on the range!"

Brother Par's lips tightened. It was the first time I had ever seen his face without his placid smile. I blushed.

"Sorry, Brother Par. Om, shanti"

"That's better. I want you to close your eyes again. Good. Now with your eyes closed, I want you to repeat: Om, shanti, shanti, shanti."

"Ohhmmm…There's no place like om."

Brother Par stood up. He waved his hand for me to stand.

"Gem, your sense of wit and laughter is always welcome in life. But if you're not going to take this lesson in earnest, then I am wasting our time."

I could tell Brother Par wasn't angry but rather disappointed. That was even worse. I sighed.

"No more jokes. I promise. But these words are kind of funny."

Brother Par sat back down. He put his right hand into his palm for a second and then nodded.

"I understand that making fun of something that is strange and new might be a way you will handle life's stresses. Yes, less jokes and I will also lighten up. 'Shanti' means peace. When we say 'Om, shanti', we are asking for universal peace. When we say 'shanti' three times, we're asking for peace in mind, body, and soul."

"Okay. Om-shanti-shanti-shanti!"

"Let's take it a little slower, Gem. In fact, close your eyes again. Good. Now, say the words slowly."

"Ommm...shan-tii...shan-tii...shan-tii..."

"Keep your eyes closed, Gem. Say the word 'shanti' only, this time."

I did. Nothing happened. I was expecting some sort of magic.

"Again, Gem."

I repeated it. Again, nothing.

"Now, Gem, I want you to say the word in your mind only."

I started to think this was stupid but when I said the word in my mind, it interrupted my thought. It felt odd. I started to think about the smell of the incense. I rubbed my nose.

"Gem, any time any thought or feeling begins to emerge, repeat 'shanti' in your mind. Keep saying the word to yourself."

I stopped thinking about the smell of the incense-'shanti'.

My stomach began to twist with nerves since I had run away— 'shanti'.

Brother Par likes me and maybe I could stay here—'shanti'.

Thoughts or feelings would start, but as soon as I thought 'shanti', I felt nothing but calm. I continued this for I don't know how long. Was I beginning to recognize God in me like Brother Par had said?

I heard Brother Par get up at some point-'shanti'.

Audrey and then Holly Ann Lark were naked-'shanti'

Dragonflies dipping into the sump-'shanti'.

Thirst—'shanti'.

Breathing slowly and heart beating calmly—'shanti'.

Mom in the casket—'shanti'. My heart quickened.

Sparkling handcuffs on Dad—'shanti'. My breath squeezed.

Bricks of Hollygrove walls—'shanti'. Tears start in my eyes.

'Shanti'. I'm falling into a tunnel—'shanti.'

I jumped up.

"Brother Par!" I screamed.

Brother Par sprang into the room.

"I'm scared, I'm scared, and I don't like this."

Brother Par held my shoulders. My breaths were rapid and my heart felt like it was going to fly out of my chest.

"Gem, it's okay. Sometimes meditation will bring on very uncomfortable feelings, but when you focus on your mantra 'shanti'—

"No. I don't want to do that again."

"You also have been meditating for nearly an hour, Gem. You are a natural at it."

I shook my head.

"What time is it?"

"A little after nine."

"Brother Par, I think I just want to go to bed now."

Brother Par nodded. He walked me to the room. One of the corner group couches was made up as a bed and ready for sleep. I noticed the secretary's little TV on the cart next to it.

"I think I just want to watch some TV before bed."

"That's fine, Gem. Good night."

I changed into the orange pajamas. The bottoms were a little tight on my legs but I think they were supposed to be. I turned on the TV and crawled into bed.

"...*Who needs wings to fly?...*"

The song wasn't in my head this time. It was coming from the TV. I looked up at the screen, and my heart began to pound.

A lady in a white dress and a white hat with things that looked like wings flew across the screen. The song went on, but this time, it was only the music, no singing. The credits started to roll up the screen and I realized it was a theme song to a TV show.

"Brother Par!" I screamed.

Brother Par threw open the door.

"What? What?"

"That show on TV. What is it?"

Brother Par squinted and after a second, he nodded.

"'The Flying Nun'. It's just a re-run."

"The song..."

Brother Par shrugged.

"It's the song that always goes through my head when I'm

scared. I remember this show from a long time ago. I have even seen some re-runs. But there were never any words to the theme song."

"It's probably just in this episode, Gem."

Brother Par nodded and closed the door. I jumped up and stared at the screen. That show. Ever since I had gotten hooked on shows like "Partridge Family", I had stopped watching re-run shows. So I had missed seeing this episode and hadn't heard the whole theme song again until now. And even stranger, I could always remember theme songs from any TV show I watched. Not this one, though. Suddenly, I saw myself sitting on a couch between Mom and Dad. The show's song is playing, and Dad is holding my arms out like Superman's, singing along with the theme. Electric bursts seemed to shoot down my back, and the TV screen began to look fuzzy. The pumping feeling started in my stomach, then wriggled up my throat until it became a thick lump. Tears gathered on my eyelids then overflowed and trickled down.

'...*Who needs wings to fly?...*'

I missed Mom, I missed Dad, and as the theme song finished, I dropped my head in my hands and sobbed. Was it all somehow my fault?

"...*Love, American style, truer than the red, white, and blue...*" The theme song played as the show ended a while later. I got up from the couch bed and went to turn the channel to the Million Dollar Movie. Just as I grabbed the dial, the news reporter Wayne Satz came on. He was sitting at the news desk with the screen behind him, and over his right shoulder was the school picture of Holly. I inhaled with surprise and plopped down so close to the TV screen I could hear it crackle with static.

"Our top story is the tragic update of the missing Torrance girl, Holly Ann Lark. Torrance Police have confirmed that a Palos Verdes horseback rider found the body of the missing eleven-year-old, just yards away from the horse trail on Palos Verdes Drive in Rolling Hills. Leo Barnham is live at the scene."

My heart pounded. I leaned forward so much that the static of the TV shocked the tip of my nose. The news reporter stood next to a white fence, his eyes and mouth meeting in a giant squint from the bright sun.

"Thanks, Wayne. The police are still combing the thick weeds, searching for any clues."

The camera moved away from the reporter and showed three police cars, and a station wagon marked 'Coroner'. The picture changed to the grassy hillside, where police officers in black stood in a half circle as two other men picked up a stretcher covered in a sheet. The reporter spoke over the picture.

"The sight was grisly earlier today when the young girl's body was discovered here in Rolling Hills, near Dapplegray Park and the Palos Verdes Reservoir, a few hundred feet down the hillside from Palos Verdes Drive. Clad only in a T-shirt, the young girl's body showed signs of sexual assault..."

My stomach twisted with fear, but I also felt a tingle in my penis when the reporter said she was only in a T-shirt. I wondered if she had started puberty like me. But I also felt like screaming.

"...Police are not releasing any more details about the molestation/murder, but witnesses in the normally quiet, upscale neighborhood here reported seeing a strange man in the early morning hours last Thursday walking this horse trail. Here is the composite sketch..."

A pencil sketch of a man with a long, white face, short, thick nose, long hair, and dark eyes gave me goosebumps.

"...Police estimate the Caucasian man to be between thirty-five and forty-five, average height and weight. Residents here are understandably further shaken by this horrific crime given its similarity to the nineteen-seventy-one molestation and murder of Tonya Lynn Phelps. Viewers may recall that the main suspect in that case, Ernest Murphy, died in an apparent murder-suicide involving his mother. Leo Barnham, reporting."

The TV picture became Wayne Satz at the anchor desk again, with Holly Ann's photo behind him. I stared at her pretty face, her big smile, and especially her eyes with so much life in them. Even though the image was black and white, I could recall her deep brown eyes. I suddenly wanted to run to the hillside where her body had been found. Seeing the last place she was alive, I thought, would bring her closer to me. Then I got angry: why would someone do that to her? Would he come after me, too? I shivered with fear, a fear that was different from Bigfoot fear or fear of the dark.

I looked at Holly Ann's picture once more. Why did that happen to her? Was she scared through it? Why was she only in a T-shirt? What did sexual assault and molestation mean? Those thoughts kept me awake all night.

Morning light spilled through the cloth shades and stung my eyes. I felt dead from not sleeping most of the night. I didn't recognize where I was for a minute. The table and corner group couch I slept on came into focus and I knew I was at the SRF ashram. My mouth was dry and as I yawned and stretched, I could hear two voices. They seemed to be in the other room—the front room of the ashram. 'So Gem…' I startled as I heard my name. They were talking about me but their words were muffled. I crept to the door and pulled it open just enough so that I could hear.

"If we could keep him here I would," Brother Par said. "He's got so much potential. I was worried he would run away again so I'm glad you came so quickly after I called."

My throat constricted and my stomach tightened into knots. Brother Par didn't want me to stay after all. I cracked the door a little further. I could see Brother Par's hands and the profile of the man with the clipboard who took the Buhlert kids away the day before. First sad, now panicked, I closed the door quietly and locked it.

I changed out of the orange pajama top and Indian pants Brother Par had given me the night before. I didn't wait to tie my sneakers. Pulling up one of the shades, the sunlight now poured into the room. I flipped open the half-moon latch in the middle of the wooden door frame and slid the frame up. It stuck a third of the way. I applied pressure with my arms and chest and the window creaked and gave way. I rolled over the sill and landed onto a hibiscus bush. The sap from the white flowers stuck to my skin but I didn't care. I stayed in the bush long enough to tie my sneakers. I ran across the lawn and down Eshelman Avenue.

I didn't know where I was going, except I knew I had to go back to the Buhlert's and get my stuff. Everything in the world to me was in the drawers of the captain's bed and I was going to need it. I ran a few more blocks to make sure no one was behind me. I turned up 253rd street and onto Cabrillo Avenue to head back to the Buhlert's. As I made my way down Cabrillo Avenue, the eucalyptus trees cast long shadows over the sidewalk. A breeze kicked up and I smelled something like cat pee. I looked around but all I saw were the tops of the eucalyptus trees shaking like wet mops. It was the trees that smelled. After checking in both directions, I crossed the street because the Buhlert's street was coming up. As I got to the curb, I jumped and landed on a grass boulevard. Something made me look behind.

The Palos Verdes Peninsula, the Hill, looked just like a giant, black whale. The morning sun didn't seem to cast any light on it. It was always scary to see, but even more since Buzz told that spooky story about cannibals and one-armed murderers. I looked at the folds and twists of the Hill, with the bushes and trees that should have been green, but at this time of day turned the Hill black. I shivered. That's where she was, that's where someone left her, that's where she was found in nothing but a T-shirt. My teeth rattled.

I couldn't look at those ugly folds and twists without imagining her. I couldn't move my legs. Then it occurred to me: if I saw where they found her, I would feel close to her. If I saw where she took her last breath, where for a second she was still a living girl, and the next second, a dead girl, I would feel so close to her.

A young girl lost her life up there. That is no place for you to go.

I didn't care what the voice said. I felt like I knew her, and I just had to see where she was left.

Slowly, I turned away from the Hill and stepped onto the sidewalk. I stared at the Hill for one last second and then I turned and walked. I would see the place where they found her. Somehow, no matter how scared I might be, I was going to go there.

I got to the Buhlert's and the house was quiet. Gerry would be at work and Dale hopefully was out placing a rescue dog. I was going to have to break in to the downstairs bathroom near the kitchen and make it upstairs if I was going to get my stuff. I went around the side of the garage and peeked through the window. I wiped away some of the crusted dust and could see that neither car was in the garage. I sneaked around to the backyard.

I turned the knob of the kitchen door but it was locked. That left me no choice but to see if I could raise or break the back bathroom window. A neighbor's golden retriever bellowed just on the other side of the backyard cinderblock wall. A jolt of adrenaline shot through me and I was sure I was caught. But whatever was bothering him wasn't me and I heard a hushed voice call him inside and a door close. Phew, all safe again. I turned back toward the house and saw that the bathroom window was open a couple inches.

The dirty screen broke into wire dust where I tugged but I didn't care. I tossed it aside and reached under the open window ledge and pushed. Stuck. These wooden sashes built in the early fifties became immovable after a couple decades of house paint. But just like the one at the ashram, once I applied all my eleven-and-half-year-old

212

strength to the sash, it gave. I was pretty sure my baseball throwing and fielding muscles helped my arms. I hauled myself up and into the bathroom. In moments, after listening to see if anyone was around, I stopped by the kitchen and grabbed a brown Hefty bag. It would be easier to haul all my stuff in one bag, I figured. I hustled up the shag stairs to my room.

I yanked open the captain's bed drawer. In a hurry, I pulled out my sketchpad and crayons. But the crayon box slipped out of my grasp and the sketchpad flew open. A couple loose pages fell from it. Crayons lay spilled on the floor. I went to pick up the sketchpad pages and saw that they were the episodes of magic TV shows I had done: Samantha casting spells in 'Bewitched' and scenes of Jeannie blinking in 'I Dream of Jeannie'. I thought about what a stupid kid I had been to believe that the magic in 'Bewitched' could be real. I left them on the floor. Sketchpad pages with drawings of 'The Partridge Family' and 'The Brady Bunch' followed. I felt hot with embarrassment: what a dumb, worthless foster kid I was.

I grabbed those drawings and with one hand pulled them loose from the sketchpad's binding. I was done with the pretend things on TV, and the dumb things they made me think about. I picked up all the loose pages and threw them into the drawer of the bed. I held up the sketchpad that was now reduced to half its original size, with twenty or so blank pages left. Satisfied, I closed it. The crayons strewn all over the floor seemed childish and silly to me, also. I picked up the lavender crayon, worn round like a bullet, and broke it in half. I threw it back down with the rest of them.

I was going to start some new drawings when I settled down. They were going to be real, not stupid fantasies. I would use color pencils as soon as I could get some, or maybe even oil pastels. I thought about trying to draw Holly Ann. Maybe I would draw Brother Par and the SRF Center, too. I dropped the sketchpad into the bag.

I emptied my paper trash bags into the bag. I had an urge to save them for some reason, but ignored it. Finally, I dumped the box of my stuff into the bag along with my baseball and mitt. I held them for a second and wondered if I could run away and join a minor league team. The last thing in the drawer was my roller skates but they were too heavy for the plastic bag. I tied the laces together and threw them over my shoulder. I grabbed up the Hefty bag—it was heavy but not too bad—and headed down stairs. Dale might be home any minute so I had to hurry. A hunger pang reminded me I needed to grab some food from the kitchen.

I knew from a TV commercial to "Eat four, four, three, and two from these groups of food as I tell you to…eat them each and every day…" I opened the fridge and grabbed a pack of Oscar Mayer bologna that was half empty—it would have to do. I grabbed up some Kraft wrapped cheese slices. I closed the fridge and noticed the loaf of Weber's Bread in its blue-and-white, checked package. I opened it and grabbed four slices. I wrapped them in a paper towel and dropped them into my bag.

I had my two servings from meat and eggs. Four servings of the bread group. I added a couple oranges and bananas and then a few boxes of raisins and a can of Beer Nuts. I looked around the kitchen once more because I had to get out. But I saw a box of Chips Ahoy and grabbed it, too. I was pretty sure I could live for a long time on all this stuff and I could sneak water from people's garden hoses. I started to leave the kitchen but hesitated: should I leave a note? Just to let them know I was okay, and to thank them? No. If I left a note, then they would know I ran away and would probably alert Maureen. That would ruin everything. Nope. Let them think something happened to me -- like I got kidnapped, like Holly Ann. I was going to miss the bright yellow kitchen and butter cream counter tiles, that's for sure. This was one of the safest places I ever lived even if it was with two wives.

I had to use the front door at the Buhlerts because the Hefty bag would not have fit through the bathroom window. There was no one around at this time of the late morning so no one noticed me leave. I paused in front of the house and regarded the mullion windows, the wood trim, and shake roof of both stories of the house. It was strange that for awhile, I lived in this two-story house, just like everybody on TV did. It didn't make me feel less sad or alone. As I walked away, I figured the people on TV probably were not any happier in their two-story houses, either.

When I got to 254th and Cabrillo, I could either turn right and walk further into Torrance, or turn left and walk toward the Hill. Since I was on my own, I decided I would head towards the Hill, toward where Holly was last alive. After that, I didn't know what I was going to do.

214

15.

Dr. Friedman pulled out a Ricola throat drop and handed it to Gem. He removed the wrapper and popped the lozenge it into his mouth.

"My throat is wracked for the day. Unless you want to take over?"

Dr. Friedman shook her head. Gem had one leg of his jeans up over the arm of the sofa and the other crossed Indian-style. His head was propped up by two throw pillows.

"I'm not the one who thought reading all this old horse shit aloud would do any good."

"We can end this if you want—you're the patient."

"No, no," Gem said.

"Did you ever try to meditate again?"

"Yeah. But see, it was really about me trying to feel God in myself. When I gave up on that idea, it just didn't seem worth it anymore."

"Too bad. You should start again. We now know that it has a significant and positive impact on the brain—the corpus callosum."

"Oh, I'll just rush right out to the SRF Center now!"

Dr. Friedman reached over and grabbed the manuscript. She threatened to smack it over the top of Gem's head. Gem threw his legs down and sat up.

"Don't try it--I'll report you for malpractice!"

"I'm suggesting something that's looking like it improves not just brain communication function but is possibly staving off dementia and you're being sarcastic."

"Me? You're Doctor Giggles, remember?"

"All right already. So I forgot about your baseball talent. You got a scholarship to 'SC, correct?"

Gem nodded and sighed.

"It was the dry spell after Coach Dedeaux. None of us were even approached to try out by any major league teams."

"Too bad. You really loved it?"

Gem stood up and stretched. He moved his closed fists together to mimic holding a baseball. He stared at it.

"The winning or losing part never mattered to me. The record we had at 'SC sort of made that moot, anyway. We really weren't very good."

He took a slow swing with his invisible bat.

"But when I was up to bat, or on the field, all that mattered was that ball and my relation to it. I kid you not that every hit was in slow motion for me, the bat contacting the ball in that sweet spot of both—and nothing else mattered at that second. Same thing with fielding. The ball hit my glove and a ballet began until I released the ball toward home plate. Again, slow motion and nothing mattered."

Gem mimicked pulling a baseball from a glove. He formed an arc with his arm and threw the invisible ball with grace and control. It was ballet to him.

"Playing ball was body and mind working like nothing else I ever experienced..."

"Even—" Dr. Friedman paused.

Gem folded his arms and knitted his eyebrows.

"Get your mind out of the Freudian gutter, Dr. Friedman. Even sex."

"Sounds close to meditation to me."

Gem shrugged.

"Dad loved it, too," he said.

Dr. Friedman slapped her thigh with enthusiasm. She checked a nail briefly to be sure her French manicure hadn't chipped.

"First mention of Dad in a long time and I didn't have to prompt it."

"Oh, goody, goody gumdrops for me! Now my anxiety will just vanish."

Dr. Friedman picked up her tablet and made a note. Gem watched her curiously as usual.

"Commitment papers for me, then?"

"Time's up. Though I really want to stay all night and finish this last part. We're more than three-quarters done and I sense we're coming up to intense territory."

Gem raised his eyebrows and smirked.

"By the way, when do I hear about all this new stuff you picked up at UCLA? Seems we're just doing the same-o analysis therapy."

"We'll get to that. Uncovering and discussing the life experiences that wired your brain for the anxiety is the first step. That's your abandonment, loss of both parents, and your mysterious dad. Managing your brain follows that. Tomorrow, then," Dr. Friedman said.

Who needs wings to fly? Who needs wings to fly? Baseball bats meeting baseballs. 'I'm alone, I'm alone!' Gem screamed. 'Daddy! Daddy!' he hollered. His father's face, red, blistered, and distorted appeared surrounded by flames. He laughed like a demon. Gem's heart pounded.

"Cupper, Cupper wake up." Kelly's sweet voice echoed and Gem woke up. The moonlight spilled through the bedroom draperies all silver and odd. Gem's mouth was parched. He sat up and felt his back and shoulders stiffly resist.

"You okay?" Kelly asked.

Gem sighed.

"Yeah. It's just more dreams. They're keeping me up."

By the time Gem pulled into the parking garage in Dr. Friedman's building the next morning, he was exhausted. The lack of sleep made the bubble of anxiety rise and rest at his midriff. He wasn't sure this whole thing was doing any good at all. His father's face, red and wounded, popped into his mind.

"Nope, nope, nope" he said. Somehow he hoped it would shake the image from his mind.

He shut off the engine and looked in the rearview mirror. His eyes were swollen and puffy. He yawned.

"Well there's my little ray of sunshine," Dr. Friedman said. She tapped her watch. "Fifteen minutes. I was getting worried."

"Can we ease off the humor for awhile? I'm dead tired from bad sleep."

Dr. Friedman looked at him over her reading glasses.

"Disturbing dreams?"

"Yep."

"The images in the dreams aren't important—we don't hold any scientific relevance in them per se. But the feelings do matter. Let's talk about them."

"I felt fearful and anxious. I really missed my dad. Something else, too."

"What?"

Gem paused.

"Guilt. But I don't want to talk about it."

"Sounds like we're getting close to something, but okay."

"Where's that damn manuscript?"

16.

Forty-five minutes later, I turned the corner onto Crenshaw. I didn't know where I going after the Hill. The late November Santa Ana winds blew their dry heat against my skin but dried my sweat immediately. I paused to cool down and started to feel nervous. How would I eat once I ran out of the food I stole from the Buhlerts? Should I just go back and face Maryvale and the next round of teenage tormentors? Did it even matter whether I was alive or dead? As these thoughts played through my mind, whipping me into a frenzy of anxiety, something else popped into my head:

"...*Who needs wings to fly?*"

The fear song, or what I now knew to be a remnant of the last happy times of my life spent sitting between my Mom and Dad watching the TV show 'The Flying Nun'. It didn't just signal that I was afraid this time. Understanding what the song was and why I remembered it now made me feel less scared. The song also reminded me of my coffee can time capsule. The sump! That's where I'd go first. I was just a few blocks away from 240th Street. Even with my feet burning as my sneakers slapped the sidewalk, and with the Hefty bag jammed with all my stuff weighing against my back, I decided I would go and dig up my time capsule. Whatever I had placed into it when I was six years old would take me back to then. Away from now, and all this nervous aloneness. Brother Par had helped me forget about some of the bad stuff, and had also reminded me of some of the good. But I didn't trust Brother Par now since he just wanted to turn me back over to Maryvale.

Each house I passed on 240th Street looked like it had been pushed through a Playdough Fun Factory with the same cutter--only

219

their colors set them apart. Bottlebrush trees drooped with their red, bristled flowers, one growing in front of each house I passed. The trees all looked the same, too, except for the lacy shadows they cast on the grass boulevards next to the curbs. As I walked along the sidewalk in front of the houses, I noticed about every ten yards or so a worn, stamped impression in the concrete that read 'Palmer & Krisel Construction 1956'. It seems they built all these houses so that was probably why they looked so much alike. The street was quiet, and I figured that empty driveways meant fathers were at work, and kids were definitely in school since it was Friday morning. The pink house with the white trim let me know that I was almost to Pennsylvania Avenue. When I saw the green house with the gray trim, I stood at the corner of Pennsylvania and 240th Street.

The Hefty bag made my right hand fall asleep as its weight pushed hard against my back. I started walking faster. I practically ran past the clapboard house with its big porch. Now I passed by the yellow house with black trim, and I rushed to get to the end of the Curtis's front lawn. At the corner of Vine and 240th, I stopped, out of breath. The sun burned my back as it got to be noon, and I rushed across the small side street and dropped my bag. There in front of me stood the locked, chain-link gates of the sump.

As I read the 'No Trespassing' sign with its warnings about Torrance Municipal code 45.1.3, the burnt toast and lettuce smell of the sump's wild weeds filled my nose. The last time I looked at this gate with its sign, I only hesitated climbing it because it had gotten so late. But now, I remembered one of my talks with Brother Par about rules kids had to follow being like laws they'd have to follow when they grew up. And since God was even in the laws, you have to honor them like you honor the God in yourself. This sign with its municipal code must have been some sort of law. But my time capsule was buried inside the sump, and if I wanted it, I was going to have to climb the gate. Screeching brakes startled me, and I jumped and looked back. A blue Mustang was stopped on Vine Street and I noticed a gray-striped cat scurry past the front wheels of the car.

I grabbed up my Hefty bag and waited to get in trouble, but the car rolled past, turned onto 240th, and drove away. I read the sign once more, and decided that God inside me wouldn't get too angry if I climbed the fence to get something that was mine. Besides, wasn't God in my coffee can, too? After all, when I buried the coffee can five years before, I had climbed the fence from my backyard. There was no sign then to stop me so I wouldn't have known that it might be illegal for me to go into the sump. I tossed my bag over the fence and it plopped onto the dirt just on the other side. Looking in both directions down Vine, I saw no one coming. I jumped onto the chain-link fence.

The fence jingled and shook as I climbed it, and at one point near the top, it warped and stretched under my weight. For a moment, it felt as if I were floating. Throwing my right leg over quickly, I rolled my torso past the top of the fence. Just as I pulled my left leg over, the inside of my left gold corduroy pant leg snagged and tore at my thigh. I jerked it free and let myself fall feet-first to the ground. When my shoes hit the dirt, pin pricks of pain shot from my heels up to my knees. The pain stopped as I brushed the dirt off my pants. I decided I could leave my bag on this side of the fence because someone would have to climb the fence to steal it and I'd hear the fence shake if they did.

As I walked along the rim of the ditch, being careful not to get too close to the edge because it was about a fifteen foot drop if I slipped, I noticed that the bottom of the ditch was dried mud made silver-gray by years of sunshine. Scattered shards of white, black, and brown trash stuck to the top layer of the mud. When a breeze kicked up, I could smell something like dead fish mixed with cow manure. The smell didn't bother me, though. I carefully made my way to the bottom of a short embankment that disappeared into thick bushes grown tall as trees and covered with leathery, black-green leaves. Those bushes spilled their branches into my childhood backyard, I remembered, so I knew the burial spot of my time capsule lay somewhere beneath them.

As I made my way into the bushes, the afternoon sun weakened into spots that punctured the blackness of the shade with weak, pale light. The shade relieved the dry heat. Half way through the bushes, with my ankles bending at forty-five degree angles as my heels sank into the years of mud and leaves, I spotted the short wall marking the boundary of my old backyard. Chain-link fence weathered to a rusty bronze capped the cinder block wall. Somewhere in the clearing between the wall and the trunks of the bushes lay my treasure.

Starting at the wall, I used my left foot as a rake and pulled away several inches of the dead leaves. I raked the leaves slowly, keeping a close eye on the surface of the ground. The mottled brown, green, and black leaves in various stages of rot made a pattern that reminded me of the granite rocks I learned about in third grade.

Continuing in a parallel pattern, I had cleared the whole area of the first few inches of leaves. The edges of the pink, plastic rulers marking the spot weren't visible yet. It took about twenty minutes to clear the first layer of leaf and dried muck, and I figured it might take a couple of hours before I could find the spot. But who cared? No one was looking for me since I really didn't matter, I concluded. I had all the time I wanted.

I kept up the raking and it took another hour before I finally got down to the dirt near the wall. My foot hurt from the continuous movement, and I could feel grit that must have spilled over the sides of my shoe and through my sock as I wiggled my left toes. I was frustrated, and then started to think that maybe this whole thing was a waste of time. After all, how far could I have dug down when I was six? I could remember digging the hole to only just below the ground level, then filling it back up with mud and leaves. It couldn't have been deep enough to protect the coffee can.

Tired, with these thoughts discouraging me and with my throat dried from thirst, I collapsed onto the ground. But instead of sinking into the dirt and leaves, my butt hit something hard and sharp. The rulers! My heart pounded as I rolled onto my knees and dug into the dirt. I spread the soil out with my right hand, and there it was: the edge of one of the rulers.

Its white-painted lines and numbers had worn off, but the plastic, slightly browned in spots with haze, sparkled mostly pink and clear. In a few seconds, I had the crossed rulers uncovered, still held together in their middles by a white shoelace stained black and frayed like twine.

"It's still here," I whispered, barely able to breathe.

I stood up and looked for something to use to dig. I yanked a thick twig from one of the bushes. Pushing the rulers aside, I stabbed the twig into the soil and twisted it. As the dirt loosened, I pulled away thick, dark, moist wads of clay. Dank and musty odors hit my nose and I paused for a second to try to remember if the sump ever had sewage in it. We would have remembered the smell, that's for sure. Satisfied it wasn't sewage, I dug back in. I stabbed the soil again and again, twisting and pulling at the dirt, until one final stab hit something solid.

"Please don't be a rock," I said.

I worked both hands into the loosened dirt and felt the cylinder shape of the coffee can. I pulled it from its brown grave, and though the can was rusted, red paint still adhered to its three latitudinal grooves. The plastic lid I had taped on with masking tape that was now beige strings was even still attached. Turning it over, I was able to make out the image of the old man in the turban chugging his cup of Hills Brothers coffee. On the plastic lid of the can were the words: "Do not open till 2000" in my best first-grade printing done in black Magic Marker. I remembered writing that, and almost wanted to bury the can back in the ground and wait the twenty-six years. But the can, rusted all over in jagged craters, wasn't going to make it till then. Five and half years was the longest it was going to be, I decided. I could feel the sharp and brittle edge of the lid as I guided my finger along to pry it off.

Are you ready to face the pain of the past?

Of course I was, I thought in response to the voice. What could be painful about a bunch of stuff in a can left by a six-year-old? Later, I would come to understand what the voice really meant. But right then, I just wanted to open the coffee can.

Using the digging stick to pop it off, I was surprised when the lid cracked and splintered like glass. A bright glint of aluminum foil sparkled, and I could still smell the faintest smell of ground coffee. I peeled back the foil, remembering that I used it because the Apollo astronauts' food was always covered in aluminum foil and if it could make it through space, it could last in the ground of the sump. It was soft, so it probably wasn't going to last very much longer, either.

The first thing I saw inside was a rolled up piece of paper with yellowed edges. Pulling it out, I realized it was a rolled page from a coloring book. I unrolled it and recognized the figure of a cartoon Frankenstein's monster standing next to a mold shaped like a body. Next to the monster was a man with a skeleton face and a black top hat. The coloring was done evenly, lightly, and carefully kept within the black lines of the drawing.

"Milton the Monster!" I hollered and laughed. I hadn't thought of that show in years.

In purple crayon at the bottom of the drawing were the words: 'I like coloring. Other stuff in my time capsule is neat. Gem O'Connell, February 19, 1969.'

I let the page roll back up on and pulled out a flat, plastic thing, almost like the mirror my Mom used for her face powder. But when I moved it, I saw violet, yellow, and green swirls of something like paint. I remembered my Fidget. I thought I had lost it a long time ago. I touched the back of the toy, and the moving colors followed the pattern I traced. Shaking it, I saw that the colors vibrated. It made me smile. I set the Fidget aside with the coloring book page.

"Playdough!" I hollered.

The yellow can with the drawing of a boy in a beret looked almost brand new. I plucked the red cap from its top and took a deep breath. The vanilla, sugar cookie dough smell of the clay gave me a shiver of joy. Sticking my finger into the red wad, I realized it had dried to rock-hard and shrunken down to a small wad at the bottom of the container.

I tipped the coffee can to retrieve the next thing and I heard something clunk against the side of the can. Reaching in, I pulled out a single, clear, light blue marble. A purie! I held it up to my right eye and squinted so that the bushes I saw through it were blue-black.

As I looked inside the can, I saw a small, gold tip pointing at me. A rocket? But when I pulled it out, I saw it was a gold crayon. I always loved the metallic crayons. If it weren't stuffed in my bag, I would have pulled out my sketchpad right there and drawn something with the crayon. But I was anxious to get the rest of the stuff out of the can.

I felt a flat, cool, metal plate and when I ran my fingers along it, I knew what it was immediately: the tarantula plate from my Creepy Crawlers kit. I remembered using the Plastigoop to make pink and black tarantulas. The smell as the Plastigoop heated—like a burning candle and Bluebird glue—there was nothing quite like it. Just to the side of the plate was a stack of baseball cards. My Detroit Tigers infielders! There was Dick Campbell, Eddie Matthews, Dick McAuliffe, even Roy Oyler. And they still smelled like Topps bubblegum.

To get the last thing out of the time capsule, I turned the can on its side and shook it. Into my hand fell a 1967 Kennedy half dollar. I saw my Dad again telling me on my fifth birthday I could either spend it or save it for something special. A lump began to squeeze in my throat and tears rolled down my face.

I did matter once, this half dollar reminded me. There was once a time when I wasn't worthless, when I wasn't just another ward of the court to be bounced from one foster family to another. There was a time when a grown-up didn't like me just because I could spell, or draw, or do math, but instead, someone loved me for just being me. This half dollar was a pressure in my palm, something sad, but it also made me feel light at the same time. I thought that was what the voice meant by the 'the pain of the past'.

As my nose filled up and then ran to meet the tears at my chin, something Brother Par said to me repeated in my head:

"...*You're a diamond in the rough just waiting for your facets to be revealed, and when they are, you'll fill the world with your brightness and clarity...*"

If that was true, why was Brother Par going to turn me into children's protective services? Because I really didn't matter, that was why. I squeezed the half dollar in my hand again. A crow cawed somewhere off in the distance.

I was tired. I lay back with the half dollar, my chest tight with sadness. I fell asleep.

Plastic tubes and eerie fluorescent light. Then Mom in the bed, so thin, like a skeleton. I tugged at my mom and she sat up and grabbed me.

"You come with me! You come with me!"

A cat howled in the corner and Mom stood behind me. The cat fought off giant ants whose bellies burned bright as comets.

"She's dead! It's over! She's dead! It's over!" I heard a voice through a choking fog. I ran to the doorway and saw a phantom. The hospital nurse stepped through the fog and held out her hand. But she now looked like a nun. The nun crossed herself.

"Pray for all sinners! Now and at the hour of their deaths!"

The nun turned and became the nurse again. But as the nurse turned back, she became Holly Ann. Holly Ann wore only the top of the nurse's uniform. She wore nothing on her bottom and she had a little hair like me.

She moved toward me, her face smiling and her brown eyes sparkling. She pushed up against me.

"Come find me, Gem! Come find me!"

I woke up. I had an erection and it felt as though I wet my pants. Now I'm a bed wetter? I never wet the bed as a little kid. I looked around and saw that I still lay under the bushes in the sump. I was relieved to discover that the urine hadn't soaked through my pants. But when I reached to pull my underwear away from the front panel of my pants to keep them from absorbing the urine, I felt a sticky wetness. I pulled my hand out and wiped it against the leaves.

I had no idea what was wrong with me. Is this what they meant in the boy-to-man movie by an "emission"? But I wasn't going to be twelve for six more months, and this wasn't supposed to happen until I was almost thirteen. A feeling of oddness spread through me, like I was outside my own body. My heart pounded, and just as sweat began to seep from the top of my forehead, I remembered the dream.

Holly Ann. Her nakedness. She's wants me to go to her. But

225

she's dead and in heaven.

Bothered by the wetness in my underwear, and confused by the mix of melancholy, arousal, and aloneness, I went to drop the half dollar into the coffee can but stopped. My dad! That was it. I would go find my dad in the desert and see if he could make everything like it used to be. It didn't matter that he was in jail. I might even find a way to help him bust out. I hadn't tried to find him since I was young, and now I was definitely old enough to find him. I hurried to the sump fence. I opened my Hefty bag, jammed the time capsule into it, and threw it over the fence.

Once I climbed over, I saw that the sun hung low in the sky. It was going to get dark in a couple hours. After pausing at the garden hose on the side of my old house and gulping the rubber-flavored water, I hurried back up 240th Street. I dodged a yellow AMC Pacer as it pulled into a driveway. Two kids were hopping with Footsies around their ankles. When I got to Crenshaw, not sure which way I should go to hunt for my dad, I looked to the left and saw Palos Verdes. A chill shot through me. Holly Ann.

After taking a second to think about it, the answer was clear: I would go to where Holly Ann was found first, and then head to the desert for my dad. I stared at the Hill.

A young girl was molested and murdered up there. It's dangerous for you to go. Leave it be.

I ignored the voice and made my way down Crenshaw, toward Pacific Coast Highway. Traffic whirred by. A subtle scent, like wet black top playground, made me wonder if the refinery storage tanks nearby were leaking. Like giant aspirin tablets with steps twisting up their sides, the white tanks loomed row upon row across the street. I felt nervous as I remembered someone telling me once that a kid drowned in one of the tanks. What an oily, black death, worse than the kid who drowned in the sump, I thought. I passed the Palos Verdes Bowl on my left and my stomach growled: Gerry had taken us bowling there once and we all got to have lunch. I had the thickest and crunchiest French fries smothered in ketchup I had ever tasted. The Kennedy half dollar flashed in my mind. My stomach growled. I had to get some fries.

When I stepped through the glass doors, the air conditioning gave me a chill. I also couldn't see well at first since the light was so dim. But I headed left toward the snack bar counter. The clock above it showed that it was three o'clock. When I stepped up to the window, a blonde lady in a yellow waitress outfit smiled at first and then frowned.

"What's with the trash bag there?" she said. Her voice sounded like she had a cold.

"Nothin'."

It was a relief to set down the bag. I opened it and pulled out the coffee can time capsule.

"What do you want, kid?" she asked.

"Some French fries, please."

She pursed her lips and nodded.

"You got the money? Forty cents?"

It was my turn to nod back.

She stepped away from the counter and I could hear a TV set. I had to walk around a brown wall splattered with spots of dirt and grease to see it. Just above a built-in, turquoise Formica table, a color set was blaring away. A news bulletin flashed on and then the bearded reporter Wayne Satz was standing outside the Torrance jail.

"The Torrance Police have arrested a suspect in the Holly Ann Lark molestation and murder. A transient, on parole for child molestation, has been taken into custody."

A photo of a scraggly, bearded man popped up on screen. I recognized him instantly and felt a shock go through me.

"Edward Joseph Ryan, thirty-two years old, was taken into custody today," Wayne Satz said over the photo.

It was the man who jumped out at me at the abandoned house a couple weeks back. It made me feel dizzy when I recalled that he told me to 'bring my sister' next time. My stomach tied into a knot.

Wayne Satz was back on screen and he stepped aside to show Ryan being led in handcuffs into the jail.

"Neighbors in the Rolling Hills area identified him as a stranger roaming the area in the last few days. Torrance Police have now focused their investigation on Ryan and an abandoned Torrance house where he had been living. The lead detective in the case will be making a statement shortly."

I suddenly felt a little queasy and no longer hungry. I dropped my time capsule back into my bag and picked it up. I headed out the side door of the bowling alley.

A small plane buzzed overhead as it descended toward the Torrance Airport, a few blocks away. Just as I got to Crenshaw and Pacific Coast Highway, where the traffic roared in the multiple lanes, the shadow from the Hill crept over me. A restaurant with a blue, orange, and yellow roof that looked like an open umbrella --the Parasol, the sign said in front-- was a bright and happy strangeness in the black-blue shadows. All I could think about now was Holly Ann.

Both sides of Crenshaw seemed to be swallowed up by gnarled trees with deep green leaves as it began to twist into the Hill. It narrowed at Dalemead, and I could feel the muscles of my legs strain as it started its incline. Even though I had now been walking for about an hour and a half since I left the sump, and it was probably only three forty-five or so, the thick growth of trees over Crenshaw deepened the street to dusk. The cat pee smell of eucalyptus trees tickled my nose as I trampled over curved, narrow leaves and leathery brown pods that looked like acorns with flattop haircuts.

About forty-five minutes later, just as I passed the South Coast Botanical gardens, my stomach twisted with hunger. My feet burned from the almost two hours of walking since I left the sump. Through the overgrowth of trees covering the street now, I saw branches of a tree reaching out like thick, green fingers over a stone wall. Orange and green blobs encrusted the limbs and as I shuffled forward, I realized the tree swelled with oranges. The tree grew between the flat stone wall and a side fence of the red house. I decided I needed to get some more fruit. I went to pull an orange from a low branch, but stopped before plucking it. Was I stealing?

As I tried to decide, feeling my feet tingle with heat from all the walking, a fly buzzed past my sweaty forehead. Following the fly's path, I watched it land and join a swarm of flies buzzing over a sickly yellow and brown mass of fallen oranges. The mushy pile of muck spread over the sidewalk and trailed off into the boulevard of gray-green crabgrass. I touched the oozing gunk with the white rubber toe of my sneaker to see if there were any whole oranges that hadn't yet rotted, but anything resembling a solid orange had dissolved into the slimy mess.

The sidewalk was public property no matter where you were in any city, I knew for sure. The branches of the orange tree spread out over it. The fruit of those branches had to be public property then, too. With that determined I pulled myself to the top of the stone wall, looked into the yard to see if anyone was on the other side, and then plucked off one orange for each hand. Balancing the two oranges between my left arm and chest, I knocked three more oranges off the tree, forcing them to fall into the cushion of the crabgrass. The soft smell of the fresh oranges made me almost dizzy as I jumped back down. I scrambled to pick up the extra oranges, and dropped them along with the two in my hands into my Hefty bag. I grabbed one out of the bag to eat right away.

I tore into its skin and juice squirted from the hole and ran down my fingers. Fresh orange aroma filled my nose as I brought the piece of fruit to my mouth. Bitter orange from its skin mixed with a sugary sweetness as I chewed. I ate the orange in four bites, spitting seeds and skin onto the sidewalk. I pulled one more orange from my bag, and got so involved eating it that I didn't realize I had made the turn onto Palos Verdes Drive. The site where Holly Ann was found lay less than a mile from me.

As I passed Rolling Hills Road, I spit the last pieces of skin and seeds from the second orange into the gutter and began to feel the stickiness around my mouth and on my fingers. Then I saw that the houses lining this street with its white, horse trail fence were so big that they seemed to stretch half a block. With their big roofs of dark wood shingles and playground-sized front lawns, none of these houses looked like each other the way the houses did on 240th Street. Some of these houses were so large they reminded me of the Beverly Hillbillies. Rich people live here, I realized.

Next to a stone house with a garden that exploded with yellow, red, and pink roses, a big green lawn opened up. Black-barked trees with dense leaves that looked like heads of lettuce cast deep shadows over park benches. This couldn't be someone's yard. I stopped at an opening in the horse trail fence and saw the small, brown sign that read 'Dapplegray Park'. Even though the setting sun made the inside of the park into a black and blue forest of shadows that spooked me, my mouth was dry and sweet. I needed a water fountain.

As I walked past the gate, I saw clumps of horse dung thick with yellow shreds of hay scattered on the horse trail on either side of the gate. A drinking fountain stood under one of the trees, and I hurried to get away from the smelly horse droppings.

I let go of my bag and felt sharp tingles in my fingers as the circulation returned to them. Bowing low over the white bowl of the drinking fountain that was dotted with rust, I turned the chrome handle and let the arcing stream hit my face. The stale, metallic water splashed into my mouth and I gulped it.

When I raised my head again, a breeze rustled the leaves of the trees all around me. I let the water hit my face to cool myself down and the cold stung. If I was going to get to Holly Ann's site, I was going to have to hurry. But then I had another problem: when it got dark in a while, where was I going to sleep? I spotted a wooden picnic bench set deeper in the park, between three of the trees. A shiver went through me as I realized I wasn't going to have much choice: that would be my bed tonight.

With sore feet and my stomach screaming with hunger, I hurried again. In about half a block, while I followed the white horse trail fence, I saw a jungle of trees growing up from behind an iron fence on the opposite side of the street. The jungle went on for more than a block, and I figured someone really rich must live there. A small road cut through the middle, and as I got closer, I saw the road wasn't blacktop but only gravel. Also, as I approached, I saw a police car and two officers talking. A bright yellow piece of plastic tied to the fence near me told me two things: the jungle across the street was the Palos Verdes Reservoir, and the ribbon of yellow plastic was police tape that marked a crime scene. I turned around quickly and headed back to the bushes nearby. I ducked in and watched. The two officers talked and compared notes on clipboards. A few minutes later, one of the officers stepped down the hillside. He reemerged from the bushes ten or fifteen minutes later. The sky was getting darker and I was ready to give up. But finally, the two officers loaded into their squad car and drove off. I picked up my Hefty bag and headed for the hillside.

Like a birthday party streamer, the crime scene tape stretched and twisted down the hillside from where I now stood. From somewhere down below, a second piece stretched up and twisted back to the fence about a quarter of a block further down. Instead of 'Happy Birthday', the yellow tape read 'Crime scene do not cross.' I jumped back from the fence like I was in trouble.

Standing about two feet from the curb, I thought I recognized the place where the Eyewitness news reporter delivered the story. Goosebumps burst on my skin. Should I go down there, or would I be breaking some law if I did?

A girl your age died down there. Go back to Brother Par.

I definitely wasn't going to obey the voice this time. But maybe I should just go back to the park, spend the night, and then start in the morning for the desert to bust out Dad. I couldn't decide. But Holly Ann's face popped into my mind. That was it.

I looked on both sides of the street and all around, and there were no cars. I knew I wouldn't get caught unless the police car came back around. Hopefully they were done here and like the news report at the bowling alley said, they were investigating the abandoned house where they found the suspect. No one was going to disturb me.

A breeze hit my back, making me feel as if I were being pushed. It would be a perfect breeze for wind skating but I wasn't here for that. The wind twirled the police tape, making it spiral like a jump rope. From down below where the two ends of the tape disappeared, I could hear a whipping sound like sheets snapping in the wind on a clothesline. My throat tightened.

I was nervous and I was about to run, but then Holly's picture popped in my head again. And this time I saw her as I had in my dreams. The police tape whipped and snapped again. I dropped the Hefty bag just on the other side of the fence. As I climbed over, my corduroys squeaked against the wood. I grabbed up my Hefty bag and started down the hill.

The hillside was thick and uneven as I made my way toward the site. Wild grass that was probably brown and green during the day reached up to my knees in gray clumps. I had to pause to pull out the foxtails now imbedded in my socks. The steeper the hill became, the more sideways I had to turn my feet to keep from tripping and falling down the hill. I didn't know how I would be able to tell when I was at the spot where she was left, especially because the grass was so tall and thick. The licorice weeds grew in wild patches all around, making the hill smell like candy, and woody bushes with dark green, circular leaves popped up in my way, too. I followed the one side of the tape, as it continued to snap and whip from lower down the hill. I wondered if someone was down below playing with the end of the tape.

In about ten minutes, after my ankles ached and the sky had turned Easter egg-blue and pink, I saw the end of the tape. It was tied to the branch of one of the woody bushes. I tried to see the end of the other piece, and that's when I noticed the flattened area of the grass. My heart pounded.

Did the police cause that from walking around, or was that where she lay? My mouth went dry and I tiptoed to the flattened grass. I dropped to my knees -- even if this wasn't the exact spot, she had to have been left nearby. Running my hand over the grass, I pretended that she lay there now, but with her eyeteeth poking over her lip in the bright smile from her school photo. I stroked the grass as if it were her long hair.

My mind flashed the picture of the stretcher: a sheet rose and fell with the contours of her kid's body. I saw Holly's mother's face pleading tearfully for her return. She had been here. These bushes and the sky were probably the last things she saw. She had probably cried here. She died here. Fear mixed with anger mixed with sadness, and my body rumbled with pain. The feelings swirled in me, and then exploded like a rushing geyser. I screamed.

"No, no, no," I cried to the dark hill, to the empty sky. "No, no, no!"

I dropped my forehead to the flattened grass. Holly Ann's death made me think of Mom. I drew my arms and my legs into my body in a hug, and rocked, tapping my forehead against the grass.

My body suddenly jerked backward as something hard hit my head. Everything went black.

17.

"Why are you stopping?" Dr. Friedman asked.

Gem's hands were shaking. The manuscript dropped to his lap and he raised his hands to his face.

"I can't do this. I need to get outta here!"

Gem jumped up and headed for the door. Dr. Friedman hustled to the door and grabbed his shoulders. Gem was a loose rag doll as she turned him toward her.

"You can't quit now. Face it, now! Face it head on or you're never going to have the peaceful life you, and Kelly, and the kids all deserve."

Gem made fists and lowered his head.

"No. My precious Kelly doesn't even know," Gem said almost whimpering.

Dr. Friedman put her hands on Gem's face and raised it toward her own. His eyes swelled with tears and confusion.

"This is your moment. You can do this. Whatever this is all about, only you and I will ever know. Okay?"

Gem leaned into Dr. Friedman. She held him a moment. He pulled away and wiped his eyes.

"This is getting unprofessional," he said.

"Yeah, don't report me."

Gem looked at the door once more. He looked at Dr. Friedman and rolled his eyes. He shuffled back to the couch, shoulders slumped. Dr. Friedman followed him and took her chair opposite. He picked up the manuscript, found his place again, and deeply sighed.

18.

My eyes popped open. Something was in my mouth and as I tried to open and spit it out, I felt something else pull across my cheeks. My head hurt, and my eyes blurred as I looked across and saw a gold light. I squinted and felt panic when I saw what appeared to be gray and white bugs in a pile near the light. Trying to run, I now felt a cord dig into my ankles, and a hard post my hands wrapped around. They were also tied. Tears built on my lids, and cleared my eyes. Was I dreaming? A man in silhouette picked up the gold light and stepped toward me.

When the silhouette got closer, I realized that the gold light was a kerosene lantern with two bright, burning mantles. As the shadowy figure held it close to my face, I could hear the purr of the lantern. The heat from the lantern began to warm me, and then the glass of the lantern touched my cheek. It burned and I knew this wasn't a dream. I tried to scream but it only came out a whimper over the gag in my mouth. The lantern moved back, and now its gold light fell on the sleeveless plaid shirt of the man who held it.

"Guess I got it too close. Sorry."

The man's face remained shadowed, with just its bearded edges reflecting the lantern light. He made a cracking and spitting sound. Was the man eating sunflower seeds? The man wiped at his chin with his thick hand, and I saw the flash of a little glass bulb in the middle of a silver ring. I flinched.

The man spit something and I was able to see that it was a sunflower seed shell. The man erupted with a deep laugh.

"I'm not gonna knock you out again. Relax. My ring left a big dent up side your head, though."

The man held up his hand again, and the hairs on his hand sparkled like short, gold wire. He wiggled his finger and I saw the glass bulb of a mood ring. It showed mixed colors of blue and green. Was that a good mood or a bad one, I tried to recall.

"I wouldn't'a' hit you at all if you hadn't a snooped. You had no right to go near that place. That's my place, and now you're in for it."

The man's voice reminded me of someone. Even though I was scared to look into the shadow of the man's face, I raised my eyes above the lantern to see if I could recognize him. The man's hairy chest and necklace of flat, white puka shells stuck out above his open shirt. But the lantern's light stopped just at the edge of the man's mean, bearded mouth. I wasn't sure, but I thought I might have recognized the man's voice from TV. But what show?

The man turned and walked away, and as the light of the lantern cast a wider glow, I saw a wall covered with red and gold wallpaper. The paper was torn in places, and caked with what looked like gray wads of dirt or dust. I could just make out fleur-de-lis designs in its pattern. A green, velvet curtain torn to shreds hung over a doorway on the left. As the man set the lantern down, planks of worn, wooden floor reflected the lantern light. The lantern also highlighted a brown sack. Then I recognized my Hefty bag. I was relieved to see it and it looked as if it were still tied closed. Looking overhead, I saw the top landing of a staircase with spindles holding up a cracked and partial handrail. Cobwebs wove through the spindles. Gray cotton candy, I thought. My stomach growled.

"That your stomach growling?" the man said over his shoulder that was so big it looked like a football.

"No food around here."

I recognized this was an abandoned house but where it was located I could not guess. A dusty, dirty smell mixed with the odor of a wet washcloth. My kidnapper now sat against the wall, cracking and flipping sunflower seed husks toward the floor. Where had I been that was *his* place? Then I remembered the last place I had been: Holly Ann's body discovery site. Chills turned my flesh to turkey skin. This must be the killer. But I thought they caught that crazy hippie. Who was this, then?

"...*Who needs wings to fly?...*"

Of course the TV theme song, my fear song, would start in my mind. As I shook with terror, a new idea struck my mind: if this man

235

did kill her, then he was also the last to see her alive. He probably touched her face, and stroked her pretty, long, blonde hair, and *sexually assaulted* her. He killed her, and then left her without her underwear. My fear melted away. I hated him! I absolutely hated him! If I could just get my hands loose, I'd kill him! I wiggled my hands but instead of loosening, the cords scraped at my skin.

"No way you're getting loose there, little fucker. Just don't get me anymore mad at you than I already am."

I didn't care what he said. I wriggled my hands again.

"You hear me!" the killer roared as he jumped up.

He tore off his shirt and I saw his muscular, hairy body that reminded me of the gladiator movies that used to come on after the 'Three Stooges'. As he rushed toward me, the puka shells bounced above the outlines of five tattoos that made the killer's chest look like leopard skin. The killer wrapped his shirt around my face, tightening it so that it smashed my nose flat.

"How you like that, little fucker?"

I was choking for breath and my chest heaved as I tried to breathe through the corners of my mouth. I shook my head to try to loosen the shirt, but instead of loosening, the material rubbed my nose raw. The gold light of the lantern made the blue and yellow plaid material stretched across my eyes glow from behind. But I wasn't scared because all I felt was anger and hate that he killed Holly.

"You don't listen to me, you nosy shit, then this is the way you're gonna die. You wanna die like this?"

I cried and struggled, and the killer pulled the shirt off my face. The killer's breath blew hot against the side of my neck and face as he spoke.

"That wasn't some goddamn public property you wondered onto. What the fuck were you doing there?"

I tried to answer but I couldn't get any words past the gag in my mouth.

"I forgot. You can't answer me too well with that."

The tightness at the back of my neck relaxed, and I felt the thick cloth in my mouth soften. I pushed it out, and my mouth ached from dryness and my tongue felt like thick beef jerky. A breeze cooled my face as the shirt was pulled off. The man was behind me, I guessed, because I couldn't see him in the round light of the lantern.

"I saw her on TV," I panted. "That's all. I just wanted to see the spot where they found her."

"Well you found the spot and you found me, too. The FBI hasn't even been able to do that."

The man chuckled oddly.

"I oughtta do to you what I did to her."

The man must have stepped closer from behind because he wrapped his hands around my throat. My knees shook.

"The little chick wasn't supposed to die. I don't kill little chicks, you understand me?"

I nodded, and began to feel very afraid again. Was I going to wet my pants? The killer let loose of my throat and stepped away. The floorboards creaked behind me as the killer stepped back up close to me. I felt his hot breath again.

"You're just lucky you're not a little chick. Sort of lucky, for awhile."

I gulped air through my mouth and a drop of saliva oozed from under my tongue.

"I'm so thirsty."

"There ain't no water here. You gotta walk to the park to get a drink, but I don't think you're gonna do much walkin'."

The man's thick fingers grabbed me from behind and I thought I was going to die again. I screamed until the killer shoved the gag back in my mouth.

"Pleashth, pleashth," I managed to get out around the gag.

"I gotta figure it all out. Now you know all of it, I don't know what to do. I didn't mean to kill her, but she kept screaming. I don't know what I'm gonna do with you. You little nosy fucker—this isn't the way it oughtta be."

The man stepped back over to the lantern, and slipped his huge arms through the shirt. His big, muscular body slid down the wall and he sat on the floor. He crinkled a plastic bag and snapped down on a sunflower seed. He turned on a transistor radio and started listening to a baseball game. Was that Vin Scully's voice? The Dodgers? For a minute, everything felt okay. But I was thirsty and my head ached badly. Pretty soon, I fell asleep.

The next morning, a searing pain shot up my arms as the man tightened the cords on my wrists. My head jerked back as the man twisted the gag from behind. When the man stepped back around, the morning light that made it through the dirty windows of the dark room struck the man's long, brown hair, and I noticed the sun's weak rays highlighted the sharpness of his cheeks above his beard. I could see that his whiskers were red and gray, but the light on the man's face turned his eyes into black holes.

"Good morning, little fucker. You're not dead yet 'cause I can't decide what to do with you after I kill you. I oughtta know but I don't yet. So this'll hold you till I get back."

The man disappeared into one of the dark hallways of the house. An engine fluttered to life, and a car drove off.

The killer left me alone. I couldn't believe it. A sharp pop of decaying wood somewhere in the house split the silence, making my heart pound in fear. From somewhere outside, a chirping mockingbird screamed at a cawing crow.

I twisted and pulled my hands to loosen the cords, but when I did, the cords tightened and dug into my skin. How I could feel the pain at all I didn't understand, since my hands had become numb and tingling lumps of flesh. I decided to scream for help. As I shrieked, using my whole chest to make the sound, the gag held back my scream and turned it into a wheeze. It also rubbed the corners of my mouth raw as I shook my head to dislodge it. My face burned hot with frustration that rolled down my cheeks as tears. For the first time in a long time, I felt like praying.

'Our Father, who art in heaven, please don't let me die this way,' I prayed in my mind. 'Please save me.' Right then, the voice said something to me that was scary, sad, and made me feel so alone:

Praying won't help. You have to save yourself.'

'Lord, please forgive the voice in my head. Please, Lord.'

If God was up there, why did he let your Dad get taken away? Your Mom die? Foster parents to hit you? Little girls to be sexually assaulted and strangled?

Yeah, why would God let such bad things happen all the time? And what had I done to deserve all this bad stuff that happened to me? The voice made sense. I agreed with the voice: why bother praying.

My tears now stopped, and I quit praying. Whatever was going to happen to me, God wasn't there to make a difference. I was all alone. My head began to feel hollow and heavy at the same time. It didn't ache. It felt more like a balloon with a rock tied to it. Did I have a concussion again like that time the foul ball bounced off my head? I felt so sleepy, and my eyes slammed shut. I floated.

Feona jumped down from a cinder block fence. She waved.

"Rock paper scissors?" she asked. She grabbed the edge of her sweatshirt

and went to raise it over her head.

"No!" I screamed at her. "No, don't do that!"

She ran across the street, but when she turned to wave at me, I saw Holly Ann's face. Her light blue T-shirt ruffled in the wind, and I saw she was naked below.

I ran to her, pulling my Hang Ten T-shirt over my head.

"Wear this around your lower area. Make it a skirt or something!"

Holly Ann smiled her school picture smile. She wrapped the striped T-shirt around her waist and ran.

Brother Par jumped out from behind a bottlebrush tree. He wore a plaid shirt with no sleeves.

"God and the universe are in you, Gem."

Brother Par was my dad; I loved him. Brother Par stepped back behind the bottlebrush tree and I saw a line of ants as big as Matchbox cars, crawling up the side of the tree. They carried my magnifying glass on their backs. I didn't want it.

My eyes popped open. Sweat dribbled down my neck, and my mouth was as dry as if I had eaten sand. My heart pounded again from the dream. I felt an odd feeling on my right: looseness, freedom.

I looked down and raised my right leg. The plastic and silver telephone cord wound around it still, but the length of it that had held me to the post dangled loosely. The dream. By running, somehow I must have moved my leg enough to loosen the cord. Were my hands loosened now, too? As I tried them, they pulled tight behind me still. My left leg was still bound tight.

I shook my right leg, and it tingled and burned as the blood returned to it. I looked around to figure where I was, and saw that the sun still shone in silver streaks far down one of the hallways. This room remained dark. Where was the killer? I relaxed a bit when and I saw the lantern hadn't been moved. He was still out.

I'd hear him drive up, I figured, and I made a plan. I was going to fake as if my right leg were still tied, just like I had seen a kidnapped person do on 'Hawaii Five-O' once. With my free leg, maybe I could kick the killer hard enough to make him fall back and hit his head. Before then, I decided I was going to make as much noise as I could. I knew it was my only way of getting help.

I lifted my right leg and slammed my sneaker against the floorboard. Even though it stung, the cracking sound it made echoed in the empty house. Someone could definitely hear that I knew. *CRACK!* I let my foot slam again. Tilting my head toward the direction of the yard, I tried to hear if anyone had responded. The crow outside screamed and that was all the response I got.

"Kkkeeeeeee—aaaahhhh---oooowwwwww!"

It sounded like a woman's scream. Then I remembered that peacocks roamed the streets of the Hill. I must be somewhere in Palos Verdes—that's it.

"Kkkkeeeeeee—aaaahhhhhh—ooooowwwwww!"

The peacock screeched again. Again, for a minute, things seemed okay. But then my bound hands burned and I was once again in this horrible place.

I let my foot slam one more time, and then stopped because the bottom of my foot ached. I couldn't do that much longer because my foot was killing me. But I pounded the floor a few more times, and each time the only response was the cawing crow. The peacock didn't even scream again. I wasn't sure how much time had passed since I started beating my foot. No one showed up, though, and with it hurting, I gave up. It must have been late afternoon, because when I looked down the hall, the sun's rays had gone from silver to orange, and now looked thin as pulled taffy.

When was the killer coming back? Where did he go? Had he spent the whole day at Holly Ann's body site? My stomach roared with hunger. I didn't care anymore about my loose foot, because all the noise it made didn't help. Chips Ahoy, that's what I wanted; some of the chocolate, crunchy sweet taste of the cookies in my Hefty bag. But it sat way over against the wall, near the killer's lantern. No way could I get to it.

I dropped my head, and that's when the chugging sound of the engine filled the air. *His* car, I recognized it, and my heart pounded again. If I didn't find a way to free myself, this man was going to kill me. Maybe it was even going to be now.

"Lucy, I'm home!" came the killer's voice from down the dark hallway.

I jerked my right foot back into the tied position on the post. I hoped he wouldn't see that it was loose. The killer stepped in from the dark hallway.

"Sure in hell's dark in here. Sun goes down in about twenty minutes, so I'll light the lantern then. Don't want to waste any fuel."

He dropped a shovel and some rope. He picked up the lantern and shook it next to my ear.

"About half full still, so we're okay. Jesus, I'm hungry enough to eat, well, you!"

My heart pounded as I shook my head.

"Calm down, I don't eat human meat. Besides, I oughtta watch my cholesterol."

The killer stepped around me and loosened the gag. My lips and mouth muscles tingled. I licked my lips a few times.

"Okay, so here's the deal: I gotta waste you now 'cause you can identify me and I'm not going back. It's the way I figure it oughtta be."

A clicking sound made me look toward the killer's hand and I saw the blade of a knife. The killer stepped toward me.

"Wait!" I screamed. "Do I get a final wish?"

The killer paused and folded his arms. A mean smirk crossed his lips.

"You watch too much TV, little fucker. I'm hungry, you're dead. It's the way it oughtta be."

"I got Chips Ahoy. In my bag over there."

The killer glanced over his shoulder toward my bag.

"You can have some," I said, feeling my voice shake. "You can have them all."

"Hmmm. I do like cookies. What the hell *is* in that bag anyway?"

The killer clicked the knife blade back into its black handle as he walked over and yanked my bag up from the ground. The neck of the bag stretched under his grip.

"This feels like trash."

"No. It's all my stuff in the world."

"What are you—some kinda' little fucker hobo or something?"

My bag clanked and jiggled as the killer tried to loosen the plastic tie. In a lunge of frustration, he tore the side of the bag.

"Shit" he yelled as my stuff burst from the hole as if the bag were a piñata. My baseball mitt and sketchpad thumped to the floor, followed by my time capsule coffee can. It landed with a tinny clank. The purie marble rolled over the wood floor into the dark corner, and the silver dollar spun on its side before falling flat. My Milton the Monster coloring book page spread out next to the can. The killer bent over to retrieve the silver half dollar.

"So you're loaded. A Kennedy half --"

The killer's body heaved with a deep breath. He snatched up the coloring book page and stared at it.

"Son of a fucking bitch! This can't be happening!"

He reached over and picked up the lantern. He rushed to me and for the first time, I saw the man's eyes. They were like my own, framed by flat, dark, bushy eyebrows flecked with gray.

"Gemmy," the killer said.

He stepped around to the back of the pole and loosened the cords from my hands. The blood rushed to my fingertips with sharp tingles, and I could barely move my hands. The killer went to untie my feet, but stopped. He sat on the floor and looked at me, shaking his head with indecision.

"I didn't know who you were. I don't even recognize you— what were you—six when I last saw you?"

The killer confused me. I guess he thought he knew me, but I didn't care what the killer was thinking about if it meant he was going to let me loose. I shook my hands and shrugged.

"Yeah. You were six when I saw you last. Don't you know me?"

I shook my head.

"My hands hurt. Can I get some water?"

The killer stood up and grabbed my hands. I went limp, thinking he was going to break them or something, but the killer extended them out in front of me and held them, gently.

"Who need wings to fly?" the killer sang.

As if a thousand math books fell on me at once, I felt my head go light. My chin dropped to my chest as my stomach crinkled up into a wad of painful muscle.

"Daddy?" The word was so foreign to my mouth that it felt like I was telling a lie as I said it.

"Daddy?"

My dad let go of my hands and raised his own to his bearded mouth. Teardrops glazed his eyes into boulder marbles. He pulled back his wild locks of graying, chestnut hair and I finally recognized my Dad's face.

I felt all the aloneness and sadness of being a foster kid all these years and I could barely stand it. A strange bubble of joy crept through those feelings because here was my dad again, my dad who had been gone, like Mom, for so long. I had questions for Dad, and things I wanted to say. My mind swirled:

"I missed you so much. I miss watching the 'The Flying Nun', 'Gilligan's Island,' the Dodgers," I said.

He molested and strangled a little girl, the voice said.

242

"Sitting on your lap at church."
He molested and strangled a little girl.
"Saturday naps between you and Mom."
He molested and strangled a little girl.
"Jokes and stories at dinner time."
He molested and strangled a little girl.

I couldn't stand the fight in my head any longer. The image of Holly Ann's T-shirt covered body. *He* did that. He *killed* her. My *dad.* A rush of cold I had never felt before tightened my whole body into a spring of fear.

"My Daddy couldn't'a killed a little girl!" I screamed.

Dad dropped his hands from his own face and walked away. He leaned against the wall, then slid down and sat.

"I gotta think, I gotta think, I gotta think," Dad said softly.

"Daddy, I have to ask you —"

"Shhh. Don't say anything. This isn't how it oughtta be."

He scared me again and so I kept my mouth shut. Dad stayed against the wall for an hour or so, long after the sun went down. At one point it was completely dark until he realized he had forgotten to light the kerosene lamp. But after he lit it, he just sat back against the wall and stared at the floor.

As that hour went by, I looked at my Dad's face and realized the awful truth and I wondered. How could he have done that to a little girl? How could he have looked into her face with those brown eyes and not seen the terror? How could he not understand the hideous thing he was about to do to her, and to her family?

How could you burn an ant? How could you hide an inhaler? How could you trick a disabled girl into showing you her breasts?

A shudder went through me as the voice said those things. Could I be just like him? Would I someday do such a horrible thing? Hate welled up in me for my dad, for what he somehow must have passed on to me. All the black rage and anger I had ever felt I now saw was in me because of him. If it was hate I was feeling for my dad, then that hate was the opposite of what I felt for Holly Ann. What I should feel for ants, and cats, Feona, and everything. By hating Dad right then, I felt something else: a love for everything that was living.

To be like him or not is up to you.

As the voice said this to me, Dad suddenly stood up, picked up the lantern and walked toward me. The mantles blinded me with their brightness and Dad was just a dark shadow behind.

"You should have never wandered there."

"What're you gonna do to me, Daddy?"

"I can't let you live -- you know who I am."

Dad reached toward his back pocket and pulled out the switchblade knife. The knife blade clicked into position.

"You're way too smart for your own good."

Dad raised the blade toward my throat. I looked into his eyes to see if there were any tears or any doubt but all I saw was a black color darker than the water of the sump.

"Please don't, Daddy. I just found you! I don't want to die."

"Shut up!" he roared. "Oh, Gemmy, Gemmy, Gemmy."

Dad pressed his whiskered face against my cheek. I felt so warm and loved and I hated it at the same time. My cheek was wet from his tears.

"Keeeeee---aaahhhhhhh---ooowwwwww!" a peacock screamed.

Dad jerked his head toward the front door. I kicked my right leg out and knocked the lantern from his hand. The black feelings of rage in me gave way, and I screamed and kicked at my father's legs. Through my hate and rage, I heard the clunk of the knife's handle as it hit the floor and skidded into the darkness.

The lamp spewed its fuel in a fiery puddle across the room and back onto Dad's pants and shirt. The flame ignited his beard and he screamed and fell to the floor howling and burning. He waved his hands frantically, trying to extinguish flames that were searing his clothes and flesh.

Save yourself!

The flames ripped into the dried bones of wood in the room, and I felt my face warm up from the heat. I clawed and pulled at the cord that held my left foot. It came free, and using my last bit of strength, I snapped the cord that held my hands to the post. The post cracked from the force and gave way. I jumped up to run as a support beam fell from the ceiling and slammed across Dad's head and shoulders. I ran toward Dad but his moans had stopped. His body and the wooden floor and walls ignited into one horrid blaze.

I ran into the dark hallway and heard a crack and rumble behind me. Silver-blue moonlight shone through the open front door and I ran out into the yard.

I looked back at the house. As it exploded into flames, I realized it must be the house of the cannibal story.

"Daddy!" I screamed.

244

A mushroom cloud of flames and heat exploded upstairs, and it knocked me onto my back.

19.

Gem closed the manuscript slowly. He handed it to Dr. Friedman and walked across the room. Dr. Friedman nodded to herself. Tears welled in the corners of her eyes.

"I need a moment to process this," she said.

Gem paced the room. He crossed his tan arms tightly over his powder blue LaCoste polo. He paused at the window and looked out over the Century City skyline and Beverly Hills. Dr. Friedman cleared her throat. She spoke softly.

"You weren't aware that he had broken out of prison?"

Gem shook his head. He stood with his back to Dr. Friedman and stared out the window. His shoulders shook as he began to quietly cry.

"They told me later that he had escaped and the FBI was tracking him like he said," Gem's voice cracked. "He and another prisoner plotted it but I never got much detail beyond that. Anyway, since they had a suspect in custody, no one linked up Dad until I told them."

Dr. Friedman shook her head. She crossed her hands, unsure of how to proceed.

"Yep. OCD, anxiety, father killer. Just your average, garden variety diagnosis, I'm sure," Gem said.

Dr. Friedman stood up and crossed over to Gem. She placed her hand on his shoulder.

"Go take a seat and let's talk about this."

Gem turned and his eyes swelled with tears. He dropped his hands to his sides and followed Dr. Friedman to the couch. She handed him a box of tissues and made some notes on her iPad.

246

"I'm just so afraid that I'm like him. I mean those thoughts coming back. Certifiable, huh?"

"Stop. We'll get to that. I have plenty of cognitive approaches to discuss. But right now, this moment, it's about your dad."

"I killed him," Gem said. He almost whispered the words as he lay back on the couch and threw his legs over the arms of the sofa.

"Burned him alive, Dr. Friedman. Couldn't I hurt my grandson or Kelly? I'm trapped inside my head with a psychopath."

"No," Dr. Friedman replied. "Facts are very crucial to therapeutic healing so listen up. You were a child saving his own life. From the very person who *should* have protected *you*."

"But what if I had gotten my hands loose sooner and just ran away from him after I kicked him? I might have gotten him—"

"We can play 'what if' all day, Gem. And just what heroic feat would you have been able to accomplish that would have erased the murder of that little girl?"

Gem shook his head. He grabbed another tissue and dabbed at his eyes and nose.

"You are not your father. Even if you have spent four decades holding on to unnecessary guilt about saving your own life, you have still managed to love, and work, and create a very good life."

"But do you understand how hard it is for me that the father I longed for was a child rapist and murderer?"

"Let's stop with the 'buts'. You are not a molester, or a murderer, or any other monster. You are a good man. The father you looked for is right here."

Dr. Friedman pointed to her right temple and smiled.

"You're it, kid. You are the father you were looking for. All the questions are inside you but so are the answers. All of us eventually lose our fathers one way or another. Our mothers, too. We eventually have to become our own parents in our minds. As your mom said so beautifully when she was dying, you carry her with you. And the good parts of your father, too. Strange as it sounds, he wasn't a complete monster. We use everything our parents taught us to become ourselves, separate from them.

"But for you there's a lot of work ahead because you have what I call a "bruised brain" from all that trauma and loss you endured. You're going to have to deal with it your whole life.

"The anxiety your dad's memory has triggered is like a cage inside your head and these intrusive and disturbing thoughts are just the bars. But the past doesn't have to possess you—you can accept and allow it. Even Mother Teresa admitted she had a 'Hitler' in herself—she probably suffered from violent, obsessive thoughts, too. Nobody has to suffer like they used to. Most of Tennessee Williams' or Eugene O'Neill's neurotic characters could be successfully treated today. And without drugs."

"There are tools to help with all this. Now that you know the source of your anxiety, we're going to help you ignore these thoughts as they come up and refocus your mind. Rewire your brain. You can do this, kid. So come on. Let's work on this together."

Gem dabbed at his eyes. He blew his nose loudly.

"Crying like a baby," he said. "But it feels okay somehow."

"You want to lie back for awhile and digest this? I can step out and catch up on some case notes."

Gem shook his head. He stood up.

"Nope. I'm good. I'm going to head home."

"You sure?"

"Yeah. I *can* do this."

"Tomorrow, then. You're on your way, kid."

Dr. Friedman looked over her glasses and smiled.

As Gem drove home from Dr. Friedman's office, he encountered the traffic jam at Avenue of the Stars once again. But instead of the usual anger and tension, he felt lightness in his chest. He could almost have confused it with the beginning of an anxiety attack, but instead, it was simply relief. Dr. Friedman had put the experience of killing his dad in clear and present terms. His dad should have been the person he believed and wanted him to be in all his yearning. And his dad should have protected him always. The guilt and shame he still felt, and would shoulder for as long as his healing required, stood in contrast to the cold, heartless facts of who his father was.

Kelly and he dined at their favorite Italian café that night, and at one point, one martini and two glasses of Chianti into his osso buco meal, he held Kelly's hand and looked deep into her eyes.

"Cupper, your face looks twenty-three again," Kelly leaned forward and said. "Are you going to ask me to marry you?"

Gem laughed and stared into the depths of her amber-brown eyes. But he couldn't bring himself to tell her about his father.

"Just wanted to look at you and tell you that you are my life."

Kelly's eyes welled up and she smiled. She released his hand

and gestured toward her mouth.

"You are my everything, too, Cupper. But you have a piece of veal in the lower left corner of your mouth."

Gem rolled his eyes and dabbed at his mouth with his napkin. They laughed.

That night, lying in each others arms naked, the lightness of relief welled up in him again. Kelly fell asleep before he did and the love he felt for her, his children, and his life rolled down his face in quiet tears. He fell asleep soon after and it was a deep, dreamless sleep.

20.

"So you all set, then?" Dr. Friedman asked the next day.

"Yep. I slept better last night than I have in months."

"Did you talk to Kelly about it?"

"Almost but I chickened out. I'm not quite ready for that."

"It's okay. There's time. Let's switch gears then and talk about some of the new stuff I picked up recently."

"I can't wait."

"Really," Dr. Friedman said.

"No, I mean it now. Let's get this going."

Dr. Friedman handed him a legal pad and a pen. Gem looked at her and shrugged.

"A souvenir? I use these at work to work up deal points for contracts."

"You'll want to take notes as we go through the process. Trust me."

"I do, Dr. Friedman."

Gem stood up later that afternoon and stretched. He felt exhausted but armed with new ways to manage his obsessive thoughts and anxiety. As he gathered up the legal pad, his keys, and iPhone, Dr. Friedman stopped him.

"Just one other thing we haven't touched on," she said. "So that boredom you mentioned a couple weeks ago—that isn't helping your anxiety, either."

"Yeah, I got it."

"What are you going to do about it?"

Gem tucked the legal pad under his left arm. He placed his fists on an invisible bat and mimicked taking a swing. He smiled and nodded.

"Gonna try out for the Dodgers—finally."

Dr. Friedman looked over her eyeglasses. Her eyebrows rose.

"Just what the Dodgers need—an AARP third baseman!"

Gem dropped his hands to his sides and knitted his eyebrows in feigned hurt. He reached up and stretched his apple green LaCoste across his belly, accentuating the flab. He looked down at it, considered it for a moment, shook his head and then shrugged.

"Maybe expand into sport representation."

"Better," Dr. Friedman said.

"Wait, wait," he said.

Gem sat on the arm of the couch. He brushed off a bit of dust. He tapped his lips with his right fingertips.

"I could bring in another partner and dial back on the agency work."

"And?" Dr. Friedman said.

Gem smiled. A rush of joy filled him.

"I've always had a fantasy about setting up a baseball camp for foster kids. Why couldn't I do that?"

"You tell me. Better yet, what does the voice say?"

"The baseball camp was the voice's idea."

"I think I like your conscience better than you," Dr. Friedman said.

Dr. Friedman held out her arms and waved Gem toward her.

"This last two weeks was a marathon. You deserve a hug."

"Doesn't seem professional, Dr. Friedman."

"Report me, then."

They embraced.

Gem pulled the car into the driveway at home. He let the car idle. 'It's not about being "positive" so much as being "pausative" he remembered Dr. Friedman saying. 'Pause to consider your uncomfortable thought or feeling at the moment, and then pause to consider everybody else's, too.' So Gem paused to consider. He hadn't made it to a Beverly Hillbillies mansion, but he had done well. Much better than he should ever have expected. But he had help: Dale and Gerry, Jennifer and Ted, Dr. Friedman, and Maureen, who ended up adopting him out of foster care when he was seventeen. She helped him apply for college and secured him a walk-on tryout for his baseball scholarship as well. And of course, Kelly, with her love and abiding belief in him. He considered himself the result of a team effort and what a team. Grateful didn't begin to describe his feelings at that moment.

And he wasn't just a good husband and father—he was a great one. He noticed the fruitless California Pepper start to ruffle and wave in the wind. He knew it would be a dry Santa Ana wind. Usually the wind put him on edge, but this time, it reminded him that this wind, his home, his amazing Kelly, the kids and new grandkid, all the friends over the years, this was all now. The shit in his head, that was all then. It was a part of now, but also, apart from now. He shook his head as he pulled into the garage, feeling confident that he not only had the tools to manage his anxiety and obsessive thoughts, but also to handle anything life was going to present. He felt a lightness in his chest as he thought about reducing his work hours and starting the foster kids baseball camp. He almost couldn't wait to tell Kelly.

When he walked through the garage service door, Kelly greeted him. She wore a soft pink summer dress and smelled of lilacs and fresh, clean air. They kissed deeply and held each other for a long hug. She pulled away from the hug and held out a stage show postcard.

"So who's Bobby Anderson?"

Gem's eyes widened.

"What about him?"

"The office sent over your mail from the last couple weeks and this was sitting on top."

Kelly handed Gem the postcard. Four glorious drag queens, one dressed in a sequined, 'I Dream of Jeannie' costume, graced the card. It read: 'The Divas Dare'—Join us for the tenth annual show benefiting the L.A. LGBT Youth Center.' Gem flipped the postcard over:

'If you're around, would love to see you. No matter what, DON'T follow the rules. XO Bobby Anderson.' An arrow extended from the signature and continued to the front of the postcard. Gem flipped it back over.

"You got something to tell me, Cupper?" she said smiling.

"Yeah. We're going to catch a drag show next week. Starring Coco Peru, Helena Handbasket, Donna Suggarz, and my old roomie, Bobby. Or better known as Beverly OFFcenter. The one in the Jeannie costume. "

"Check those abs," Kelly said.

252

"I know, he must be fifty-one."

Gem looked at the postcard a moment longer and shook his head. Kelly grabbed the postcard back.

"You gotta come upstairs and check out who's staying the night. Maureen and Bruce are going to be coming over to meet their grandchild, too."

Kelly took his hand and led him up the maple hardwood stairs with the cherry wood and wrought iron railing. They stepped quietly into the room just across from theirs. The cream wallpaper embossed with lambs stood out between the mulberry and powder blue stripes. Gem walked up to the edge of the antique cherry crib. Little Tyler lay in a yellow onesie sound asleep. His tiny pink hand curled into a fist at his mouth as he sucked his thumb. Gem reached out and stroked his grandson's belly. The warmth of the deepest love moved like a wave from his gut to his head and made his eyes well up.

Never he heard the voice say.

Kelly's iPhone rang with its bamboo bell tone. She pulled it from her dress side pocket.

"Curt's calling?" she said quietly.

Gem nodded and she stepped out into the hall. Gem rubbed Tyler's belly for a few minutes while Kelly chatted with Curt. Gem leaned over the edge of the crib and kissed Tyler's forehead that smelled of baby oil. Kelly stepped back in quietly and touched Gem's back.

"Well, I'm glad we didn't touch Curt's room," Kelly whispered. Gem sighed.

"What now?"

"Best Buy let him go. Something about down-sizing."

"He's got to stand up on his own two feet this time. We're not going to be around forever. What do you think?"

Kelly shrugged. She shook her head.

"He and Shana want to come over and discuss their moving in for awhile so that they can save money for the baby—blah-blah-blah."

"What are a mother *and* father for, anyway?" Gem asked.

Gem placed his arm around Kelly's waist. They both smiled as Tyler slept.